Rethinking Single-Sex Teaching

Rethinking Single-Sex Teaching

Gabrielle Ivinson and Patricia Murphy

 Open University Press

Open University Press
McGraw-Hill Education
McGraw-Hill House
Shoppenhangers Road
Maidenhead, Berkshire
England SL6 2QL

email: enquiries@openup.co.uk
world wide web: www.openup.co.uk

and Two Penn Plaza, New York, NY 10122289, USA

A catalogue record of this book is available from the British Library

ISBN 13: 978 03352 20403 (pb) 9780 3552 20410 (hb)
     10: 0335 220401 (pb)   0335 22041 X (hb)

Library of Congress Cataloging-in-Publication Data
CIP data has been applied for

Typeset by BookEns Ltd, Royston, Herts.
Printed and bound in Poland by OZGraf. S.A.
www.polskabook.pl

The **McGraw·Hill** Companies

Contents

For Tony and Catherine with love and thanks (GI)
For Syd and Pat with love and thanks (PM)

Series Editor's Introduction

Educating boys is currently seen – both globally and locally – to be in crisis. In fact, there is long history to the question: what about the boys? However, it was not until the 1990s that the question of boys' education became a matter of public and political concern in a large number of countries around the world, most notably the UK, the USA and Australia.

There are a number of different approaches to be found in the literature to troubling questions about boys in schools. The questions concern the behaviours and identities of boys in schools, covering areas such as school violence and bullying, homophobia, sexism and racism, through to questions about boys' perceived underachievement. In *Failing Boys? Issues in Gender and Achievement*, Epstein and her colleagues (Epstein et al. 1998) identify three specific discourses which are called upon in popular and political discussions of the schooling of boys: 'poor boys'; 'failing schools, failing boys'; and 'boys will be boys'. They suggest that it might be more useful to draw, instead, on feminist and profeminist insights in order to understand what is going on in terms of gender relations between boys and girls and amongst boys. An important question, they suggest, is what kind of masculinities are being produced in schools, in what ways, and how do they impact upon the education of boys. In other words, there is an urgent need to place boys' educational experiences within the wider gender relations within the institution and beyond.

This series is one that falls squarely within the last of these broad categories. In the plethora of rather simplistic and often counter-productive 'solutions' (such as making classrooms more 'boy-friendly' in macho ways) which are coming from governments in different parts of the English-speaking world and from some of the more populist writers in the area (e.g. Steve Biddulph), there is an urgent need for a more thoughtful approach to the issues raised by what are quite long-standing problems in the schooling of boys. Approaches by policy makers for advice and by teachers and principals responsible for staff development in their schools to researchers in the field of 'boys' underachievement' are an almost daily event, and many have already tried the more simplistic approaches and found them wanting. There is, therefore, an urgent demand for more along the lines suggested here.

This is not a series of 'how to do it' handbooks for working with boys. Rather, it draws upon a wide range of contemporary theorising that is rethinking gender relations. While, as editors, we would argue strongly that the issues under discussion here require theorising, it is equally important that books in the area address the real needs of practitioners as they struggle with day to day life in schools and other places where professionals meet and must deal with the varied, often troubling, masculinities of boys. Teachers, youth workers and policy makers (not to mention parents of boys – and girls!) are challenged by questions of masculinity. While many, perhaps most, boys are not particularly happy inhabiting the space of the boy who is rough, tough and dangerous to know, the bullying of boys who present themselves as more thoughtful and gentle can be problematic in the extreme. We see a need, then, for a series of books located within institutions, such as education, the family and training/workplace and grounded in practitioners' everyday experiences. These will be explored from new perspectives that encourage a more reflexive approach to teaching and learning with reference to boys and girls.

We aim, in this series, to bring together the best work in the area of masculinity and education from a range of countries. There are obvious differences in education systems and forms of available masculinity, even between English-speaking countries, as well as significant commonalties. We can learn from both of these, not in the sense of saying 'oh, they do that in Australia, so let's do it in the UK' (or *vice versa*), but rather by comparing and contrasting in order to develop deeper understandings both of the masculinities of boys and of the ways adults, especially professionals, can work with boys and girls in order to reduce those ways of 'doing boy' which seem problematic and encourage those which are more sustainable (by the boys themselves now and in later life). Thus books in the series address a number of key questions. How can we make sense of the identities and behaviours of those boys who achieve popularity and dominance by behaving in violent ways in school, will find themselves in trouble when they are young men out on the streets? How can we address key practitioner concerns about how to teach these boys? What do we need to understand about the experiences of girls as well as boys in order to intervene effectively and in ways which do not put boys down or lead them to reject our approaches to their education? What do we need to understand about gender relations in order to teach boys and girls more effectively? How can we make sense of masculinities in schools, through multi-dimensional explanations, which take into account the overlapping social and cultural differences (of, for example, class, ethnicity, dis/ability and sexuality) as well as those of gender? What are the impacts of larger changes to patterns of employment and globalisation on the lives of teachers and students in particular schools and locations? The series, as a whole, aims to provide practitioners with new insights into the changing demands of teaching boys and girls in response to these questions.

This is the last book in our series and we are fortunate to have such a remarkable contribution to thinking about Educating Boys, Learning Gender to cap it off. Since concerns arose about the boys' achievements at school in the mid-1990s it has become something of a fashion to separate boys and girls into single sex classes within co-educational settings. Education professionals involved in some of these projects invited Gabrielle Ivinson and Patricia Murphy to research what was happening in these classes and to offer advice. They have done an intensive, qualitative study exploring not only the impact of single sex teaching on achievement and the making of gender but also how the nature of subject knowledge is affected by the different modes of pedagogy adopted. The result is a theoretically nuanced, yet highly practical book. It offers much to teachers, policy makers and academics alike.

Debbie Epstein
Maírtín Mac an Ghaill

Acknowledgements

This book would not have been possible without the help and cooperation of the teachers and their students in our case study schools. We owe them much and thank them for giving us their time, insights and support for our work. We would also like to thank Debbie Epstein for her support and sound advice throughout. We would like to thank Anna Graham, Alicia Stubbersfield, Valerie Walkerdine and Tony Ivinson for reading the text and making insightful suggestions. The research was funded through the Faculty of Education and Language Studies Centre for Curriculum and Teaching Studies. Gabrielle would like to thank her colleagues at the Open University for their companionship while she undertook the fieldwork and for Patricia's continuing intellectual inspiration. Barbara Adam, Catherine and Tony Ivinson, Jan, Valerie, Katie and Daniela gave me personal encouragement including numerous wonderful dinners, plentiful glasses of wine, walks and pub visits while the book was being written; Gabrielle would like to extend her heart-felt thanks and love to them. Patricia would especially like to thank Gabrielle for working alongside her over the years and for all she has learned through that process. Her thanks also to Siobhan Murphy for her love, laughter and support in managing the present and re-imagining the future.

Introduction

Constituting the problem: the role of cultural beliefs

Policy debates and initiatives in England about gender and education are interesting for what they demonstrate about enduring beliefs regarding gender. Historically-rooted ideas about gender re-emerge and experience something of a renaissance as they reconnect with contemporary cultural mores when societies confront perceived disruptions to familiar social orders – the 'ways of being' in the culture.

The dominant cultural belief about gender is in the binary divide between males and females which places them in oppositional relationships – what one is the other is not. This indicates a social representation of gender that is biological, innate, fixed and dichotomous. Associated with a biological view of gender is the cultural belief in male superiority and female inferiority, which has its roots in Greek philosophy. These beliefs have been drawn on throughout history to justify the exclusion of women from the public realm. They have also shaped educational policy and continue to do so. However, this is rarely acknowledged because these beliefs are embodied in our thinking and inscribed in our routines and behaviours. They are taken-for-granted common sense beliefs, or 'cultural illusions' as McDermott (1996) refers to them.

For example, in post-war Britain the labour shortage meant that for the first time in an era of peace women were encouraged to enter non-traditional areas of work such as industry and engineering – i.e. those from which they were previously excluded. The concern with students' participation in the physical sciences emerged first and foremost therefore as an economic problem for which girls were the perceived solution.

Ameliorating initiatives, which included single-sex teaching groups and skills training, were predicated on a deficit view of girls who were seen to lack the essential experience, knowledge and skills to engage effectively with these subjects. The initiatives were designed to compensate for this. They did not challenge the accepted epistemological order about the selection of knowledge and ways of knowing involved in the construction of the subjects. When the solution failed to emerge through the 1970s and 1980s, the problem was recast as an educational one. What became targeted for action were girls' inappropriate attitudes to maths and the physical sciences, which explained their failure to choose to study these subjects. The solution was therefore to change the girls (Manthorpe 1985). That girls might struggle to identify with these subjects and imagine a future in relation to them, given the historical construction of these subjects as 'masculine', and the legacy of exclusion from the physical science curriculum that girls inherited, was not, however, considered. To do so would have changed the perception of the problem, challenging assumptions about gender as an attribute of an individual and direct attention to the construction of the subject, what types of persons were associated or dissociated with it historically, and how this was manifest in its teaching. Unsurprisingly girls continue not to choose to study physics post-16 (Murphy and Whitelegg 2006).

Along with beliefs about the innate nature of gender, education is also deeply influenced by the belief in the normal variation of innate abilities. In a meritocracy where there is an overt social justice agenda, the assumption is that sex groups will achieve equally, albeit not necessarily at the same level, yet according to a normalized view of the world in which some are able, the majority is average and the remainder below average or less able. This belief informs much of the policy on gender and education as it is assumed that if overall educational outcomes are equal for populations of girls and boys then the system is functioning in a gender-neutral way. This view is congruent with a social representation of gender as innate but conflicts with the historical and social construction of male superiority. The influence of both views is evident in the response to, and representation of, the 'problem' of boys' literacy performance relative to girls.

The use of league tables in the 1990s in England as a mechanism for accountability made public individual and school national test and examination results. This allowed simple comparisons of boys' and girls' overall achievements to be made. The unequal outcomes in literacy, with girls outperforming boys throughout compulsory schooling, were immediately identified as a perturbation that undermined the assumption of equality of outcome and therefore became a matter for action. The emergence of the problem as a concern for boys of lower achievement was not supported by careful analyses of the results, which suggested that the gap between girls' and boys' performance was at the top end of the grade profile (Gorard 2000). However, the achievement gap had become associated politically with concerns about male antisocial behaviour, criminality and unemployment –the 'laddish' culture (Jackson 2002). This was the 'real' problem and its source could not be attributed to high achieving boys in a cultural context where to be male carried with it a historical legacy of superiority.

Indeed the problem generally was attributed to the environment and the neglect of masculinity resulting from the advantages given to girls by the curriculum, its teaching and its assessment. Not only were boys not to be perceived as deficient, girls' superior achievements were constructed, through media representations, as the product of bias.

Through headlines such as 'Male brains rattled by curriculum oestrogen' (*Times Educational Supplement*, 15 March 1996), an educational environment hostile to masculinity was depicted. Perhaps more disturbing was the coalescing of media views that girls and women had not only invaded the public sphere, which they increasingly were required to do, but were beginning to limit boys' access to it when it was historically their rightful space. This perceived rise in female prowess has to be understood in the context of a history of feminist mobilization in education that lasted into the 1980s (Arnot *et al.* 1999). This resulted in some national and regional initiatives that focused on the disparity in uptake and achievement in science, maths and technology of girls relative to boys. These drew on feminist critiques of epistemology that questioned the ways of knowing that were legitimized in the selection of valued knowledge in these subjects and sought to legitimate a broader array of ways of knowing. These initiatives had some visible presence in schools although much less influence than was imagined. It was not until 1988 with the advent of the National Curriculum in England that girls and boys were granted equal access to the full range of core and foundation subjects. By the end of the 1980s, discourses about girls as the victims of patriarchal structures within 'modernist institutions' (Epstein *et al.* 1998) were fading as girls' achievements in examinations at ages 16 and 18 began to overtake those of boys, representing a major disruption to the social order. The threat to the belief in male superiority can be detected in the media responses to this differential performance: 'Boys become the weaker sex in education' (*Guardian*, 29 August 1998).

In the media response, female teachers and their domination of the teaching profession were targeted, as was the proliferation of teaching and assessment methods that were associated with feminine qualities such as collaboration and diligence rather than competition and risk-taking: the former were seen to advantage girls in coursework, the continuous assessment component of external examinations that is conducted without time or place constrictions, whereas the latter masculine attributes were seen to be better served by examinations, despite the fact that there was no evidence to support these assertions (Elwood 2001).

The solution that emerged, supported by the Education Secretary at the time, was to separate boys from girls. The belief in essential difference and the dichotomous nature of gender is evident in the following proposed solution and manifest in the media responses:

Blunkett to bring back single-sex education.

(*Daily Telegraph*, 20 August 2000)

Team spirit, discipline and a motivating master put boys on par with the girls.

(*Guardian*, 14 January 1998)

Single sex lessons plan to counter laddish culture.

(*Guardian*, 21 August 2000)

Single-sex organization and views of gender

The retreat in England to a particular pedagogy believed to be fostered in single-sex organizations reflects a long history where educational policy and practice has made explicit the belief that sex groups are different in both how they learn and what they should learn. When education first began to be extended to the bourgeoisie, provision was predominantly single-sex schooling. The curriculum offered was defined by society's construction of the male and female spheres, which located males in the public domain and females in the private domestic domain (Delamont and Duffin 1978). When the working classes gained access to education, scarce resources ensured that single-sex schools were not feasible. Nevertheless, single-sex organization was common and a differentiated curriculum the norm, maintaining the public/domestic divide and the continuing belief in the fundamental differences in female and male social roles (Arnot *et al.* 1999).

In education currently, there is no longer a clear gender demarcation between public and private spheres, though while females have increasingly been required to, and have chosen to, enter the public domain, the same cannot be said about males and the domestic sphere (McDowell 1990). Furthermore, those parts of the public sphere females can gain access to remain heavily gender differentiated, reflecting continuing stereotypes of 'men's work' and 'women's work'. Therefore, in advocating single-sex organization of teaching and learning, educational rhetoric and policy maintains a difficult tension between a belief in innate gender differences and a belief in equality, though all too readily the former can dominate the latter.

For schools encouraged to take on board a policy directive to take up single-sex organization, the rationale for doing so was explicitly one of equity and entitlement. This often masked a market forces argument, where schools saw the practice as a means of attracting a particular social group who associated single-sex teaching with elite education and the means to enhance their child's social and cultural capital. To implement the policy, learning environments had to be orchestrated to reflect the gender differences believed to exist between girls and boys in their learning. Gender differences have been challenged consistently in sex difference research into cognitive abilities, which continues to show that differences between sex groups for the vast majority of the population are small and fragile in comparison with within-group differences (Eagley 1987; Halpern 1992). Consequently, in enacting single-sex settings schools had to draw on cultural beliefs about the nature of these differences. In so doing they looked to the gender dualisms embedded in social representations of gender such as those that circulate in newspaper headlines. For example, a classic gender dualism opposes aggression with passivity, associating the former with masculinity and the latter with femininity. Hence the need for boys-only pedagogy to emphasize 'discipline' as noted in the headline above, whereas girls are represented as passive and biddable, and hence discipline is not an issue.

Although seen as supporting a more conservative and informed response, the education media were equally influenced by the gender dualisms in the solutions they emphasized, for example, 'Boys should sit next to girls' (*Times Educational Supplement*, 9 January 1998).

Such a solution, referred to as 'gendered seating', is predicated on similar assumptions about girls' passivity and conformity, which are seen as a civilizing influence on boys, perpetuating an ancient cultural view whose source can be traced to Greek and early pagan philosophies. In this view the metaphor of dominion was associated with masculinity and nurturing with femininity, which underpins the social representation of females as the gentler and more civilized sex. Associated with aggression and dominion is the masculine attribute of competitiveness, which is contrasted with 'collaboration', a feminine attribute – hence pedagogies that advocate 'team spirit' as an essential aspect of masculinity, to be fostered in boys-only settings.

The theoretical framing: gender and learning

In this book we challenge the retreat to single-sex teaching on several grounds. Not in the sense that it is inherently a less effective approach to teaching but in terms of it as a 'solution' to gender. 'Gender' cannot be 'solved' in that there is no possibility of gender-neutral systems, nor is there an overarching 'female' or 'male' gender essence that pedagogy can address.

The media and educational discourses about single-sex teaching take a dichotomous view of gender, in which it is represented as a static and unchanging attribute of an individual. In this view how we act and how we are perceived, and the sense we make of things, are the same across contexts and over time. What is more, all who are like us (i.e. share the same transparent category of gender) are imagined to experience the world and act on it in similar ways. Differences between us, within the binary categories of male and female, are attributable to our innate genetic qualities and not to anything outside of us. Underpinning such a view of gender, and of the world, is a particular conception of the human mind and of knowledge. If all females and – separately – all males, experience the world in the same way this is congruent with a view that argues that people and the environment are separate. In this view people are separated from the reality of the world which is external – a given, objective world. The symbols used to represent this reality – knowledge – are mirrors of that reality (Bredo 1994). This in turn supports a view of learning in which knowledge about the world has to be transmitted from outside and received and internalized by individuals.

Fundamental to this view of learning and of knowledge is that there is no process of meaning-making on the part of the learner, and knowledge is stable across people. Therefore our experiences in the lived world, including experiencing the world as a 'female' or as a 'male', do not impinge on the meanings that are available to us. The learner is a passive receiver. Any constraints on learning can be attributed to learners and their innate qualities. Therefore, gender differences in learning are due to biological differences between the sexes. Social and cultural influences, which are external, do not influence cognition. Such beliefs taken up in practice in schools deny the way that cultural systems shape individuals, make demands on them to be certain kinds of persons, and position them differentially depending on how gender values are privileged in subject communities in schools.

In this book we challenge this view of gender and the concomitant view of mind, and of learning. Our concern is to recognize complexity in the gender mediation of learning and to make aspects of it visible, so that gender does not continue to be an unintentional and invisible constraint on learners' access and engagement. To do this we draw on an alternative conception of mind that recognizes that people and the environment are never separate and that 'mind cannot exist save for culture' (Bruner 1996: 3). In referring to environment we imply much more than the physical and include the historical, social and cultural surroundings. Vygotsky's (1994) theorizing about learning argues for a unity of the social and personal. This approach acknowledges that our ways of thinking about the world are construals of the world – it is not just the stimulus world, instead the world is what we make of it. Meaning is not pre-existing, rather being a human is to engage constantly in a process of negotiating meaning, as this is how we experience the world. Hence mind is agentive, not passive, constructing and negotiating meaning through dialogue and discourse with others.

Human understanding of the world develops through a process of associations between characteristics of objects, people and experience. These associations lead to objects and people gradually acquiring 'ever more eccentric and intense degrees of significance' (Greenfield 2000: 52). In this way people and events acquire differential degrees of importance for individuals. The world is a personally-felt one, referenced by the individual. In this view, because the personal and the social are indivisible, then the meanings that we negotiate are necessarily distributed and not properties of individuals: 'Meaning exists neither in us, nor in the world, but in the dynamic relation of living in the world' (Wenger 1998: 54). Lave and Wenger (1991: 33) describe this as agent, activity and the world mutually constituting each other. Humans are social actors, reflexively and recursively acting upon the world and creating it at the same time. Learning and knowing is, therefore, better understood as relations among people in activity, 'in, with and arising from the socially and culturally structured world' (Lave and Wenger 1991: 51). Consequently, learning is an aspect of all activity and activity is always situated in a social, historical and cultural context and is dialectically constituted in relation to that context. In other words, activities do not exist in isolation but are part of broader systems of relations and social structures, in which they have meaning and in which gender is embedded.

Gender in this view of mind is both an aspect of the social order incorporated within symbolic networks, and a dimension of social situations. As part of the social order, gender is a historically produced discursive construct which acts as a resource to constitute gender identities (Kotthoff and Baron 2001). We referred to enduring beliefs earlier, and an important aspect of our understanding of gender that flows from a sociocultural perspective is that time cannot be segmented: 'The present extends through the past and future and cannot be separated from them' (Rogoff 1995: 155). Thus the shared symbolic networks within a culture regarding what it is to be 'male' and 'female' circulate as ideas that become manifest through social conventions and social practices. In this way, cultural beliefs about what it is to be male and female are 'conserved, elaborated and passed on to succeeding generations who maintain the culture's identity and way of life' (Bruner 1996: 3), and become sedimented in expressions of gender dichotomy such as those we have referred to. Hence vestiges of previous world-views remain as part of the gender culture we inherit and can be revitalized as social dilemmas and social needs ebb and flow.

Perceptions of gender set up expectations of what it is to be identifiably masculine or feminine that are more or less stable norms of a culture. Learners locate themselves within and through these social gender category systems. Davies (2003: 9–10) talks of children's need to 'get it right': 'Getting it right means practising the culture in an identifiably individual way and to do this students have to know the ways in which cultural practices can be varied'. In this sense a gender identity as such does not exist – rather, a *capacity* exists to learn to provide and to read depictions of masculinity and femininity (McDermott 1996, citing Goffman). The meaning of gender-social categories varies across subject settings. Learners develop different relational identities in subject settings because they are afforded different positions in them depending on whether they are a boy or a girl, a high achiever or a low achiever etc. Gender therefore has a dynamic dimension as an aspect of social situations, and can be understood as a 'moment in action', as people negotiate and commit to meanings and positions while participating in activities within subject contexts (Penuel and Wertsch 1995).

The study

We undertook research[1] in two schools where gender and learning had been problematized for a variety of reasons. The schools responded in two ways. In one school, Monks School, single-sex teaching was taken on across the curriculum. This was partly in recognition of market forces, as we noted earlier, where single-sex organization is associated with elite practice, as historically it was a key feature of private selected schooling. Furthermore, it addressed continuing concerns that at particular ages it was appropriate to keep the sexes apart until such time as physical maturity was reached (Arnot 1983). In another school, Palmers School, the focus was on boys and literacy. The concern was to improve the achievement of some and maintain the achievement of others. This was addressed by two forms of organization: gendered seating, where girls functioned as role models and peer tutors for low

[1] The research was funded by the Centre for Curriculum and Teaching Studies, Faculty of Education and Language Studies at the Open University.

achieving boys and a civilizing force; and single-sex groupings to provide average and above average achieving boys with the ideal pedagogic environment for them to continue to succeed in English. In this school there was explicit recognition of essential differences between males and females, but what this might mean was up to individual teachers to determine. In both schools we observed ongoing classroom practice in 'girls only', 'boys only' and, in some cases mixed, groupings. We observed across a range of subjects that included English, drama, science, design and technology, art and mathematics. The activities that we focused on were those orchestrated for students in ongoing practice in subject settings.

To understand learning in school subjects, attention has to be paid both to the forms of social agency that shape individuals – teachers and students – and to individual and group agency. This view had implications for our research, as it required us to take account of both the personal and the social, for to understand one, account has to be taken of the other. Culture, gender and cognition (Lave 1988) exist at different levels of the sociocultural order. Rogoff (1995) refers to three planes of analysis: community/institutional; interpersonal; and personal. These planes are inseparable and mutually constituting and can become the focus of analysis at different times. The community plane foregrounds the institutional structure and cultural technologies of intellectual activity. The interpersonal plane is made up of the events of everyday life and focuses on the engagements and arrangements of intellectual activity. The personal plane is concerned with the process of appropriation, which occurs in the process of participation. This way of analysing learning has implications for how events are researched. It focuses attention on looking at similarities and differences across varying sociocultural activities and tracking relations among aspects of events from the different perspectives offered by the planes of analysis.

To understand the learning process we analysed students' agentive acts, paying attention to the complex interplay among cultural tools employed in activities in subject settings, and the sociocultural and institutional context of the activities and their embedded purposes (Penuel and Wertsch 1995). The research also recognized that students bring to subject settings in school multiple identities constructed in the multiple communities to which they 'belong', including social identities such as gender and their identity as a learner within a particular setting. Holland *et al.* (1998) talk of the way people are caught in the tensions between past histories and present discourses, and images that they associate with or which impinge upon them. It is in the resolution of these tensions in the flow of activity within subject settings that there is the potential for mediated agency. We therefore focused on the flow of activity and students' improvisations within that to understand the nature of their mediated agency and its consequences for their learning and belonging in a subject.

The focus

This book is concerned with how gender is recognized, understood, represented and reconciled in teachers' and students' interactions in educational settings where subject knowledge learning is the primary goal. Our stance is that to understand gender mediation you have to concern yourself with both girls' and boys' experiences, particularly as the common assumption is that there is equality in what is made available to learn and, if there is not, then single-sex organization achieves this. Central to the book is the recognition that subjects, and the cultural tools and resources associated with them, have values attached to them that reflect their sociocultural legacies. These historical roots continue to influence the values attached to resources and practices that are made available to students and provide them with clues about what are legitimate ways of acting in subject classrooms. These value systems affect how individual girls and boys feel positioned, distancing them or connecting them to the practices of the subject and extending to them what Wenger (1998) refers to as an identity of participation or non-participation.

In understanding subject learning as occurring as students participate in activities in subject communities, we recognize that learning is not just about appropriating ways of knowing and acting that are valued in different subjects, but essentially about the formation of an identity: becoming a competent schooled person within that subject. Hence, learning is a process of transformation in which learners take on new identities through their participation (Lave 1988). Students' and teachers' perspectives on the positioning of learners in subject communities by virtue of their gender have implications for their participation and learning, and we believe this to be problematic. While gender mediates all social contexts, we argue that in single-sex classrooms there are different possibilities for the way students' responses are read. Our pilot work indicated that teachers' practices shifted so that they instantiated knowledge differently when faced with either a group of boys or with a group of girls. Therefore, single-sex organization simultaneously provided interesting contexts to make visible how gender mediates individual learning and how this mediation differs across contexts, and allowed reflection on the strategy itself as an ameliorating solution to gender inequity.

Looking across subjects, and settings within subjects, our data allows us to consider how the meaning and organization of gender varies between subject contexts, and importantly, how this influences the possibilities for learning for particular students. As we have researched within schools where gender was identified as a problem, and pedagogy as the means to address perceived inequity in subject achievements, we were able to consider how teachers understand gender in relation to their subject and their learners. Thus we recognize the teacher as a 'key agent in regulating and reproducing (or contesting and transforming) the gender order of the classroom' (Dixon 1998: 148). By focusing on teachers' practices, and discourse within these, as well as students' experiences, we gained insights into the ways that hegemonic masculinities and femininities become privileged or disrupted in particular settings. In focusing on gender mediation as a 'moment in action' we borrow from McDermott the idea that each interactional moment produces new possibilities and constraints. Therefore each 'moment in action' is constantly on the verge of being something else (1996: 290). It is 'what that something else' might be that interests us in working with gender. Looking across these examples our intention is to offer further understanding of gender and its action in the world and, importantly, what can be changed in a setting so that students' agency is extended rather than constrained.

In Chapter 1 we look in more detail at single-sex organization, its historical roots in the structuring of education and the challenges raised about it as an effective educational approach. We consider the mediation of policy on single-sex organization since the 1970s, and current discourses about gender and schooling in relation to it, to establish the context for its re-emergence. We then examine the current evidence available about the impact of single-sex organization on students' learning.

In Chapter 2 we use an excerpt from a single-sex setting to introduce the conceptual tools we find helpful in analysing and interpreting practice. We look at what is understood by practice and learning through participation and explore agency and identities in more detail. We consider identities as trajectories that incorporate the past and the future in the process of negotiating the present (Wenger 1998). The process of reconciliation is the work that learners engage in to belong in a subject and to maintain some kind of coexistence between multiple memberships or trajectories of identity. We look at what might influence this process and make it effortful for learners in different subject settings. Finally we revisit cultural beliefs about gender to reflect on the historical roots of teachers' and students' perspectives on gender in relation to their subjects and themselves.

In Chapter 3 we look at the community and institutional planes, examining teachers' practice and how knowledge is instantiated for single-sex groupings. As part of this we explore teachers' representations of their subjects; their beliefs about gender in their accounts and how these beliefs emerge in practice. Identification is central to how students are positioned and feel positioned in subjects, and depends on the images they can build of the world and themselves in relation to it (Holland *et al.* 1998; Wenger 1998). The discourses in school subjects are constantly reproduced and reconstructed in settings, regulating and legitimizing ways of knowing and being. These discourses are pivotal in the processes of identification, which involve making connections across time and the social landscape, and enable learners' identities to take on new dimensions.

In Chapters 4 and 5 we foreground the interpersonal plane, looking at interactional moments in activity. In so doing we consider how students experience agency in different settings and relate this to the possibilities made available for their learning through teachers' practices within and between different settings.

In Chapter 4 we turn to subjects with a masculine historical legacy and focus primarily on data from settings involving 'girls only' and 'boys only' groups in mathematics, design and technology and science. We examine how teachers' discourses and practices open up or close down practice for girls and boys, students' reactions to this, and the consequences for their learning in the present and the future. We also consider how the association of 'competence' in these subjects aligns with historical legacies of masculinity which constrain some boys' and girls' agency, and the consequences for their evolving identities in the subjects.

In Chapter 5 we focus on drama, English and art to examine the notion of positional identities in subjects that have a feminine historical legacy. We explore how teachers' practices change as they attempt to open up practice for boys in subjects that they may experience disconnection from, because the practices and products give value to expressions of interiority and symbolic resources that are associated with 'feminine' ways of knowing and being. In so doing we consider how notions of a gender hierarchy can lead teachers to subvert their subject in order to empower boys in a setting. We consider how girls, in comparison, are positioned through the tasks that teachers select, and the consequences for their participation and subject learning.

In Chapter 6 we look at the personal plane and student accounts of the process of reconciliation as they manage a gender-subject identity. We focus on four students, a girl in design and technology, a boy in English and a boy and girl in drama. We return also to a boy we introduced in Chapter 2 as we consider what needs to be in place to expand rather than close down possibilities for learning. We consider the process of reconciliation, and although this is personal and typically invisible we look at students' improvisations through their dialogue, actions and products and then at the influence of peer group culture on this.

In the final chapter we discuss the implications of our research for pedagogy, for single-sex organization and for learning in subject settings. Our research in single-sex settings helps to make visible historical legacies that have aligned subjects and the identities they extend to learners, with traditional social representations of gender. By opening up teachers' and students' experiences and practices within single-sex settings we hope to support a critical awareness that can be used to develop practice to resist historically embedded gender patterns and open up subject domains to a wider range of learners.

Chapter/**One**

Schooling and the curriculum: a history of single-sex organization

The two co-educational comprehensive schools, Monks School and Palmers School, introduced single-sex classes at the end of the 1990s. In naming 1999 'The Year of the Boy', the headteacher of Palmers School was reacting to an international debate about globalization and shifts in labour markets. Fears surrounding de-industrialization, the decreasing importance of the nation state, and hence government's power to influence and control social life, burgeoned towards the end of the millennium. In times of transformation consensual ideas about what constitutes a desirable future for society, and therefore the purpose of education, become elusive and conflicted. As the ability to imagine the future becomes clouded, societies delve back into the past to find ways to make sense of things. In some respects the resurgence of interest in single-sex classes in co-educational comprehensive schools and the re-emergence of gender as dichotomous and oppositional can be seen as part of the search to find and stabilize an aspect of the cultural landscape in shifting times.

In the Introduction we argued that the retreat to single-sex organization to address gender differences in achievement reflected a retreat to a particular view of gender. This view ignores within-group diversity and focuses on beliefs about between group differences. These cultural illusions about what it is to be male and female, expressed as bipolar categories, were drawn on to articulate the pedagogic strategies that were believed to appeal to boys in the twenty-first century and, by default, to girls. The historical roots of the single-sex organization of education, however, had less to do with pedagogy and much more to do with curriculum, that is, the knowledge which groups should and could have access to. Furthermore, from the mid-nineteenth century in the UK, while gender was a central educational preoccupation, so too was class – as together they defined the relative roles and status of males and females. Three class-based strata were identified: the upper classes (i.e. those with substantial capital and/or land); the middle classes (i.e. professional and managerial workers); and the working class, which included craft artisans as well as unskilled labourers. Representations of masculinity and femininity varied within these three strata. Sara Delamont (Delamont and Duffin 1978) describes how the struggle for access to education varied according to the social roles made available in the three spheres. Thus for upper- and middle-class women the issue was the right to an education to enable them access to the public domain of professional work. For the working classes, on the other hand, the struggle was for access to education and the freedom from poverty that this right allowed.

What is significant for our concerns in this book is that the problem of differential achievement articulated as one of gender and pedagogy has deep curriculum roots wherein particular knowledge is associated with particular categories of people. For centuries, education was seen as the sole preserve of upper- and middle-class men and the specified curriculum drew on Greco-Roman perceptions of educational purpose. The academic curriculum for schools evolved with only these groups' needs in mind. To recognize how cultural legacies re-emerge in classroom practices we retell the story of education and, as we do so, it will become apparent that in many respects it has been a history based on single-sex organization.

As we argued in the Introduction, the cultural legacy that associates subjects with certain groups is significant in both understanding current beliefs about the benefits of single-sex organization as a pedagogic strategy to address inequality, and to understand subject teachers' approaches to it. In this chapter we consider in very broad terms the historical development of the institutionalized curriculum, what became selected as valuable knowledge and for whom, and therefore the purposes that education was seen to address and for which groups. Alongside this we chart briefly the development of the organization of schooling. We next examine some of the rationales for a single-sex strategy to ameliorate disadvantage and consider these in relation to the policy position that emerged in England. We conclude by considering the evidence base that is available about the relationship between educational benefits and school organization.

Knowledge and the school curriculum

Historically the status attributed to knowledge has reflected the categories of people that are associated with its use and production. In broad terms this aligned femininity with labours of the body, which Hannah Arendt ([1958] 1998) distinguishes from work of the hands and mental work (personal communication, Barbara Adam). Mental work is the product of human reasoning about the world and about people, and can be realized as texts. Texts transcend the life of the author both in the present and in the future, providing a lasting trace and making a bid for eternity. For these reasons text-based knowledge was accorded high status. Work of the hands involved craft knowledge realized in artefacts such as jugs, swords and buildings, rather than texts. The products of this knowledge were seen to lack the transcendent properties of texts but nevertheless extended the impact of the maker into the near future. Therefore the knowledge associated with craft was significant, yet lower status, knowledge. Work of the body such as how to care for others, make meals and stave off decay had to be constantly redone and therefore left no tangible trace. Women have traditionally undertaken this kind of work and the knowledge associated with it has been least valued. The alignment of high status knowledge with masculinity and scholarship influenced how the curriculum of institutionalized education evolved, the status accorded to subjects and, importantly, who was given access to them.

The education of boys from the upper and middle classes

For centuries education was in the control of the Church and the first schools were attached to monasteries and cathedrals and not in separate institutions. Greek educational ideas were taken up by Christian theologians around the fifth century (Ovitt 1987). Knowledge was imagined to already exist (Adam 2004), yet in an esoteric realm. In the Middle Ages the economy, which was largely agrarian and craft based, did not depend on an educated mass, and consequently illiteracy among the majority of the population was unproblematic. However, there was an increase in demand for education premised on the Hellenic view that education was for the gentry and professional men, as they needed to be free to think. This need was met by a gradual increase in fee-paying public schools and the establishment of the first universities in the twelfth century. The purpose of education at this time was to improve the mind and was not intended to address social or economic needs. The Greeks believed that a scholar had to learn to think before applying knowledge, establishing a hierarchy between theory and practice. The university curriculum was, therefore, dominated by conceptions of abstract text-based symbolic knowledge, namely the 'trivium' consisting of rhetoric, logic and grammar, which was accorded a higher status than practical knowledge – the 'quadrivium' of geometry, arithmetic, astrology and music. The functional knowledge of the artisan was not recognized as having symbolic value and any knowledge associated with the body was similarly considered inferior and female.

The fourteenth century saw an expansion in education through the introduction of the first grammar schools for boys (Jarman 1963). Like the universities, the grammar school curriculum was based on the trivium. There was still no institutional educational provision for girls. Working-class girls typically entered domestic labour at age 8 and were taught skills such as spinning, cooking and sewing, in preparation for marriage. The education of upper-class girls was mainly through home tuition by governesses and was restricted to the social skills of music, dancing and sewing, as befitted their role as wives (Purvis 1991). Only elite men were expected to be educated to fulfil roles in the public realm. Historically the single-sex organization of schooling reflected which group was considered worthy of education and could afford it.

The Greek spirit of enquiry dominated education in the Renaissance period of the fifteenth century, and scientific enquiry flourished. Under the Act of Supremacy in 1534 the king became the head of the Church of England and the state, via the Church, took control of education. A small number of cathedral schools were established which gave free education, and later cathedrals were ordered to support a free grammar school, and this provision extended through the Elizabethan period. This, however, had little impact on the provision of education to the vast majority of the middle and lower middle classes, the working classes and girls generally. This period saw a significant shift in the status of art, originally associated with lower status craft knowledge, which still had no place in the academic curriculum. Painting and sculpture became 'an' art. The social status of artists increased and their knowledge was distanced from that associated with the manual labour of the craft-person (Mason and Houghton 2002).

The purpose of education remained to train and discipline the elite male mind. Hence classics and theology still dominated the institutionalized curriculum in England (Jarman 1963). Although this curriculum had its critics, Church control prevented any reform. One such critic was Francis Bacon who, in the seventeenth century, launched an attack on university and school curricula for being moribund and rooted in the past. This denied a role for new understanding to become part of the canon of symbolic knowledge, the aim of Bacon's new mode of enquiry, the scientific method. He advocated a change in the conception of knowledge to include knowledge creation based on experimental sciences. Comenius (1631) similarly proposed an expansion of the curriculum to include mathematics and physics. The debate in England about what constituted knowledge and, in particular, what sources could be accorded symbolic transcendent value, focused entirely on what it was to be an educated man. The two conceptions of knowledge, one rooted in the ancient texts of the past, and the other based on the scientific investigation of physical matter remained in opposition. Bacon also reinstated the importance of physical education. The body had been viewed as the site of original sin and monks were expected to suppress bodily desires in pursuit of spiritual knowledge. The struggle to control the body was man's attempt to become closer to God to cultivate the ideal rational non-emotional mind, and to distance himself from woman. Consequently femininity became associated with the negative, the non-Godlike characteristics of humanity (Davies 2003). A focus on physical education did not necessarily constitute a return to mind-body harmony, however. The male could be 'mind' only if the body had been brought under control and physical education could be the means to achieve this. At this time, with the exception of a small number of noblewomen, there was little opportunity for girls to gain access to high status knowledge.

In the seventeenth century, the invention of the stagecoach and the development of roads led to an expansion of boarding schools, allowing boys from country districts access to education. The same development had an impact, although smaller, on the provision for girls. Many grammar schools closed and while some schools like Harrow were intended to extend education to working-class boys it was the upper and emerging middle classes who benefited (Archer 1921). Conditions in boys' boarding schools were poor. The child in Christianity symbolizes innocence, to achieve manhood is therefore to separate and become distanced from innocence. As John Locke observed, to send a boy to school 'is to sacrifice his innocence to the attainment of confidence and some drill of bustling for himself among others, by his conversation with ill-bred and vicious boys' (Archer 1921: 13). The view emerged that masculinity, en masse, was seen to carry the 'uncivilized aspect of nature', while femininity en masse 'the civilized aspect of nature'.

The association between masculinity and uncivilized behaviour has deep cultural roots. This belief, as we noted in the Introduction, emerges in debates about the advantages and disadvantages of single-sex groupings and underlies such strategies as gendered seating, where girls are placed alongside boys. The complementary roles of masculinity and femininity resonate with earlier beliefs in which man was imagined as a steward placed on earth to protect 'feminine' nature. However, the increasing awareness of natural disasters and the industrial revolution rendered this image untenable and man was re-imagined as the 'controller' of nature. Hence masculinity became associated with aggression and manipulation and femininity with protection and stability (Rothschild 1983).

In the eighteenth century, the moribund curriculum that Bacon had attacked became associated with university life, characterized by drunkenness, absurd dress and little work (Archer 1921). We can see vestiges of 'the dilettante', who was seen to achieve without effort, re-emerge in our present images of 'the lad' (Epstein 1998: 98). While the university curriculum continued to serve the interests of men studying for professions in the Church, law, medicine and academic school-teaching, the possibility for curriculum reform began slowly to emerge. For example, the ability to speak French was increasingly seen as desirable for both upper-class gentlemen and ladies; nevertheless, science up until the nineteenth century was treated as a hobby carried out by the eccentric few. Royal Commissions and the increase of state grants to schools gradually loosened the ecclesiastical stranglehold on education, which in turn allowed reform of the university curriculum. Although classics and mathematics continued to have high status, the curriculum broadened to serve the needs of the sons of the manufacturing and the mercantile classes. However, it took until the mid-nineteenth century before law and science became full university degree subjects (Delamont and Duffin 1978).

The school curriculum dominated by classics and mathematics also came under attack, but the overall purpose of school subjects to train and discipline the mind remained. The Clarendon Commission, which reported in 1864, although critical of the public school curriculum, argued that classics should maintain its high status and take up about half the curriculum. However, it also broadened the curriculum to include a small amount of science, more mathematics, foreign languages, music, drawing, geography, history and English composition. This shift in what an educated male should know brought with it tensions because it gave status to subjects hitherto regarded as 'feminine'. Consequently, both what was taught and how it was taught began to be distinguished for boys. The study of French became an object of scorn as too much exposure would 'damage ... the intellectual tone' (Cohen 1996: 129, citing Butler). The Taunton Commission (1868–9) established in 1864, reviewed all schools including girls' boarding schools that had extended provision for middle-class girls. However, much of girls' education was unavailable for review as it was either conducted in the home or in private schools not on public record. The Commission generally focused on the education of boys and maintained the emphasis on the training of the mind. For example, French teaching was valued if it emulated that of the ancient languages and focused on grammar, the scientific treatment of the language (Cohen 1996: 130). The Commission proposed a three-tier system of fee-paying schools based on divisions within the middle class. It reinforced the longstanding view that the upper middle classes would be prepared for university education and therefore receive the curriculum advocated in the Clarendon Report. The middle stratum, the sons of the mercantile and trading classes, would be schooled until 16 years of age in non-classical subjects as would lower middle-class boys who, it was expected, would leave school at age 14. This reinforced the distinction in status between abstract and functional knowledge.

The education of girls of the upper and middle classes

In the first half of the nineteenth century the education deemed appropriate for girls reflected societal views about sex differences. Catherine Manthorpe (1985), writing about the development of science in the school curriculum, cites Maria Edgeworth's (1795) views about the appropriateness of chemistry for girls. She suggested that it is:

> well suited to the talent and situation of women; it is not a science of parade, it affords occupation and infinite variety; it demands no bodily strength; it can be pursued in retirement; it applies immediately to useful and domestic purposes; and whilst the ingenuity of the most inventive mind may in this science be exercised, there is no danger of inflaming the imagination because the mind is intent upon realities.
>
> (p. 368)

This quote reflects enduring beliefs about the feminine intellect and nature. The association between physical work and versions of masculinity (Paechter and Head 1996) is one argument advanced to exclude women from certain domains of activity and learning. The argument that education endangered women's health was rooted in the belief that mental activity aligns with masculinity and not with femininity. The potential of a subject to inflame the female mind derived from the belief that femininity was associated with passion, rather than reason, and with an absence of control.

The purpose of education for upper- and middle-class girls was further influenced by the strict demarcation of life into the public and private realms advocated by the social contract theorists of the seventeenth century (Pateman 1988). As Sara Delamont (Delamont and Duffin 1978) noted, this resulted in an education designed for acquiring a husband and the culturally valued accomplishments required to entertain his friends (Purvis 1991). These included conversational knowledge of some foreign languages, the ability to play musical instruments, to sing and to embroider. The greater the extent of her accomplishments, the greater a woman's cultural capital would be in the marriage market-place. Girls received their education either from governesses or in girls' boarding schools, which continued to spread during the first half of the nineteenth century.

By the 1850s, one section of middle-class women began to challenge the social construction of women's restricted roles (Manthorpe 1985). They agitated for an education that would equip women to support themselves should the need arise or should they choose to. However, in the struggle for access to the elite curriculum, single-sex organization was assumed because it mirrored that of boys' schools. Elite girls' education was characterized by two conflicting discourses, which Delamont argues restricted girls in two ways. The dominant discourse of masculinity positioned women outside the public domain. However, women's access to education and the public domain threatened the social order and the heterosexual regime that underpinned it (Watson 1997). Therefore to achieve success educators had to uphold the highest standards of 'ladylike' behaviour to demonstrate that schooling would not de-feminize girls. This meant that teachers and girls had to take on board the gendered discourse of what it was to be identifiably and socially accepted as feminine. This conflict between accepting the social mores of femininity while fighting for access to the 'masculine' public domain limited the extent to which feminist educators were able to challenge cultural myths of gender and knowledge.

In the debates over girls' curriculum two factions emerged (Delamont and Duffin 1978). One faction, the 'uncompromising' minority, argued that girls were equal to males in ability. Rather than challenging the 'male' university curriculum consisting of classics, mathematics and later the sciences, this faction insisted on girls' access to it as well as to the same examinations as boys. The other 'separatist' faction argued that women had different, yet equally valuable, social roles to men. Consequently they rejected the male curriculum and assessment and argued for courses suited to girls' futures as teachers, nurses and mothers. Girls' public schools, which were established in the second half of the century, reflected the same stratified system advocated in the Taunton Report for boys. The first girls' public school, Cheltenham Ladies College, run by Miss Beale, was established in 1853 and catered for the 'daughters of gentlemen'. The next development was girls' day schools, which were owned by shareholders and catered for the middle and lower strata of the middle classes. Miss Buss established North London Collegiate and Camden School for this purpose. Under the auspices of the Girls' Public Day School Trust, more high schools were established, which catered for girls across the middle classes, and in the later part of the century more public schools for upper-class girls were opened. Many of these schools were anxious to maintain an education for girls that mirrored that available for upper-class boys. Initially they had to deal with parental concerns about the potential negative impact of a masculine curriculum on their daughter's future marriage aspirations and health. To address these concerns, for example, Miss Beale introduced science under the guise of geography, a subject that was given little priority in the male curriculum (Manthorpe 1985).

By the end of the century the curriculum in girls' high schools had developed in different ways under the influence of limited resources, an absence of trained female staff and continuing resistance to girls studying the same courses as boys. Some schools maintained the uncompromising position of teaching the academic 'male' curriculum, including physics, whereas others taught a separatist curriculum including physiology, hygiene and later biology and domestic science, and excluding physics. Other schools accepted parental pressures to emphasize a literary and accomplishment-based curriculum. Education offered upper- and middle-class girls either the role of the celibate successful professional or accomplished educated wife. While there were advocates of co-education, it was generally accepted that elite education needed to be differentiated by gender and class, ensuring that single-sex organization remained well into the twentieth century.

The education of the working classes

Only a minority of working-class children were in schooling at the beginning of the nineteenth century, and for girls it was approximately 10 per cent of the female population (Purvis 1991). A variety of schools were available such as dame schools, Sunday schools, charity schools, factory schools, schools run by philanthropists or the Church of England and a few schools run by religious dissidents. Dame schools were small private home-based schools usually run by one woman for both boys and girls. The curriculum consisted of reading, spelling, sewing and knitting. Needlework was an important skill because it could supplement the family income. Being able to read the Bible was considered a social requirement, as was learning to bow and curtsy to one's betters (Purvis 1991). The education of the working classes became a matter of concern in this century as the franchise was extended to more men who needed to use their vote wisely. Education was also seen as a civilizing influence in the homes of working-class families. Crime was linked to levels of illiteracy, as it is today, and education for both sexes was seen as a solution to this. Boys were educated to take their place within the brotherhood, which Carol

Pateman (1988) refers to as a male fraternity and therefore the social order of the school reflected that of public life. Girls were educated to become the guardians of the domestic domain, ensuring the health and well-being of the population without which, it was believed, society could not function.

A separatist philosophy dominated mass education and there was no feminist challenge to this. The 1870 Education Act introduced a state system of national elementary schools. The Act made no attempt to define the principles of education equality. Boys were educated according to an occupational hierarchy and girls in relation to a sexual hierarchy of family life in the private sphere (Arnot 1983). Hence, when science was introduced into the elementary curriculum, girls were given lessons on domestic economy along with needlework and laundry work (Skelton 2001). Industrial craft and domestic science were seen as pre-vocational training for boys and girls respectively. When education was made compulsory (1880), and free (1891), the expansion which followed created a demand for larger schools. Financial constraints necessitated co-educational schools, though typically they had separate entrances for girls and boys. The curriculum continued to be taught along strictly gendered lines so that even when subjects like science became compulsory later in the century, the content of girls' lessons remained very different to that of boys', with girls studying nature and the body and boys the physical sciences. At the beginning of the century, the girls' curriculum developed to take account of the employment opportunities in office work. Craft education for boys was introduced into grammar schools in 1902 in the form of metalwork and woodwork. However, this did not signal any shift in the value placed on functional knowledge. As Rachel Mason and Nicholas Houghton (2002) point out, although manual work was recognized in the examination system from 1917 it was 'scorned' by universities. Art, however, maintained its status as a subject through which the middle classes could develop aesthetic sensibilities, imagination and creativity.

Less than a quarter of secondary schools were single sex by 1919 (Arnot 1983). The 1944 Education Act introduced the tripartite system, which provided state education to all through selective grammar, secondary modern and technical schools, which ostensibly were accorded equal value. In practice the system reinforced the policy emphasis on a tailored curriculum to meet class- and gender-based conceptions of need over and above school organization or pedagogy. In the tripartite system, for example, technical education for girls in science became domestic science and secondary modern education emphasized biological science. The selective grammar schools maintained the academic curriculum and the emphasis remained on the physical sciences. Boys continued to have greater access to academic grammar schools, being allocated more places than girls in the belief that differences in physical maturation rates advantaged girls. The small number of technical schools reflected the limited funding made available and the low status the state attached to practical knowledge. The system soon became essentially bipartite with practical, 'technical' activities restricted to the secondary modern curriculum of lower 'achieving' students.

After the 1944 Education Act it continued to be more economical to place boys and girls under the same roof. Nevertheless, separate boys' and girls' classes accommodated the differentiated curriculum believed appropriate to sex groups. The tripartite system reinforced the low value attached to the practical arts and the continued valuing of symbolic knowledge for males and, to a lesser degree, females of ability. The status divide between theory and practice, academic and vocational knowledge, and by direct association sex groups and social classes was, therefore, maintained and enshrined in school structures. In the next section we consider the challenge to single-sex organization and the views about gender that underlie arguments for and against it.

Reasons for the single-sex strategy

Dale's (1969, 1971, 1974) research is generally heralded as a major influence on the move away from single-sex schooling. It focused largely on grammar schools between 1947 and 1967. Dale argued that co-education was the 'natural' state for secondary education and challenged previous essentialist views about gender. These views assumed that boys and girls matured at different rates and that until maturity was achieved the presence of the opposite sex would serve as a distraction and limit the potential for learning (Arnot 1983). Dale's research concluded that co-educational grammar schools provided a happier school ethos for both staff and students than single-sex schools and did not impair academic achievement. Several criticisms have undermined Dale's conclusions, not least his argument about what is 'natural', which his research failed to demonstrate. Dale's argument paid little attention to the evidence about subject polarization in co-educational schools. As Bone (1983) has pointed out, he prioritized social justice goals over issues about access or academic goals. However, Dale's research conclusions resonated with policy concerns at the time about increasing educational opportunities, as he had argued that co-education provided an authentic educational experience that reflected life outside school.

The introduction of comprehensive schools in 1965 led to a dramatic decline in single-sex schools. Many grant maintained grammar schools became independent and this limited access to single-sex education for the majority of state educated students. During the 1980s falling numbers saw the amalgamation of numerous single-sex boys' and girls' schools and the then Secretary of State for Education and Science warned local education authorities that they should retain their single-sex provision.

Comprehensive co-education was premised on egalitarian arguments and evidence of the gender polarization of subject choices within comprehensive schools brought into question its efficacy. This polarization was evident in single-sex schools but to a lesser extent. In 1975 the majority (87 per cent) of state comprehensives were co-educational, whereas the majority (74 per cent) of state grammar schools were single sex. The Department of Education and Science survey (1975) revealed that gender differences in subject choices were compounded by option structures in the curriculum organization of co-educational schools. The Sex Discrimination Act of 1975 did not challenge school organization, but nevertheless served to highlight gendered access to curriculum subjects. Schools were cautioned, but not required, to provide equal opportunities and the onus was placed on parents to take complaints to court (Arnot *et al*. 1999). Nevertheless it has been argued that the threat of legal action was effective in reducing sex differentiation in the curriculum (Carr 1985). The polarization in subject choices in co-educational schools meant that girls failed to gain access to mathematics and sciences in the same way as boys did. This fuelled concerns about the effectiveness of co-education in providing equality of educational opportunity (Deem 1984) and rekindled interest in the potential of single-sex organization to offer equality in an unequal world (Shaw 1984). This was in spite of a review of evidence published by the Equal Opportunities Commission that showed that the type of school rather than school organization influenced subject choices and academic achievement, when prior achievement and social background was taken into account (Bone 1983).

A feminist mobilization to raise awareness of girls' restricted access to science, technology and mathematics fuelled a resurgence of interest in single-sex organization. Numerous initiatives to enhance girls' participation invoked single-sex organization as one of a number of effective pedagogic strategies. Some studies, though not in England (Hoffmann 1997; Parker and Rennie 2002), offered evidence that adopting single-sex groupings enhanced achievement in science but this depended on a number of pedagogic conditions being met. Research demonstrated that the strategy had to be accompanied by changes in curriculum and assessment to provide girls with opportunities to relate science content to familiar everyday experiences. Single-sex organization also reduced class size and increased teacher-student interactions.

The personal support of teachers has been found to be a key determinant of attitudes to science for both boys and girls (Krogh and Thomsen 2005). Teachers' awareness of, and commitment to, gender issues was also crucial (Berge with Ve 2000).

Perspectives on single-sex organization

The implementation of single-sex teaching reflected distinct understandings about the nature of the problem underlying students' subject choices and achievement. In England the dominant perspective was a liberal feminist one, which advocated single-sex organization as a compensatory strategy to provide girls with a secure environment in which they could access experiences within contexts that they were familiar with and develop knowledge and skills that they were believed to lack. It was argued that single-sex classes would allow them to gain the competencies and confidence to choose to participate in subjects on equal terms with boys. Thus the strategy was a short-term one rarely used in isolation. For example, such initiatives also typically involved visits from women role models, which was intended to help girls extend their imagined futures (Whyte 1985). The ability to imagine new futures is part of the process of identification, as Wenger (1998) describes it, relies on personal visions of future possibilities that include mathematics, science and technology. To achieve this, girls needed to be able to create new images of the world and of themselves and in so doing make 'connections that can be envisioned across history and the social landscape' (Wenger 1998: 194). Role models were effective in changing many girls' views of the possibilities for women's futures but rarely changed personal views (Murphy and Whitelegg 2006). The liberal feminist position represented a limited understanding of gender as a social construction emerging in social interaction, as we discussed in the Introduction. The single-sex strategy gives access to subjects but does not challenge the values that are embedded in their practices.

A more radical feminist view argued that co-educational schools were the key means by which patriarchal relations of domination were reproduced; thus single-sex settings would subvert this (Sarah *et al.* 1980), on this premise any single-sex setting would benefit girls. Janice Streitmatter (1999) made a similar case for single-sex classes in the US context to provide reparation for girls who were 'short-changed' in co-educational classes (American Association of University Women 1992). Reparation in the form of single-sex classes for girls is considered illegal in the USA due to Title IX, the legislation created to uphold the principle of equality. Streitmatter's argument revolved around a distinction between equality upheld by Title IX and equity understood according to Jacklin's definition as 'treatment that is fair to women both in form and result' (cited in Streitmatter 1999: 120).

According to Streitmatter, girls are deficient not due to any innate attribute but due to a culture that arises in classes where there are boys. Single-sex classes are advocated because by excluding masculinity the culture inside classrooms changes. All girls are targeted because the cultural legacy of femininity is one of oppression. She argued that masculinity both as a cultural legacy and as an emergent characteristic within classroom practice provided a hostile environment that prevented girls from realizing their academic potential. All boys were viewed as the carriers of masculinity, realized through their talk, their bodies and their behaviours in classrooms. Teachers, according to Streitmatter, respond to these manifestations to the detriment of girls. Sarah et al. (1980) on similar grounds advocate an all-female staff for girls. In the Introduction we argued that a gender identity does not exist; rather there is a capacity to learn to provide and to read depictions of masculinity and femininity, which all students have to do. In this view gender is immanent, fluid and a feature of interaction rather than an individual characteristic. From a sociocultural perspective the physical removal of boys cannot remove the influence of representations of masculinity from a social setting as activity is situated in a social, historical context and is dialectically constituted in relation to that context. As Jane Kenway and Sue Willis (1986) argued, the belief that removing boys removed negative influences operating on girls is to misunderstand the gender mediation of social structures and practices and girls' readings of these.

Research investigating the dynamics of social relations between girls demonstrates that girls create hierarchical structures within peer groups and invoke a 'masculine gaze' to impose versions of femininity on other girls (Holland et al. 1998; Gulbrandsen 2003). There is a great deal of literature on the various versions of femininity that girls can adopt (e.g. Lloyd and Duveen 1992; Renold 2000; Frosh et al. 2002). This literature demonstrates that girls do not simply create 'academic cultures' once boys are removed. Both positions discussed failed also to consider the values and practices of the teacher as a key agent in regulating the gender order of the classroom (Dixon 1998). This we argue is because it is rare in work on gender to investigate relations between learning, knowledge and gender.

The most radical, and the most rare, initiatives during this period of amelioration for girls tended to treat single-sex organization as one of several pedagogic tactics for use as and when teachers considered it helpful. The emphasis in these initiatives was to challenge the social construction of the subject domain and to use social situations rather than science topics or concepts as the structuring units of the curriculum. This altered what was valued as learning outcomes, which was also reflected in the methods of assessment used (Hildebrand 1996; Whitelegg 1996). This approach built on the liberal feminist approach, which changed contexts and in this sense created cultural bridges between girls' worlds and the science world. However, the liberal feminist approach did not incorporate this cultural knowledge into the subject domain. The more radical approach redefined the learning goals and purposes of physics and had a significant impact on access and achievement. Underlying these initiatives was a relational view of gender and knowledge, which recognized that the phenomena of subject choice and achievement were embedded in broader discourses of masculinity and femininity such as we have articulated in this chapter and elaborate further in Chapter 3.

The debate about single-sex organization in relation to girls' access to subjects was overtaken in England by the introduction of the National Curriculum in 1988 which saw science and mathematics introduced as core subjects for all students from the ages of 5–16. The removal of choice appeared to address the problem of differential access. This, however, was to take a simplistic view of access. We argue a social practice theory of learning where practice is understood as a shared history of learning in a subject. The legacy of girls' dissociation from mathematics and many aspects of the physical sciences and technical subjects will continue to position girls differently to boys in these domains in that their facility and legitimacy to negotiate meanings will differ. The ability to negotiate meaning in a subject is fundamental to participation and therefore learning (Wenger 1998). Without teacher action to disrupt this, girls more than boys may struggle to experience a sense of legitimacy in their participation, undermining their agency.

It is curious how little the recent history of interventions to address gender inequalities has been drawn on in the resurgence of interest in single-sex organization. In the Introduction we described how the problem of girls' participation in science, mathematics and technology was characterized very differently to the problem of boys' achievement in literacy and this may, in part, explain this. We turn next to consider the social context, which saw gender return to the policy agenda and the re-emergence of single-sex organization as an ameliorating strategy.

The position in England

Throughout the Anglophile world education is based on the principle of equality that emerged in the post-war consensus about citizens' rights to equal provision. In the UK the Sex Discrimination Act (1975) and the National Curriculum established a legal framework to protect the right of equal access to the curriculum for all children. Single-sex teaching takes place within standards debates on the one hand and aspirations concerning diversity on the other. By placing our discussion of the current rationale for the advocacy of single-sex organization within the context of other contemporary positions we aim to make visible how the learner and gender are perceived. The reporting of national assessments of individuals at three key points in their educational careers (ages 10–11, 13–14 and 15–16) and their publication in league tables according to overall levels and grades of performance achieved by a school, made public aspects of differential performance between boys and girls. The validity of comparing performance based on changing assessments year on year is questionable in itself. However, for the purposes of this book the main issue is the *form* of reporting. The evidence suggested that the gap between girls' and boys' performance overall was narrowing in science and mathematics and was no longer significantly different, whereas the advantage girls had overall in English and modern languages was sustained. Girls were also achieving more and higher qualifications than boys. The form of reporting masked the evidence that progression year on year was occurring for both groups and that the overall findings did not occur consistently across all subjects or aspects of subjects (Murphy and Whitelegg 2006), or across all boys and girls, or schools. The literature on gender, achievement and schooling is considerable (e.g. Mahoney 1985; Kenway *et al*. 1997; Datnow and Hubbard 2002) and the forms of reporting have been the focus of much critique (Gorard 2000; Skelton 2001; Connell 2005). For our purposes we want to focus on the debate only in relation to single-sex organization as the solution to the problem.

The evidence of boys' relative performance to girls overall, and specifically in English, was not a new phenomenon in England or in other countries but it, along with single-sex organization, took on a new dimension because of the convergence of a number of socio-historical and political factors. The oil wars in the 1990s, the collapse of the industrial base, the emergence of post-Fordian working patterns and the globalization of the economy created a renewed sense of social transition at the end of the millennium. The need to compete in the international arena set alongside increasing fears about the futures of boys dispossessed within the labour market heightened the significance of literacy. The historical development of the curriculum had from the beginning valued symbolic labour, which is epitomized by literacy. A literate workforce was judged essential to compete in the knowledge economy. Symbolic manipulation had become the desired capital and it was the subject in which boys were failing most obviously in comparison to girls. Therefore the need for action in relation to boys became paramount.

A further influence was the recognition of the success of intergenerational mobilization by the middle classes in promoting their girls, and of feminists in challenging the social construction of women's restricted realms, which reinforced beliefs that the co-education system was biased. Current evidence and historical precedent indicated that single-sex organization could ensure an effective learning environment for boys. Therefore, as with the liberal feminist approach, single-sex classes were advocated as a form of repair or compensation within what had become imagined as an overly feminized school environment. As we noted in the Introduction, the reported differences in achievement challenged not only the current cultural belief that as groups boys and girls were equal but also the longstanding belief in male superiority associated with a history that saw education as the birthright of upper- and middle-class males. There was also concern that the public domain, hitherto where males held dominion, was now being overtaken by females (Yates 1997).

At the same time educational reform policies established an accountability framework in which schools were responsible for student performance, and parents were positioned as clients, ostensibly with the right of choice in relation to provision though not necessarily with the means to mobilize that right. Genuine choice relies on groups having the social and financial resources to exercise it, and therefore it is not distributed equally across social groups (Apple 2000; Ball *et al.* 2000; Whitty 2002; Ball 2003; Ball and Vinvent 2006). Together these educational policies were part of a larger reworking of education underpinned by neo-liberal theorizing. One assumption therefore was that parents would choose schools with the best performance record and that this would serve as a means to raise standards by placing schools in direct competition. This presumes that meanings and values are similar across social class groups and fails to recognize that class shapes meaning-making, in much the same way as we argue that gender does.

This shift towards a decentralized, market driven education system and the resultant commodification of education created pressure on schools to acquire distinct identities for marketing purposes. The belief in the superiority of single-sex schools through the historical association with elitism, fuelled by league table results that could not, in their manner of reporting, reflect adequately differences between school populations or schools, provided one potential marketing ploy. This was the ploy that underlay the move in Monks School to instigate single-sex organization, which did indeed see intake rise as a consequence. Therefore the aim of single-sex classes in

England is somewhat Janus-faced. Schools use the caché of the single-sex label to market themselves on the one hand and yet use a rhetoric that suggests that they will provide reparation for the feminine bias that is believed to exist in schools. Hence the take up of the strategy may say more about which parents rather than which students are being targeted by the move to single-sex organization.

Arguing within a civil liberty framework, Cornelius Riordan (1997, 2002) adopts a position, in his advocacy of separate classes for minority group boys in the USA, that raises questions that apply equally to the position on single-sex organization current in England. For example, in line with liberal feminists he sees the approach as *compensatory*; to redress the unequal social positioning experienced by minority groups of boys (Riordan 2002). Riordan argued that co-educational schooling failed minority groups, evidenced by their poor achievement in public examinations in comparison to other groups. Therefore he advocated removing minority-group boys from white boys as well as from girls.

According to Riordan, minority groups become sucked into subcultures that are deviant and which come to dominate in co-educational schools. In this deficit view Norma González (2005) argues that culture is seen as a holistic configuration of traits and values that presumes 'rules of behaviour' for diverse populations. This denies individual agency and positions groups' social and cognitive resources for learning as deficient, rather than as different, forms of competency. School cultures, according to Riordan, can counteract youth cultures if they maintain an 'academic culture' such as he observed in his research in Catholic single-sex schools. The separate class strategy for Riordan achieved a dual purpose. First it provided spaces for minority-group boys. Second it ensured that those specialist spaces deployed pedagogic practices that encultured boys into an academic culture rather than a black youth culture, which Riordan believed carried a masculinity oppositional to academic masculinity; the latter being the route to acquiring cultural capital. Neither Riordan nor Streitmatter engage with what an academic culture might mean in different subjects and how the historical legacies that we discussed above position individuals and mediate their participation. Streitmatter's position assumed a feminine academic culture would flourish once the conditions of a masculine free space were achieved. Riordan, on the other hand, placed the burden to produce the academic culture on two sources, the teacher and the parents' right to choose the school.

Riordan's focus on the proactive choice of parents is an important move in his argument that distinguishes his position from that of Streitmatter's. It aligns him with the same individual liberal assumptions that underlie educational policy in England in which parents are assumed to value achievement as a form of cultural capital and choose schools that will provide their children with academic success, thus separating them from 'others' (Ball 2003). Riordan's argument is therefore particularly pertinent. He based his belief on the evidence that the impact of single-sex schools on educational achievement was strongest in societies in which they were a minority type of school and therefore part of a highly selective situation; findings corroborated in the English setting (Gillborn and Youdell 1999). In seeking equality for minority boys, Riordan gives value to a system that is predicated on the differential valuing of students by schools. This same conflict we suggest underpins the advocacy and take up of single-sex organization in England. When parents opt into a school of their choice the assumption is that they are in agreement with the values, pedagogic approaches and curricula maintained by that school, which generates a shared relationship between parents, teachers and students (Riordan 2002: 20). The future imagined within this position remains market-dominated and the minority-group boy is reconfigured in line with white academic masculinity.

It is useful to speculate on the pedagogic assumption in Riordan's argument. The rationale for single-sex organization in England has identified lower ability males as the target group and so there is a similar need to be alert to essentialist views of culture and a cultural deficit approach. Younger and Warrington (2002), in a study of four co-educational comprehensive schools in England all attempting to address underachievement, particularly that of white working-class boys, suggest that 'street' culture which emphasizes a hegemonic masculinity of 'laddism' is prevalent among boys who drop out. They argue, in a similar fashion to Riordan, that the values embodied in this version of masculinity are oppositional to an academic culture, as learning and achievement are perceived as not 'cool', which corresponds with Epstein *et al.*'s (1998) research findings. The strategies to address this perceived conflict tended to focus on providing support to boys to resist peer culture pressure and to take risks in adopting behaviours that transgressed peer culture values and ways of being. This approach allows space for boys to reflect on and reconstruct versions of masculinities but it is less clear how this articulates with pedagogical approaches in subject classrooms, which similarly allow for different subjectivities. The authors recognized that pedagogic approaches were less developed in the schools and highlighted the need for these, but give little insight into what effective pedagogy might entail.

Riordan's position on the other hand suggests that, through pedagogic intervention, identities can be supplanted. This, we argue, conflicts with sociocultural understandings of identities and human agency. As we noted in the Introduction, meanings are negotiated and distributed rather than being the property of individuals. A sociocultural approach recognizes that individuals have multiple identities that are neither bound nor stable, but constantly evolving and are developed through membership of, and engagement in, each of the communities to which an individual belongs (Wenger 1998). Giving recognition to individual agency is not to deny group agency. As Pedre Portes and Jennifer Vadeboncouer (2003) argue, membership of some groupings, like class and gender, and their associated values, routines and scripts, cuts across other communities and in some settings, for some individuals, can take priority. Group agency becomes proximal and social and educational priorities distal as the tools and practices of the group commodify the participants. It is the nexus of multiple identities that helps individuals to sort out what is and is not important – i.e. salient in a setting (Wenger 1998). Therefore to enculture students into an academic culture requires recognition of their multiple identities and how these influence their perceptions of salience and therefore their ability to identify with the practices and purposes in a subject culture. Teachers have to work with them and embrace them in the process of negotiate meaning in a subject setting.

This pedagogic device of cultural bridging requires a considerable amount of expertise from teachers to identify the forms of competency that students bring to subject settings that bridge to the practice and forms of competency valued in the subject. For example, Carol Lee and her colleagues working with minority groups of boys explored the structure of African-American languages including rap (Lee and Majors 2003) and drew on these cultural forms and hybrid speech genres to bridge students' understandings of literary texts studied within schools. This pedagogic approach allowed students to draw on their knowledge of talk and rap to recognize, identify and empathize with literary structures within school texts. The approach created classroom interactions that extended the practices and tools of the subject culture to the students in examining arguments and problems related to academic texts. In so doing it also extended to individuals an identity of participation and competency as they recognized themselves in the co-production of the academic argument. In this way identities are transformed and subject learning identities evolve. What is more, through interaction the academic subject culture expands to accommodate vernacular speech genres, reflecting the stance that agent, activity and the world are mutually constituting (Lave and Wenger 1991).

Cultural bridging in a sociocultural perspective is key to learning for all learners and the usefulness of single-sex organization, we argue, relates to the extent to which it supports this. Where cultural bridging is not enacted because of the absence of alternative pedagogic principles, teachers tend to draw on historical legacies of gender when faced with groups of boys in single-sex classes and the implementation of the strategy is undermined. Elizabeth Woody (2002) identified single-sex schools attended by minority group boys that were set up to extend choice and meet differential needs, and found that they were reminiscent of military academies, with a 'boot camp' mentality. Traditional pedagogy in boys' schools used extreme forms of disciplining and training en route to developing academic approaches. This reflects the Christian legacy enshrined in the curriculum for boys where the development of the mind necessitated the suppression and subduing of the body.

Single-sex organization as a pedagogic reform to achieve equality of opportunity articulated in educational policy proposals is based on an inadequate understanding of performance by sex group, and a limited understanding of how gender operates within and without school and across subjects and individuals. It was seen as the solution in itself, which Kenway and Willis (1998) describe as the curriculum-as-usual version of single-sex classes that lack a gender reform agenda. They contrast these with single-sex groupings that are used strategically (Rowan *et al.* 2002) to deconstruct readings of gender and reconstruct them, as for example in the work of Kruse (1996), Peyton Young (2000), Martino and Meyenn (2002), and Parker and Rennie (2002). Research into the strategic use of the single-sex strategy has, like the policy, tended to focus on boys, framed within the new field of masculinity studies and critical pedagogy. It draws attention to the transformation rather than the reproduction of gender culture and the diversity of social gender identities (Mills and Linguard 1997; Linguard and Douglas 1999). Yet other research, often eschewing the single-sex strategy, has explored the problem raised about literacy learning, providing detailed insights into ways in which boys can be facilitated to move more deeply into classroom literacy practices (Rowan *et al.* 2002). Our focus is somewhat different as we adopt a complementary sociocultural framing to explore what teachers do when faced with a national policy position taken up locally without regard to evidence about the efficacy of single-sex organization or any professional development support. In the next section, therefore, we look briefly at the evidence for the effectiveness of single-sex schooling and the current research that exists into the success to date of the single-sex grouping strategy.

Evidence, beliefs and benefits

The reliance on measurable outcomes in looking at performance and in turn the gender mediation of schooling has been widely criticized (Weiner *et al.* 1997; Raphael Reed 1999). However, even this narrow focus provides little evidence to substantiate the belief in the effectiveness of single-sex organization in supporting girls' and boys' learning in comparison to co-educational organization. Reviews in England and elsewhere point to the need to treat with caution the findings that single-sex organization on its own is a significant factor associated with enhanced achievement. Social, cultural and institutional factors have to be taken into account as well as the prior achievements of the student populations (Smithers and Robinson 1995, 1997; Arnot *et al.* 1998; Elwood and Gipps 1999). The American Association of University Women Educational Foundation (1998) concluded that there was no evidence that single-sex education in general 'works' or is 'better' than co-education and the long-term impact was not known. Furthermore, single-sex education was very broad and therefore defied generalization as one single-sex environment may be very different to another. Mael's (1998) extensive review in contrast suggested that there was evidence that females benefited particularly in mathematics and science from single-sex education, though again the findings were mixed. Spielhofer *et al.*'s (2002) study looked at the evidence at student level in England, taking account of prior attainment and some social variables, and concluded that girls in single-sex comprehensive schools achieved better results than their peers in mixed comprehensive schools, and that this was particularly striking in science. Smithers and Robinson's (2006) summary, which took account of the evidence above, and that of other international studies, reported an emerging consensus across countries that there was little evidence of consistent advantages for single-sex schools (p. 5). While noting the difficulty of comparing like with like they felt able to conclude that ' "good" schools were not good because they were single-sex' (p. i).

Because of the inconsistent findings and the difficulty of controlling the multiple factors that influence achievement in school, proponents continue to disagree about the relationship between single-sex schooling and achievement. Therefore a number of beliefs about its efficacy continue. One such belief was evident in the feminist challenge to co-education in the 1980s – i.e. that girls in single-sex schools were more likely than their peers in co-educational schools to choose to study non-traditional subjects such as mathematics and science. Early studies did find fewer polarizations in student subject choices in single-sex schools (Bone 1983; Stables 1990), and this is supported by later studies (Spielhofer *et al.* 2002). Other studies in contrast suggested that gender differences in subject preferences continued irrespective of school organization (Colley *et al.* 1994; Francis *et al.* 2003). The findings about subject choice and school organization are limited and inconsistent and what is not known is what happens at classroom level to influence students' choices and the role of teachers, parents and social class in these decisions.

Another belief is that single-sex schooling has a positive impact on self-concept. How self-concept is understood, however, varies between researchers. Smithers and Robinson (2006) define it as 'what a person holds to be true about his or her personal existence' (p. 21). We use the idea in relation to belonging and identity in that self-concept is about students' images of themselves in relation to a subject, both in terms of the present and the future possibilities they can imagine for themselves. A study in Belgium found that girls in single-sex schools reported a greater sense of belonging and integration in school than did their peers in mixed schools, and socioeconomic background did not affect this finding (Brutsaert and Van Houtte 2002). The American Association of University Women (1998) review concluded that there was some evidence of more positive perceptions of cognitive competence and higher self-esteem for girls in single-sex education. In contrast Dale (1969, 1971, 1974), as we noted, reported an advantage for co-educational schooling for both boys and girls and this is supported by other studies examining self-concept (Marsh et al. 1988). Co-education is generally believed to advantage boys more than girls but evidence is limited and again inconsistent (Dale 1969, 1971, 1974; Brehony 1984). Sara Delamont (Delamont and Duffin 1978) referred to the 'double conformity' which middle-class girls in the nineteenth century faced and Susan Watson (1997) in her large-scale study of school choices in New Zealand argues similarly that the desire for a single-sex school is a 'double-edged sword'. Single-sex organization gives girls access to academic success free from the distractions of the opposite sex but at the same time has to produce 'particular types of "girls" who can operate in the constraints and demands of heterosexual desire' (p. 380). There are several studies that report no effect of school organization for girls or for boys and given the problem with the construct itself there remains little evidence to substantiate the belief.

Researching the factors that influence learning in single-sex class-rooms is as difficult to do as comparing different types of school organization. Typically studies are qualitative, vary in subject context and in how effectiveness is judged, and can therefore inform about particular instantiations of single-sex settings. Michael Younger and Molly Warrington have carried out the most extensive research into single-sex classes in co-educational schools in England. In one study (Younger et al. 1999) of eight single and co-educational schools, teachers professed beliefs in differences between girls and boys but many believed they treated girls and boys the same or did not differentiate between them. This was not borne out by observations. Boys received more attention and more questions from teachers than girls did as part of a management tactic to maintain boys' participation. This is in line with Kelly's (1988) meta-analysis of teacher-student interaction studies. Girls tended to dominate in initiating questions and seeking teacher support. In a study of one mixed school that since the 1970s had established single-sex groupings across subjects, which places it outside of the more recent policy context, Kelly found students and parents were very supportive of the strategy. Teachers on the other hand considered the strategy advantaged girls more than boys. Lower ability boys were singled out as least likely to benefit from single-sex teaching, which is of particular significance given the tendency for them to be targeted by current policy as most in need of the strategy. Teachers in advancing this view invoked the cultural legacies discussed earlier of the unruly 'laddish' boys who en masse were uncivilized and who therefore missed the support and civilizing influence of girls (Warrington and Younger 2001). This provides further support for the concern expressed by many feminist writers that the strategy of curriculum-as-usual boys' classes may not challenge but exacerbate laddish cultures (Kenway and Willis 1998; Jackson 2002). The majority of teachers in the school reported that they did not consciously change their practice to meet the needs of single girls' and, separately, boys' groups but rather that practice evolved. This finding corresponds with that reported by other researchers (Sukhnandan *et al.* 2000; Jackson 2002; Younger *et al.* 2005).

In another article about the same school, Younger and Warrington (2002) caution about the dangers of implementing the strategy without associated staff development programmes. They argue the need for teachers to take into account the 'varying perspectives, views and feelings which girls and boys can differently bring to certain topics and issues' and caution against essentialist approaches (p. 371). The teaching strategies that they identify as beneficial, practised by teachers who explicitly attempt to differentiate practice for girls and boys, included for example variations in pace, use of group work, short-term clearly defined tasks with achievable targets and the valuing of collaboration and competition. None of which suggest an approach that emphasizes cultural bridging or any challenge to the construction of academic domains. The authors do emphasize that the strategy will only be effective when 'differential approaches to the teaching of boys' classes and girls' classes are systematically planned, and explicitly implemented' and evaluated (p. 371). It is perhaps surprising that they do not comment on the absence of these approaches given the time that the strategy had been in practice and therefore why they remain optimistic about its potential. There are other smaller scale studies (e.g. Martin 2002) which claim like Younger and Warrington a positive effect on achievement but do not (and indeed cannot) attribute this to the strategy alone.

Berge with Ve (2000), describing the use of single-sex organization in

Sweden, argue that it has been enacted in a very different context to that in England and remain tentative about its efficacy if used alone. A fundamental difference between the contexts of use is the absence of a commodified approach to education at the time of the study and the continuing support of a welfare state and community in Sweden. The educational aims the strategy was intended to address and the perception of teachers also differed. However, in both countries teachers have experimented with the strategy. In Sweden teachers were encouraged to experiment with pedagogic approaches as the tools for achieving equality. Single-sex groups were mobilized occasionally and for limited amounts of time and in specific subjects of the curriculum. Both boys and girls were targeted, and the aim was to change futures. The strategy went beyond curriculum-as-normal groupings and involved gender transgressive activities to expand the range of activities and ways of knowing available to boys and girls, in order to break down traditional gender patterns of work and relationships within the public and private spheres.

Berge with Ve found that teachers' commitment to equal opportunities practices was strongest when it was informed by personal transformative experiences that provided opportunities for deep reflection about gender norms in society, a finding echoed by Parker and Rennie (2002). They argue that teachers who had a reflective understanding of gender as a cultural legacy were more able to provide explanations to students about why they were being asked to undertake particular activities. When teachers did not have such experiences the authors found that they were ill equipped to challenge gender norms and address student resistance, and their pedagogic practices, even in single-sex classes, reflected gender cultural legacies. Martino and Meyenn (2002), in their study of single-sex organization in English classes, found only one teacher whose pedagogy was not mediated by normalized biologically based assumptions about boys, and attributed this to her knowledge of the social construction of gender.

There is little to suggest that there are clear advantages to single-sex organization from past and current research, yet the difficulty of researching it cannot be overlooked in making that statement. What has emerged over time and among very different studies is that there are merits in its use. However, which students are targeted, and when it is used, has to be carefully considered. We argue that the use of single-sex groups needs to be informed by an awareness of the influences of gender legacies on practice and an understanding of the interconnections between gender and subject cultures. Who teaches in single-sex classes and what kinds of support they receive are key.

Pedagogic futures

Single-sex classes have been advocated as compensatory or ameliorative strategies to address perceived inequity in subject achievements, and this policy position glosses two important levels of analysis: historical legacies and immediate classroom practice.

Cultural legacies are carried into classroom practice, yet not in simple ways, and it is in the complexity of this relationship that pedagogic strategies have to be developed. In England the learner targeted for single-sex provision was the boy and arguably the working-class boy. Single-sex classes were imagined as spaces that would restore a normative and dominant social representation of masculinity, weakened through contact with feminized environments. Such arguments invoke common sense ideas about biological difference. There are strong common sense ideas about gender that circulate and exert a powerful influence within classrooms, as we have indicated in this chapter and elaborate further in the following chapters. We can, as Rowan *et al.* (2002) argue, acknowledge where students are positioned to develop cultural bridging practices, without accepting masculinity or femininity as innate attributes of a boy or a girl. Students actively create culture and bring their cultural knowledge with them into the classroom. Sometimes this is recognized and sometime it is not. Learning takes place when what the student already knows is recognized and provides the basis for new sociocognitive constructions and, as part of this, for new ways of being to emerge. If the pedagogic discourse on offer provides no space for self-recognition or identification then learners' agency and potential to learn is undermined.

Pedagogic discourse is a discourse of aspiration; it projects students forward into what they do not yet know and into what they have not yet become. In imagining the future, teachers draw on ideas and world-views from within the culture of their specialist subject and like everyone else they also draw on dominant ideas that circulate in the press, in the pub, the café as well as those generated among participants in schools. Because the logic of the school is to produce future citizens, this aspiration is imbued with morality. In the historical overview we demonstrated how the moral aspect of schooling has changed across eras. Even so, the groups who have been excluded from schools historically are still controlled in ways that reflect that history. In taking students forward, deeper into the practices of their subject cultures, what kind of future is imagined by the teachers and what kind of spaces does that open up for learners to act, behave and produce according to the knowledge that they brought with them from other settings? We start to answer these questions in the following chapters. In the next chapter we introduce the tools that we use in our analysis of practice through an example from Palmers School to demonstrate how new constructions of meaning emerge in everyday classroom practice.

Chapter/ **Two**

Understanding the knowledge-gender dynamic in classroom practice

In the Introduction we explained in broad terms our way of understanding and researching the gender mediation of learning. In the first section of Chapter 2 we draw on one excerpt from our data to explore in greater detail the conceptual tools for analysing and understanding our observations, and teachers' and learners' accounts of their behaviours and experiences, and why we find them useful.

Palmers School: the response to gender and learning

Palmers School had instigated an initiative called 'The Year of the Boy', planned and carried out in the period 1998–2000 when our fieldwork took place. This was in response to the national concern about the disparity between the proportion of boys compared to girls gaining five A* to C grades in the General Certificate of Secondary Education (GCSE). (The GCSE is the examination taken by students at age 16 when they complete compulsory education in England. 5 A* to C grades is the national standard by which schools' performance is compared in published league tables.) In Palmers School the examination results revealed a 20 per cent gap between the number of girls and boys passing English language and literature, which compared with a national gap of 15.6 per cent in language and 14 per cent in literature in 1998 (Inter-group Statistics 1998).The headteacher of the school had requested that each subject department provide an agenda for addressing boys' needs that would close the achievement gap between boys and girls at GCSE. The English department was particularly vulnerable as the government and media focus highlighted a crisis for boys' literacy, associating inadequate levels of literacy with a range of disparate social anxieties. The pedagogic strategies and approaches that were deemed suited to boys, which we referred to in the Introduction, were therefore targeted in particular at teachers of English. These strategies reflected a return to traditional pedagogic approaches, which were circulated through the media, for example a return to a prescribed narrow curriculum – 'the three Rs' (*Guardian*, 14 January 1998); make 'boys read for an hour every day' (*Sun*, 6 January 1998). Other back to basics techniques endorsed in the media and in policy documents were to ensure a tightly structured learning experience to keep boys in control and on task. These included the use of writing frames, time limits on tasks, dividing information into bite-sized chunks for effective transmission and processing, and quick, sharp assessments, all of which reflected not only a particular view of gender but also of knowledge and learning, as we described in the Introduction. The school visit from the English adviser for the local education authority reinforced and legitimated these pedagogic strategies and techniques. Mrs Sharp, a teacher we observed teaching an all boys group, described the changes the English department had made. She explained that the key to raising boys' achievement was pace and high expectations:

> English is an exciting subject; let's make it exciting and ... in order to get high expectations the output has got to be high and you can't get that if you are not well planned, not well resourced, if you're not pushing them through. It is also a control; today you saw it when I said you have 20 minutes with your partner to build up those stories. 'Can't we have five more minutes?' 'No, that is your time limit', and they've produced within that time limit. If you gave them an extra five minutes they would take it but not produce anything more.

Understanding the social mediation of teachers' beliefs about pedagogy and what constitutes effective practice is an essential aspect of our research.

A social practice view of learning

We introduced our perspective on learning and knowing in the Introduction: learning occurs through participation in practice as people engage together in ongoing activity using the tools of their cultural community (Rogoff 2003). These cultural tools, or mediational means, shape activity so that understanding of individual action is always in relation to the mediational means in use (Wertsch 1991). Practice is therefore a social process of shared learning, thinking and knowing in relations among people in mediated activity. A social practice theory of learning assumes an agentive mind, and emphasizes the negotiated character of meaning, and the mutually constitutive relationship between context, people and activity. People and the world are therefore eminently flexible and continuously changing as the process of negotiating meaning constantly changes the situations to which it gives meaning and affects all participants (Wenger 1998: 53). Thus learning arises from the socially structured world and cannot be understood in isolation from it. Consequently we cannot separate Mrs Sharpe from social influences if we are to understand her practice and interpret our observations; the same is the case with students.

Context and arenas

We had to consider how to address social context in the interpretation of our data. Lave (1988) used the relationship between arena and setting to deal with context, where a setting is 'a relation between acting persons and arenas in relation to which they act' (p. 48). An arena therefore encompasses a setting and is public and durable in that there are enduring practices, i.e. taken-for-granted ways of behaving. The term 'arena' used in such a way is particularly appropriate when considering a school. It is within the arena that practice occurs and communities emerge. Here we are thinking of communities of subject learners. A school is defined by such factors as the buildings, its geographical location, the demographic distribution of its catchment area, and the local social and economic situation. It is also defined by other elements such as ethos and the relationships between school members, which become instantiated in particular practices such as wearing a uniform, and structures such as assemblies and timetables that might, for example, involve ability groupings. These features or practices of an arena are not directly negotiable by the individual and therefore transcend the experience of the individual, both the teacher and the student. An arena 'is outside of, yet encompasses the individual, providing higher-order institutional framework within which setting is constituted' (Lave 1988: 151). The arena of school, although providing this higher-order framework is itself situated and exposed to practices beyond its boundaries (Bruner 1996). In our research, what was of particular interest was the policy and media response to boys' achievement relative to that of girls. The influence of the headteacher and his view of the school and its values were very significant. Through his actions he represented to the teachers and the students that boys' achievement was problematic – but only *some* boys – and that the solution lay with the teachers. The adviser, and her views of the subject and policy in relation to it, was also a significant external influence. Without her legitimation what emerged in Palmers School may have been very different. In addition the timetable structure at the school allowed the English teachers to split groups in order to put into practice the gendered seating strategy.

Within an arena, practice and communities emerge. We therefore differentiate between communities within a school, looking at subject departments as potential arenas too, to account for discontinuities between the practices of different subjects, which have an enduring public nature. For example, in design and technology workshops there may routinely be more talking allowed than in other subject classrooms, aspects of uniform may be relaxed, but then aprons may have to be worn. A radio may be allowed to create a relaxed workshop environment; all taken for granted ways of behaving that teachers believe make the subject one within which students of a wide range of abilities can feel a sense of 'belonging'. Within the same school, entering maths classrooms may reveal a much more formalized set of practices. One can imagine, irrespective of the teacher, desks, which are separate, students with heads down working individually, very little movement and possibly an air of silence. To move would not be legitimate in a maths classroom and permission is usually required to do so, as in many other subject classrooms, whereas to move is essential in a design and technology workshop. Wenger (1998), recognizing the discontinuities of practices within large institutions, introduces the notion of a 'constellation of interconnected practices' (p. 127). We see the constellation as the school arena and the interconnected practices as the subject department arenas.

Context and settings

So what is a setting? The setting is constituted out of a person's activity and at the same time generates that activity, which is what is meant by activity being dialectically constituted in relation to context. Unlike an arena, a setting and an activity do not exist in a realized form but emerge between people and allow them to foreground subjective experiences. Subjective experiences are by their nature dynamic and transient in that the experience has happened and is never repeated. What endures is what individuals appropriate from that experience, though this is open to change as soon as new meanings are negotiated. Setting therefore functions as an index of time. In other words, as students continue to engage with settings in an arena – for example, a maths lessons in a maths department within a school – they develop their sense of what it is to 'do' a subject and to become a learner of maths. In this way students develop 'forms of competence' or identities as learners (Wenger 1998). We can think of students' subject identities as a 'trace' of their participation in subject settings (Holland *et al.* 1998). The arena, setting and its participants are engaged in a continuing dynamic.

We focus on the dynamic, the 'moment in action', in our data collection but the implications of this for the evolving identities of learners are also considered. The use of arena and setting is appropriate to our research concerns as it 'reformulates relations between the level of analysis of social practice in the everyday world and that of the constitutive order in relations with which experience in the lived world is dialectically formed' (Lave 1988: 171). Thus through arena and setting we can look at the context of activity in classroom settings and at the same time consider the context of that – i.e. the department, school and beyond – and how this shapes the dilemmas experienced by learners undertaking the activity. The concept of community (Wenger 1998) emerges in the intersection between the arena and the setting as experienced by the individual. By investigating the community it is possible to understand teachers' practices within that community, and the learning that is made available and to whom.

Learning as formation of identity – power, negotiability and identification

If we return to Mrs Sharp, what she brings into the setting is key. So in understanding observations in a setting we pay attention to the teacher as part of the participatory framework. However, the teacher has a very different role in the setting to students. Teachers supply the structuring resources for learning and access to what is learned is mediated through the teacher's participation and an external view of what knowing is about in a subject. Access to what could be learned is further mediated by teachers' understanding of gender in relation to learning. In Mrs Sharp's words:

> ... when people say that the boys are naughty, that they lack concentration, that they are messy, they are casual about their homework, casual about bringing books, presentation of their work and pride in their work and they are not really interested in pursuing the ... pursuits of language and literature study, they have to be made interested by [an] all singing all dancing teacher. I actually think a lot of that is complete myth. I don't believe it at all. What we don't do enough of is focus on what boys do have the success of.

[We] term what we deem as disruptive, for example a boy making a lot of noise means he is disruptive, could actually be twisted around to the boy ... is making some witty, articulate contribution to the conversation, or to the discussion that is already taking place. This desire [of the boys is] to please.

It matters greatly if teachers resist or embrace hegemonic cultural perceptions of gender and extend these to students through their practices. We also recognize the difference in power between teacher and students and between students. Practice is a shared history of learning in a subject and students have to be enabled to 'catch up' with this shared history (Wenger 1998). The teachers' responsibility is to open up practice to students. Issues of power in a social practice theory of learning relate to the ability of participants to negotiate meaning in a setting and to form identities as learners of subjects. Negotiability, according to Wenger (1998), is the facility and legitimacy to take responsibility for shaping meanings within the setting. To open up practice to students the teacher has to recognize the extent to which students feel able to negotiate meaning and this in turn depends on their ability to feel a sense of legitimacy in their participation in the setting, that is, their right to belong. Mrs Sharp's concern is that others' interpretations of boys' behaviour dissociates boys from English, and limits their ability to make connections with the practices of the subject. Because their way of doing English is not recognized it makes it more difficult for them to imagine doing English, and this limits the possibilities for their identities as learners of English to take on new dimensions. Identification is how this process is described and it can work through association and opposition by connecting or disconnecting students in subject settings. Identification depends on the pictures of the world and of ourselves that we can build (Wenger 1998: 194). Learning as identity formation and identity as 'forms of competence' are central to how we interpret our observations and teachers' and students' accounts. We also consider the processes of negotiability and identification in understanding how students experience agency in different settings. To elaborate this we turn to Mrs Sharp's classroom at a particular moment in time – i.e. when a particular setting was orchestrated.

Agency and identity

Assumed throughout this discussion is the notion of the agentive mind, which is proactive, constructive, selective and directed to ends to which learners and their teachers are committed (Bruner 1996). We refer to 'mediated agency', as in a sociocultural view all individual action is shaped by mediational means, the tools of the culture. Agency relates closely to power, in that it is the realized potential of people to act on their world purposefully in interactions where different courses of action are possible and desirable, depending on the participants' points of view, which includes the teacher in our research. If we think of students' subject identities as a 'trace' of their participation in subject settings it is also a 'trace' of their experience of agency (Holland *et al.* 1998). In our analysis of the learning dynamic we do not *assume* agency, but consider how students' agency is mediated and whether this is empowering and extends their agency or disempowering and constrains it. Our concern is to make visible the mediational means employed in settings and the implications for students and their future learning. To consider agency and identities in learning we briefly consider aspects of Mrs Sharp's practice and one student's (Steven) experience of and response to it.

THE SETTING

The class Mrs Sharp took was a Year 10 single-sex boys' class. It included those boys who were seen to be achieving well – i.e. average or above average – and the issue was to nurture and maintain their achievement and extend their identity as people who do English. Mrs Sharp was the head of English and, therefore, had status within the school which was recognized by the boys. She set a creative writing task exploring different genres in novels. The students were asked to create three novel openings that would eventually contribute to the course-work element of the English language GCSE examination taken at age 16. The task took three lessons and each setting was observed.

The pace of interaction in Mrs Sharp's class was fast, energetic and challenging. Competition, autonomy and rivalry were continuously enacted among the boys, and humour was a common vehicle for their delivery. They did, however, defer to Mrs Sharp's authority. She used her verbal dexterity to maintain that authority, using the same forms of interaction that the boys did with each other. To the clearly inattentive Luke she jibbed:

> *Mrs Sharp:* Luke are you OK?
> *Luke:* Miss, I'm thinking.
> *Mrs Sharp:* No, you are thinking like you've turned your brain off mate.

She pointed out when the boys had not been clever enough or fast enough on the uptake, and used their forms of rebuke such as, 'James, shut up!' She also used their threats which invoked fear of exposure, such as when she singled out a boy with a 'mock' humiliating comment, 'I am going to embarrass you by making you stand up if . . .'

In the second lesson, after discussing genres and looking at examples, the students selected a genre and drafted a novel opening. Mrs Sharp used the strategy of asking all of them to read out an example to signal the worth of each of their contributions and to enable them to learn from each other. Steven was recognized and labelled with an identity of competence in creative writing in English, more so than other boys in the class; he was 'good'. This is not an easy identity for boys to manage as this creative expressive aspect of English does not align with 'masculinity' in subject discourses, as we noted in Chapter 1 and discuss further in the next chapter. Furthermore, being 'academic' in a 'laddish culture' is not deemed 'cool' (Jackson 1998). Wenger (1998) refers to identities as trajectories in constant motion that incorporate the past and the future in the process of negotiating the present (p. 153). They help us sort out what is important and what is not – i.e. what contributes to our identities. Individuals have a multitude of selves that are neither bounded nor stable but constantly changing and are developed through membership of, and engagement in, the practices of each of the communities to which an individual belongs. How an individual behaves in each community may vary as we 'construct different aspects of ourselves and gain different perspectives' (Wenger 1998: 159). Thus there was a tension for Steven between his needs to maintain his identity as an obviously identifiable and acceptable boy within the peer culture and his concern to maintain his identity of participation as a learner of English.

Reconciliation of these tensions is an active, creative and very personal act that is, by its nature, invisible. What is observable is the product, the improvisations students undertake to allow goals to be achieved. This is the outcome of mediated agency. These twin notions of reconciliation and improvisation allow us to think about interactional moments, where the process is the product (Wertsch and Stone 1979: 21), and the possibilities and constraints that they create for individuals (McDermott 1996: 290). The requirement for a public performance of reading out a draft was salient in Steven's work of reconciliation. He trod a line in producing his text that he felt allowed what was important to him in maintaining face with his peers and what was in his view identifiable as 'good' English. Davies (2003: 9–10) talks of children's need to 'get it right', which means practising the culture in an identifiably individual way. This requires students to understand the ways in which cultural practices can be varied.

'The deformed banana', Steven's novel opening, revolved around a central character, a banana, that was misshapen and in seeking friendship experienced rejection by other characters. Steven used two devices to maintain his position in the peer culture. One was to deploy humour and absurdity. The humour arose from the way human emotions were attributed to a banana and was emphasized by the nature of Steven's performance. Jokes are a form of display by boys, for boys (Filer 1997). Steven played to the crowd and built in pauses for the boys to recover from their fits of laughter before delivering the next absurd and hilarious twist of the tale. The second device was to use the banana as a vehicle for his voice, which allowed his expression of emotions related to deformity to be distanced from him. As we discussed in Chapter 1, interior knowledge that is creative and flows from the person outward is aligned with the body and femininity. Scientific knowledge, on the other hand, is associated with the mind and reason separated from, and external to, the body and aligned with masculinity. Objective/subjective is a classic gender binary and the creative writing element of English tends to be associated with texts which describe interior subjective knowledge rather than exterior objective knowledge. When a student produces a creative writing text there is a general expectation that it reflects something about the person who produced it. Thus being a boy in an English class and making visible your interior knowledge is a high-risk activity that requires the boy to find a 'masking' strategy, a common way of handling transgressive identities. As one boy in the class commented: 'I think it is harder to write about real things because if you were writing about them, then if people read them they would like know what your thoughts were about things. Whereas if it is just a fantasy thing it is not going to reveal anything unless you want to reveal it.'

Wenger (1998) considers identity to be the pivot between the individual and the social. Lloyd and Duveen (1992) and Abreu (1995) similarly insert social identities as a pivotal structure in the dynamic of learning. In talking about their strategies for maintaining identities the boys interviewed spoke about the pressure they felt from peer group banter, and from the need to present themselves in a range of ways that was policed by other boys. In interview Steven revealed that in crafting his novel opening he was working for a positive reaction from his peers: 'Yeah I wanted to get a reaction from somebody who was reading it you know ... You understand that when someone says "Oh that's really good" or somebody's laughing.'

The text demonstrated Steven's expertise at English in his depiction of the emotions of rejection and shame experienced through his character. He chose in his writing to express his thoughts about a serious issue such as deformity, as he understood this to be a legitimate practice for English. In interview he described this practice: 'It's like putting on a different pair of shoes, experiencing something that would not normally happen. You train yourself into different scenarios.'

Other boys also spoke about creating alternative realities in texts in order to explore emotions by expressing them through an imagined, alternative world (Murphy and Ivinson 2005). The language Steven used was sophisticated, witty and funny. However, Mrs Sharp's reading of the text was influenced by the performance of it. She controlled the classroom ethos and Steven, playing to the crowd, in some senses infringed her authority, an authority she saw as essential to enable boys to be boys while also ensuring they were controlled and on task. This emerged as Mrs Sharp described the subject matter of Steven's text as somewhat 'immature'. In our interpretation it was the influence of her working to align her practices and discourse with what she understood to be traditional or hegemonic masculinity that led to her particular reading of the performance. This in turn mediated her reading of the text. From talking with Mrs Sharp after the lesson it was clear that she had not recognized Steven's central theme which was not about humour and deformity but about the emotion of rejection. For Mrs Sharp the vehicle of humour dominated, and the content of the story was not salient to her. While Mrs Sharp carefully picked up on features of the 'boys' world' as motivational strategies she did not recognize that Steven, like many boys, was experimenting with emotions within imaginative scenarios.

Steven knew the risk he was taking; he was socially competent in that he knew both how to appear unremarkable within the terms of the identities extended to him in the setting, and that he had to conform to the knowledge boundaries and the acceptable forms of knowing in English, which were policed by Mrs Sharp. He was quite clear that the novel opening was primarily aimed at his male peers in a way that would reinforce his popular social identity. This is what we understand as mediated agency, as the text constrained Steven's expression of English to meet the goal of maintaining a social gender identity. He also competently read Mrs Sharp's evaluation as a clear indication that in her terms his text did not represent 'good' English – it transgressed the academic code. His solution was to reject the novel opening for submission in his coursework portfolio. Our concern is with the degree of effort required of students like Steven in creating improvisations in order to maintain positions in subjects, and as part of their work of reconciliation, realizing that the product of such effort may be valueless in the subject because of a gendered perspective.

Gender mediation of learning

We argue that there are complementarities between social practice perspectives of learning and poststructuralist views of subjectivities which we can usefully apply to understand the gender mediation of subject knowledge construction. For example, the notion of multiple identities reflecting membership in multiple communities links to the notion of multiple recognitions and commitments that underlie the process of subjectification. Conceptualizing identities as trajectories in constant motion highlights similarities between this view of identities and subjectivities. Both are seen as achieved in relation to others, constantly evolving and shaped by mediational means, such as ways of speaking and making meaning in specific contexts or settings in which particular discourses are employed. Wertsch (1991) refers to the way that schools instantiate social categories such as 'masculine' or 'feminine', 'normal' or 'special', to reduce ambiguity and increase clarity. He argues that schools have always created categories simply because everyday life is more complex and ambiguous than institutional resources can cope with. As we noted in Chapter 1, when discussing the re-emergence of single-sex organization, the external pressure to formalize, categorize and clarify school life has increased in the UK, driven by the need for accountability and indeed an accountancy culture in the creation of educational markets. The drive towards classifying and then counting students' 'output' in terms of achievement has made social categories very salient within school cultures. The categories, and the processes through which they are deployed and worked, are features of institutional life, and institutional uses of such categories 'construct' the identity of a student in relation to socioculturally situated assumptions (Wertsch 1991: 37), in the same way that the process of subjectification is described as constituting and reconstituting people through the discourse and the practices they have access to (Davies 2003).

Sociocultural perspectives of learning and poststructuralist understandings of gender do not segment time; histories are understood to influence the present and the present influences how we understand the past. Therefore, as part of our analysis of the process of gender mediation we consider some potential historical influences to help understand teachers' practices and how these reflect their representations of their subjects in relation to gender. We also consider students' perspectives of their positioning in different subjects to help interpret their actions and understand what mediates their agency.

In looking at potential historical influences we are concerned with the way hegemonic perceptions of masculinity and femininity emerged and were characterized, because of the cultural legacies that align subject knowledge and gender, as we suggested in Chapter 1. Central to the process of identification, which connects and disconnects learners with subject communities, is the notion of positionality (Holland *et al.* 1998). Teachers' practices and discourses draw on gender-subject narratives and through them associate girls and boys differentially with subjects, extending to them identities of participation or non-participation. In this sense knowledge is proprietary, associated with categories of people, and teachers' practices cue this identity. Students may therefore develop different positional identities in different subject settings because they are afforded different positions in them (Holland *et al.* 1998). This experience of positionality, as we noted with Steven, mediates students' experiences of agency, and of identification, and therefore their potential to develop expertise. To understand Steven's actions in using the banana as a medium for his voice we referred to the historical legacies that align interiority with femininity and exteriority with masculinity. When Steven disguised the exploration of the emotion of rejection behind the amusing character of the deformed banana he was aligning his writing with cultural legacy of 'the man of reason'.

Similarly, to understand Mrs Sharp's classroom practices we recognize that she drew on symbolic elements (Zittoun *et al.* 2003) from social representations of gender (Duveen 2001), distributed across culture to help her achieve her aims. She rejected some of the contemporary hegemonic representations of masculinities such as those captured by the term 'laddism' that labelled boys as naughty, unfocused, messy, casual and disorganized. She had an intuition that by working with the positive aspects of masculinity that were culturally available at the time she could enhance boys' achievement in English. The fast pace, the witty repartee, the focused attention given to each boy illustrates how she adapted her practices in line with her beliefs about boys' ways of working. She reinforced the values of independence and individuality by ensuring that every boy was given a turn to read out his novel and by giving them choices, albeit limited, such as 'you can write notes if you want to but you don't have to'. In adopting some of the shared common sense conventions of the boys' world, Mrs Sharp was actively working with cultural legacies of masculinity.

Cultural legacies of contemporary pedagogic practices

The stories that societies develop to explain humanity's relationship with the world, as we suggested in Chapter 1, are closely bound up with cultural legacies of masculinity and femininity. In each era the stories that societies construct about gender have incorporated and rearranged earlier ideas (Williams 1984; Arendt [1958] 1988). For example, the early Christian spiritual framing of social life constituted a break with the Greco-Roman era of high antiquity (Arendt [1958] 1988) and yet ideas about feminine inferiority inherited from the Greeks were re-appropriated by Christian churches (Kung 2001) and influenced dominant ideas and discourses about gender in the medieval era.

Current debates about single-sex organization have, as we discussed in the Introduction, revitalized the biological metaphors, which hold the gender polarity in place and re-engaged education in debates about alternative pedagogic strategies. Scientific metaphors are continuously absorbed into everyday discourses (Moscovici 1988) and offer frames of reference for understanding and talking about masculinity and femininity. These metaphors reinvigorate cultural legacies, which positioned women relative to, and inferior to, men. The press headlines, which we referred to in the Introduction, depicted gender as biological, innate and fixed. However, this genetic image of gender can be viewed as just one of the many metaphors that have been used down the ages to describe and explain gender difference. As Davies (2003: 12) comments: 'New discourses do not simply replace the old as on a clean sheet. They generally interrupt one another, though they may also exist in parallel . . . undermining each other perhaps, but in an unexamined way'.

Our analysis of the newspaper headline stories about boys' relative achievement to girls detected chains of signification through which a disparate range of social concerns coalesced into an increasingly unified story about 'the troubled boy' and which, once formed, appeared to have an indisputable ring of truth about it (Heider 1958; Jodelet 1991; Moscovici 2001). 'The troubled boy' then acted as an attractor as well as a crucible for a series of deeply felt anxieties that were accompanying the run up to the end of the millennium, a time when societies take stock, reflect on the past and imagine their futures. Once the social representation of 'the troubled boy' had gained the status of common sense truth it was almost impossible for teachers to object to directives voiced from every strata of society to design pedagogic interventions to address boys. Yet as self-appointed consultants emerged there was very little sound education research available for teachers to draw upon to help them understand gender. Therefore, common sense beliefs about gender imperceptibly informed pedagogic interventions.

'The Year of the Boy' in Palmers School can be seen as a local response to a perceived problem of boys being excluded from the public realm. Deadlines are associated with the public world of business and by giving boys tight deadlines as part of her classroom practices Mrs Sharp was enlisting and revitalizing the historical idea that aligns masculinity with the public realm: 'Sometimes it takes guts to stick with your time limits because you think, oh what if they don't finish – but they always do, always, especially boys; they hate missing a deadline.'

The idea that boys are destined for the public realm, and not girls, forms part of the long tradition of gender culture that was revitalized, though not in a deliberate or conscious way, through Mrs Shaw's pedagogic practice. In effect, the past was drawn into the present (Dewey 1934; Jodelet 1991; Bruner 1996) and historical legacies were embodied and enacted through voices, texts and gestures.

To retain a view of the history of gender culture we intersperse descriptions of classroom practice with gender stories and start by telling two in this chapter. These reflect significant cultural shifts, which form part of the gender heritage, which we have argued serves as a resource to constitute gender identities. In both stories a cultural shift is reflected in a change in the discourse, either directly as in the first story, or indirectly as in the second, through the association of oppositional gender dichotomies with particular practices and relationships between people and the physical and social world. As Carol Merchant (1983: 101) notes, 'Because language contains a culture within itself when language changes, a culture is also changing in important ways'.

The first one is about how the public and private domains were created and is based on Carole Pateman's (1988) book, '*The Sexual Contract*'.

Gender story 1: the public and the private

The social contract theorists, Hobbes, Locke and Rousseau, re-framed the basis of social participation extant in the medieval period, by disconnecting civic society from the rule of God the Father. They suggested that social participation was founded on an original contract entered into freely. Their argument aimed to persuade people that it was in their best interests to submit themselves to the authority of the state and be bound by civil law, in exchange for the securities, benefits and rights of social life. Such an argument could have formed the basis for a society where there was equality between the sexes; however, the social theorists had no motivation to disconnect women from the rule of the husband, quite the opposite. To maintain women's low status with respect to men, rationality was conveniently put to one side and public and private life were separated. The construction of the public realm served to separate the sexes in order to perpetuate a hierarchical relationship between men and women. This allowed the argument to be made that marriage was not subject to the same rules as the social contract because it belonged to the private realm and was politically irrelevant. Under the social contract men enjoyed superior rights to women purely by an accident of birth, which gave them immediate access to the brotherhood of men (fraternal patriarchy), who enjoyed the political status of individuals, which was withheld from women. At the same time as being accorded autonomous political status men were given dominion over the private realm in compensation for working for the state in public life, such as in politics, paid labour and defence.

The public domain retained the links with work, war and objective reasoning. As we mentioned in Chapter 1 the public/private characterization of social life ensured that education became one of the instructional mechanisms through which girls and women were taught to know their place in society and, in particular, where they were trained to become wives and mothers. The contract theorists set up the social foundations that legitimated women's exclusion from communities where knowledge was produced. This also cemented associations between femininity and features such as caring, empathy and subjectivity. Such legacies re-emerge in everyday practice as individuals appropriate symbolic resources to resolve immediate problems. Educational strategies aimed at boys can be read as attempts to clarify, once again, what the public realm is and to ensure that boys reclaim their positions within it. We can see this reflected in the fears that were fed by media stories at the end of the twentieth century that schools had become contaminated by femininity.

Steven drew upon the symbolic resource of a 'deformed banana' in his creative writing text to impress his peers. Yet, his practice of masking emotion through the use of absurdity and humour aligns with deep cultural legacies of masculinity as rational, objective and disengaged from emotions. The epitome of the 'man of reason' was the scientist who expelled subjectivity, affectivity and personal engagement when he wrote texts. These features of masculinity were reinforced when particular developments in the practice of science emerged around the same time that the contract theorists were clarifying social transitions, which we now characterize as those that took place between the Middle Ages and the Age of Enlightenment.

The scientific method described by scientists such as Francis Bacon worked in exactly the opposite way to the deductive logic of textual analysis found in the monasteries, and later in the grammar schools of the fourteenth century, which relied on deductive logic. Knowledge was distilled from sacred texts by referring back to what had already been written, so that the particular followed from the general and the general was laid down in ancient books. Bacon's inductive method, in contrast to Aristotelian deductive reasoning, saw knowledge as empirically rooted in the natural world. For him science 'derived axioms from the senses and particulars, rising by a gradual and unbroken ascent, so that it arrives at the most general of axioms last of all' (Bacon 1620: aphorism 19). In contradistinction to his predecessors, Bacon imagined abstract reasoning as objective and unsullied by subjective, social and cultural influences. To maintain this perception of objectivity the process of 'coming to know' was portrayed as neutral, and the knower as necessarily separate from the known. Bacon was one of the first to write about the inductive method, and while controversial even among scientists at the time, it became one of the predominant views about how science is practised (Williams 2006). The next gender story draws on Merchant's (1983) essay 'Mining the earth's womb', which we use to demonstrate that as the world-view was changing, different metaphors – for example, about nature – emerged that related to gender.

Gender story 2: a new system of investigation

The notion of the living 'female' universe to be nurtured and protected emerged in Greek and early pagan philosophies. The image and language of nature or the organic conceptual framework brought with it an associated value system and ethical constraints. But as the economy became modernized and the scientific revolution proceeded the dominion metaphor spread beyond the religious sphere and assumed ascendancy in the social and political spheres. By the sixteenth and seventeenth centuries, the tension between technological development in the world of action and the controlling organic images in the world of the mind had heightened to such an extent that old structures were incompatible with new activities. Thus, whereas in the nurturing organic metaphor those who mined mother earth were portrayed as uncivilized brutes 'raping the passive receiving earth'. This was no longer a tenable image when societal needs necessitated unprecedented access to the earth's resources and the means for shaping them. At the same time the devastating effects of natural disasters and diseases directed human inquiry towards finding the means to control the outside world. Francis Bacon extended the metaphor from miners shaping the earth on the anvil to scientists and technologists. Scientific inquiry was no longer forbidden. By digging into the mine of natural knowledge mankind could recover the lost dominion. In his depictions of nature Bacon drew on images of nature 'in error', and 'recalcitrant' nature, characterizing an earth that imposed natural disasters on humanity. Bacon maintained the association of nature with femininity but now this was a femininity that was problematic. This was reflected in the female imagery deployed by Bacon to describe matter, as the 'common harlot'. As matter, the known – the feminine, was separated from the knower and by implication the knower was associated with man. The natural state was to be controlled and consequently the discourse invoked imagery which simultaneously strengthened a hierarchical relationship between masculinity and femininity. The notions of nature in 'bondage', 'bound into service' and put 'in constraint' depicted man operating on nature for the human good. Within this discourse miners, smiths and scientists became heroic figures. The new method of interrogation was not through abstract thought but through scientific method. Previous social constraints now became sanctions as the language of the culture shifted for human good. Scientific method and mechanical technology would create a new system of investigation that unified knowledge with material power.

Gender story 2 could have given us an alternative historical legacy to the one we have inherited. At the same time as the scientific method was being articulated Descartes, through his new philosophical method of radical doubt, reinforced the image of the separation of mind and body and mind and matter (Lloyd 1989). In *Meditations* (1641) Descartes depicted thinking as more 'real' than the bodily sensations. The world was viewed as mechanistic and divided into two realms, the internal world of the mind and the external world of natural phenomena. Knowledge was presented as objective. The gap that Descartes' method of radical doubt opened up between human reasoning and the structure of the material world had to be closed by invoking the existence of a veracious God. This endowed human reason with a quasi-divine character (Lloyd 1989: 115). Descartes' writings could have been seen as a liberating philosophy for women, separating the mind from the enfeebled female body. However, reason came to epitomize scientific practice and femininity became associated with the world outside the reason and logic of science. Descartes' legacy merely served to further associate man with, and dissociate woman from, reason. Scientific intuition was to remain free from 'the blundering constructions of the imagination' (Lloyd 1989: 116). A conceit grew that it was possible to know the 'true' nature of the natural world including that of woman and of man through empirical observation. While the monk had to repress temptations of the flesh to attain spiritual knowledge, the scientist had to suppress passion, sensuality and emotion in order to attain objective knowledge.

The need for boys and men to mask emotion belongs to a long cultural legacy that aligns emotions with femininity. When Steven told a story that masked emotion, he was not being perverse. He produced a text that he knew would appeal to the other boys because they would

University of Chichester

Borrowed Items 19/01/2016 14:56
XXXX9295

Item Title	Due Date
* Behaviour in schools : theory and practice for teachers	26/01/2016
* Better behaviour	26/01/2016
* Rethinking single-sex teaching	16/02/2016
* Motivating classroom discipline	16/02/2016
* School management and pupil behaviour	16/02/2016
Solving behavior problems in math class : academic, learning, social, and em	16/02/2016

* Indicates items borrowed today

www.intellident.co.uk
email support@intellident.co.uk

recognize absurdity, humour and outrageous fictional scenarios as masculine features of his writing. The assumptions that the boys shared and jointly recognized were grounded in gender culture rooted in the past. These markers of masculinity are culturally specific and draw on deep historical legacies (Willis 1977; Kessler *et al.* 1985; Connell 1987, 1995; Walker 1988; Mac an Ghaill 1994; Sewell 1997; Mills 2001). In enacting witty repartee, humour and jokes, these boys played out a contemporary version of masculinity. While symbolic markers of masculinity such as humour (Filer 1997) are recognized by many groups and individuals, the way they are taken up, used and deployed varies from person to person and from situation to situation. Later in the book we describe incidents when girls drew on symbolic resources, such as humour, that had masculine gender markings. We show that girls' uses of humour were not salient to teachers and remained invisible to them. Some boys were more adept at using symbolic markers of masculinity to achieve specific aims, effects and personal expressions than others and the same applies to girls' uses of feminine and masculine marked symbolic resources. Gender culture provides ubiquitous symbolic resources that individuals appropriate and use in a wide variety of ways. Therefore, gender has to be understood as a reservoir of symbolic resources that can be differentially appropriated and deployed by any individual, boy, girl, teacher or student. The effect of using symbolic resources that have recognizable gender markings, however, is not arbitrary and has social consequences that are borne out of the differential valuing of masculinity and femininity across time. In the next chapter we explore more fully the different cultural streams that constitute the elements of the school curriculum. We describe how the teachers who took part in the study responded to single-sex groupings and in the process how they managed the historical legacies of their subjects and the knowledge-gender dynamic within them.

Chapter/ **Three**

Reworking knowledge: teachers' beliefs and practices

Understanding practice

Participation or 'taking part in' is inherently social and assumes relations among people. These may be proximal, as when students and teachers engage in classrooms, or they may be distal. For example, when you read this sentence you may be alone but are trying to make sense of what we mean in the context of being involved in a shared educational concern. 'Shared' in this sense does not assume agreement but rather an assumption of mutuality that meaning can be negotiated in a joint enterprise for, as we argued in the Introduction, negotiating meaning is how we experience the world. If we imagine classrooms, workshops and school laboratories we know that what goes on in them differs. The similarities we might envisage reflect the enduring practices of the school arena. Even when these make the spaces appear similar in the organization of tables and chairs and a collective focus on a whiteboard or a text, we know that the meanings sought, the tools used, such as the texts, and the ways of interpreting and representing meaning differ. Wenger (1998) describes practice as collective learning and distinguishes it from 'just doing'; it is what we do in particular contexts with a particular history. The subject settings that we analyse are in this sense indexes in time of communities of learners engaged in particular practices. The use of the term 'community' in a school context is contentious as it is argued that, unless students elect into such a community and relate to and realize the collective motive, they do not reproduce practice, and evidence suggests that many do not (Roth and Lee 2006). We use the term here as a means of understanding learning and so take it to represent that collectively, in specific contexts such as school subject settings with particular pedagogical relations, meanings are negotiated with a specific prescriptive target practice in mind (Lave and Wenger 1991).

Teachers' practice includes all the resources and cultural tools that they draw on to 'do their job', which is to take students forward into the futures they imagine for them in relation to their subjects. Reifications are products of a community and serve as 'the way a certain understanding is given form' (Wenger 1998: 59). A community of practice, for example a group of professional scientists, produces: abstractions such as terms, concepts and formulae; instruments such as ammeters, pipettes and burettes; and processes which include ways of representing, decoding, interpreting and classifying. These become the focus for negotiation of meaning. Teachers draw on these mediational means, in their practice and in the discourse that they use, in personal ways. The history of the subject, teachers' representations of this, and their understanding of the goals of learning for their students mediate these ways. The department and the school exert influences too and the requirement to separate students by gender is one such example of this influence. Wider social influences, in particular the accountability that teachers face within and beyond school to achieve national standards and to maintain intake across social strata to resist the possibility of a school entering a cycle of decline, are another fundamental source of mediation of practice. The single-sex strategy in Monks School and the gendered seating in Palmers School were responses to these influences.

Knowledge-gender dynamics

Each subject of the curriculum can be viewed as a community with a particular historical lineage. We imagine subjects as cultural streams that are intertwined with gender. The discourses in a school subject are constantly reproduced and reconstructed in classroom settings. In looking at teachers' orchestration we focus on their discourse and practice, and how this reflects historical legacies. We consider how students may be orientated towards it and the consequences of this for their ability to feel that they can engage mutually in practice. In so doing we also consider assumptions made about access to and competency in the use and understandings of the subject's reifications, the cultural tools for thinking and acting, and the extent to which these extend to individuals an identity of participation. In this chapter we want to demonstrate how teachers manage the historical legacies of their subject and bring forward from Chapter 1 some of the beliefs about knowledge that became associated with certain subjects and certain groups. Our interest is in the proprietary nature of knowledge (Holland *et al.* 1998).

One such belief was that knowledge is objective, which derived from the primary belief that knowledge was pre-existent, which accorded it a symbolic value external to nature. The early association of God with rationality further compounded this view. As God is necessarily separate from the body, the struggle to be more God-like meant that the mind had to be divorced from the body. Early associations of everyday practices with forms of knowledge aligned women with work of the body, distancing perceptions of femininity from rationality and its pursuit. During the Enlightenment period, as we noted in gender story 2, with the ascendance of the scientific method rationality, the mind's ability to render ideas into delineated mental items corresponding to the structure of reality, became the property of man. As Guy Claxton (2000: 32) observed: 'The Enlightenment of the eighteenth century picked out just this one way of knowing and, in raising it to a high art, implicitly ignored or disabled any others: those that were not so clinical and cognitive, and were instead more bodily, sensory, affective, mythic or aesthetic'. So we can imagine how the opposition of mind and body became linked to the oppositions of objectivity and subjectivity, and exteriority and interiority, in discourses about the nature of valued knowledge and how these in turn mapped onto gender dichotomies. In Chapter 1 we described how a shift to include other subjects in the school curriculum such as modern languages and drawing saw these subjects redefined and restricted to include only those aspects that disciplined the mind. There was direct condemnation of learning to express oneself, which girls excelled at in French; therefore, value was given to correctness over fluency and grammatical knowledge over accent (Cohen 1996 citing the Taunton Commission).

The nature of school subjects has been transformed in many ways in recent times – however, teachers as members of communities of practice share a history of learning. In our analysis of teachers' practice and discourse we consider the masculine-objective/feminine-subjective associations as a potential influence mediating teachers' representations of their subjects. Since the historical legacy of, for example, the physical sciences aligns with versions of masculinity we might anticipate that boys and not girls are imagined as the legitimate inheritors of this knowledge domain. Drama, on the other hand, which relies on self-expression and values emotive, intuitive and passionate response, may be perceived as a subject where girls by right of gender are extended an identity of belonging. In this way we imagine subjects as cultural streams carrying forward gender identities sedimented in discourses, conventions and practices that teachers can unwittingly revitalize through their practice. We suggest that this happens in particular when teachers are confronted with a need to respond to gender as an emergent aspect in their setting and when they have no other resources to draw on to inform their actions.

Another dimension of curriculum knowledge that we identified was the association of functional knowledge with particular groups and the low status it was accorded compared with symbolic objective knowledge. This is not a strict demarcation, in a similar way to which objectivity and subjectivity cannot be seen as such. For example, we noted how knowledge of painting and sculpture became transformed and separated from other craft or artisan knowledge. The association of knowledge with vocation was the significant feature here. Art was not studied historically to become a professional artist but to improve the mind if one was male, and as an accomplishment, a pastime, if one was female. Sewing, domestic science and industrial craft (and later handicraft) were, however, viewed as pre-vocational training and not as education. The vocational element is significant because this associated forms of competency with gender and class groups. Again we can anticipate that the historical association of particular vocations with particular forms of practical knowledge might position girls and boys as groups differentially in teachers' practices.

As our intention is to provide insights to inform practice we were also concerned with the extent to which knowledge-gender alignments might create barriers to change for teachers. In practice, where knowledge is treated as objective and learning is the reproduction of knowledge, the mind is necessarily passive. The person has to subordinate her or his subjective understanding and conform to the rules and principles of the subject. Meanings are imposed from the outside (Moscovici 1984; Bernstein 1996, 1999). This in Wenger's terms gives primacy to reification over participation in teachers' representations of their subjects, which undermines the possibility of negotiating meaning and therefore human agency. Giving value to the subjective response assumes learning to be a process of knowledge creation as opposed to reproduction. Knowledge is dynamic and changing and the mind is agentive and recognized as constructing meaning. In this representation of a subject, participation is prioritized.

Why is this important? If a cultural legacy of belonging in a subject is attributed either to a boy or to a girl, and in the practice of a subject this is assumed, then an identity of participation and of competency may be extended to a group by right of gender, and withheld from others. As Dorothy Holland and her colleagues (1998: 135) point out, 'Teachers will take some students' groping claims to knowledge seriously on the basis of certain signs of identity. These students they will encourage and give informative feedback. Others, whom they regard as unlikely or even improper students of a particular subject . . . are less likely to receive their serious response'. This is problematic in all subjects but particularly so, we suggest, in subjects where a belief in objectivity, or a group's inherent incompetence closes down practice and the possibilities for negotiation of meaning, as those who are marginalized are doubly disadvantaged.

The implementation of single-sex groupings and gendered seating in Monks and Palmers School was premised on the curriculum-as-usual approach at school level. We have noted in the literature how such a strategy cannot only fail to challenge cultural legacies but reinforce and heighten them as teachers fall back on their beliefs about gender and about knowledge. In the next section we exemplify what this meant in practice in two settings orchestrated by a teacher.

Overt gender shaping in practice

In the following two extracts, Mr Hunt introduced the topic of 'joins' as part of a module on resistant materials, part of the design and technology curriculum, to a boys' and a girls' class respectively. The boys' lesson on joins was highly successful from Mr Hunt's point of view as the boys, a challenging Year 9 middle set (neither high nor low ability) were all engaged and committed. Mr Hunt invited us to observe him introduce the same topic to a parallel girls' class. The girls' lesson, however, went badly wrong. Mr Hunt could not account for this and expressed his disappointment and confusion. We compare the two lessons in order to throw light on how gender emerged in Mr Hunt's pedagogic practice.

Mr Hunt teaches boys about 'joins'

Mr Hunt introduced the boys to the topic of joins using a chronological narrative that began with the earliest known joins made with twine and progressed systematically to modern joins made with screws. He started by saying:

> *Mr Hunt:*   The idea of joining materials together goes way back.

His initial examples were from the Stone Age. He explained that the first joins allowed hunting weapons to be made by fixing stone flints to pieces of dowelling using twine. He used the whiteboard to illustrate a spear made with flint and wood. He said that when man became more sophisticated he needed fixtures that would be strong and permanent – for example, to make bridges across rivers. He explained that the joins used for the surface of early roads were temporary.

Mr Hunt:	Can you give some examples of joins that can be taken apart?
Sam:	Nut and bolt.
Peter:	Nail.
Rob:	Staples.
Mr Hunt:	What about permanent?
Kev:	Welding.
Mr Hunt:	Welding makes one piece, you can't unjoin it.
Nathan:	Glue.

He then described how man made primitive buildings with joins made from string, leather and bark. When man started to travel the high seas in rafts, he required flexible joins:

Mr Hunt:	On the high seas you might want your raft to be springy and flexible so that it does not come to harm; that kind of join goes back possibly 3000 years.

He explained that early man learned the technique of splitting logs to make wedges. As he spoke he sketched a three-dimensional drawing of two wooden wedges suspended above a block of wood with cut-away grooves where the wedges would be inserted. The boys listened as they copied the diagram into their exercise books. There was a fair degree of chat and spontaneous interjections as the boys made witty comments or responded to their teacher's questions, such as:

Sam:	The Tudors and Victorians would have not used wedges?
Mr Hunt:	Yes, the Tudors probably would have because most of the roofs were made of thatch but by the time we get to the Victorians most of the roofs were not. They used nails, I will draw a nail for you. [Mr Hunt draws a nail with a right angle bend in it]
Mr Hunt:	A blacksmith would have made that. Why was it shaped like that?
Tom:	To bang in a wall?
Mr Hunt:	No.
Wayne:	It's a tent peg.
Mr Hunt:	Right area. Think about the ground and a house.
Tom:	I don't know.
Joe:	Will you find out?
Mr Hunt:	I will find out for you. [Mr Hunt draws a diagram of a French nail]
Mr Hunt:	Could be bought at B&Q and a French nail is made of wire. Imagine a machine hits the top of the nail, it spreads it out. The technique is called 'upsetting'.

Alec: Whacking.

Mr Hunt: Yes, it is basically whacking. We don't use iron too much these days; we add something to it, not a metal, carbon. It's a black powder that makes the metal harder than iron, steel an alloy. Nails made of mild steel, not what we use for ... that sort of nail.

Mr Hunt's narrative assumed mutual engagement and a joint enterprise, and he made this explicit by engaging the boys in the history of the community of craftsmen who used joins. By mentioning the eras in which each join was invented the boys were invited to feel connected to a linear historical chain. Mr Hunt addressed the boys as the imaginary agents who built, travelled and invented, for example he said, 'If *you* were to take sandpaper', and 'That is the one *you* get now from B&Q'. He actively offered the boys 'images' that they could relate to and provided them with connections across time to their current lives, both within school and outside of it, to enable them to perceive salience in their activity. In these ways he enabled the process of identification with the subject. He spoke about the metal nails invented in the Iron Age and the modern, mass-produced screws used in contemporary DIY activities. At the same time he engaged them in a range of practices and ways of representing them using drawing, a cultural tool, and introducing them to techniques and terms. He said that if the boys went to B&Q they would not find the kind of hand-made nails that a blacksmith would have used to shoe horses, but mass-produced ones made by machines that 'looked like this', and he drew one for them. He explained that wood was a primitive material and it was only much later that man discovered that he could use metal to make things. He used and explained terms such as 'slotted steel' and 'countersunk'. Importantly, he approached joins as a 'concept' with overarching meaning and highlighted affordances between different types to allow the possibility for the boys to take forward their understanding to new situations. The boys were recognized as competent and he extended their agency by providing them with new resources to negotiate meaning in the subject. The history of joins was the history of man and the masculine valence of the lesson aligned with the historical legacy of resistant materials or handicrafts as a male domain.

Mr Hunt teaches girls about 'joins'

Mr Hunt started his lesson with the girls in a very different manner. He tried to create salience for the girls by structuring the lesson around objects in the domestic realm. He started by telling the girls:

Mr Hunt:	The posh name for glue is adhesives.

His delivery was much slower than it had been in the boys' class. He explained that the traditional material used for making furniture was wood:

Mr Hunt:	Wood is a traditional material. It is old fashioned; it could go back 5000 years. There are two things to worry about with wood. There are frames and carcasses. [He spells out the word] c a r c a s s e s. An example of a frame is something you are resting on at the moment – a table. Could you please do everything I say unless I say otherwise. What do you think a carcass is? How would you describe a wardrobe?
Bella:	A box.
Mr Hunt:	Yes.
Anna:	What about a chest?
Mr Hunt:	Yes, a chest of drawers would be a very good example. I notice that in the test you were spelling drawers wrongly. Let's talk about the test. Most of the drawing will be in three dimensions, which you will like.
Carol:	I don't like that.
Mr Hunt:	Notice when I start my drawing I start a little further down from the top. It is because of space. How would you show it was wood?
Kim:	There you see the veins, rings.
Mr Hunt:	What letter has the shape of a rectangle?
Bella:	L.
Mr Hunt:	Yes, why?
Sara:	Because it is half cut out?
Mr Hunt:	Yes.
	[Mr Hunt draws a three-dimensional table and a carcass on the whiteboard]
Mr Hunt:	The trouble is you have to hold that together with something. [Pointing to a join on the drawing of a table] What would you use?
Anna:	Glue.
Mr Hunt:	Yes glue. I know you are not very happy about three-D drawings, but they are not that bad. I suggest you do it very lightly.
	[A girl throws a rubber across her bench to another girl]
	That way you do not have to throw rubbers across the room, especially if you cannot catch it.

	[At this point some more girls throw rubbers to each other]
Melanie:	Sir, I can't draw them.
Mr Hunt:	What might tables be made out of other than wood?
Helen:	Polyvinyl table.
Mr Hunt:	Can you spell that?
Jane:	p o l y v i n a l.
Mr Hunt:	P o l y v i n y l a c e t a t e. I would appreciate it if you would not talk, you are stopping me from doing my job.
	[Later in the lesson]
Mr Hunt:	Have you ever seen your dad doing that, or your mum?
Gale:	[Laughing] Her mum? Have you seen her mum?
Alicia:	My mum!
Carol:	My mum wouldn't do that!
Mr Hunt:	It's not absolutely essential. If you want to be critical Carol, I can take it. I told you to move, now do it.

Differences between the boys' and girls' lessons

The narrative Mr Hunt generated for the boys included the heroic feats of man, community practices and male inventors from France, Holland and Germany responsible for developing the 'Pozidrive' and the 'Phillips screw'. He had no such history to call on to create a narrative for the girls. The slow pace of the girls' lesson in comparison to the boys' lesson reflects this absence. Mr Hunt aligned the girls with the domestic private sphere and treated them as users of technology rather than as producers. His attempts to turn this around and suggest practices that girls or their mothers might engage with ran counter to his own understanding of the subject and to that of the girls. To understand this we need to recall the discourses that were circulating when technology and its value in society was shifting (see gender story 2).

Joan Rothschild (1983) describes how the emerging discourse, which sanctioned technological activity, placed aesthetics in opposition to the technical and characterized femininity as passive and masculinity as dynamic. The female role was to stabilize by holding, protecting and preserving. Males were portrayed as the manipulators, the doers assaulting nature. In this way ideas about gender and ideas about technology became associated in industrial society. As Ruth Schwartz Cowan (1997: 218) observed: 'They [society] all agreed that there was some natural and necessary connection between working with your hands, being skilled, being independent, and being a good man'. This construction of masculinity affected the practice of technology; men could invent machines and women and children could operate them. However, when there was a struggle to maintain control over access to machinery, men appropriated skilled work and 'women's work' was restricted to the unskilled and routinized (Wajcman 1991). Consequently, 'technical competence' was seen as integral to masculinity and women were positioned as technically incompetent. David Layton (1993: 33) notes: 'We have tended not to think of what women do as in any sense technological, despite their involvements in survival technologies since the dawn of history'.

If we consider how the feminine has been construed in relation to technology we can begin to understand Mr Hunt's lesson with the girls. The historical legacy that aligns women with the home and 'outside' of technology is reflected, we suggest, in his positioning of the girls as users rather than as practitioners, and this mediates his practice. This is evident in his initial sentence where he refrains from using the terminology of the subject and makes explicit his belief that girls are more comfortable with everyday language than specialist language. Thus he denies them access to the reifications of the community and constrains their participation as a consequence. His focus on spelling extends to the girls an identity of incompetence in the subject, and more generally. He addressed the boys as agents while in the girls' class he invoked their fathers and future husbands in DIY activities, reinforcing their role as users. He addressed the girls as if they were observing items of furniture rather than making them. For example he said, 'Just imagine having a drawer of cutlery or jewellery'. By treating girls as users he limited his practice to artefacts as opposed to practices that transcend artefacts. His perception of the girls' realm was narrowly interpreted as 'home furnishings' and further limited their access to artefacts, materials and joins.

Further evidence of Mr Hunt's perception of the girls as outsiders who could neither manage the practices nor access the repertoire of the community was evident in his approach to their three-dimensional sketching; a common tool of the community for communicating ideas. Rather than opening up practice by engaging the girls in the use of the tool he drew attention to the 'difficulty' of the practice for girls. It was not surprising that Carol resisted Mr Hunt's suggestion that they would like three-dimensional drawing. Carol was reacting to Mr Hunt's framing and recognized how she was positioned. He kept suggesting that they draw 'lightly' in case they made mistakes and in this way encouraged the girls to be hesitant. At one point he said, 'before I do [draw on the whiteboard], I just want to say that this needs a lot of skill', and a few minutes later, 'This is not easy, not an easy one just to make, because of all the angles'. Another time he said, 'For those of you who feel they can handle the three-dimensional drawing, I would like you to try . . .'.

For Mr Hunt the key issue was that the subject was problematic for girls. Consider Mr Hunt's first reference to the girls about joins: 'The *trouble* is you have to hold that together with something [pointing to a join on the drawing of a table]'. It would seem likely that the breakdown of the lesson we observed reflected the girls' recognition of the outsider status extended to them by Mr Hunt. Mr Hunt, in responding to gender as a consequence of the school's single-sex teaching strategy, attempted to change his pedagogy and introduced many unintended effects into his lesson, which we suggest have a number of sources. The historical legacy of resistant materials provided an ample stock of masculine symbolic elements to draw upon and there was an absence of feminine symbolic elements. Hence, Mr Hunt, in attempting to create a girl-friendly pedagogic space, fell back on stereotypical beliefs about femininity in his practices in the girls' class. While the boys seemed to be flattered by the identity that Mr Hunt extended to them it was probably as unrealistic as the identity that he extended to the girls and which the girls resisted. However, Mr Hunt lacked the personal resources for reflecting on gender and its historical legacies in relation to his practice and treated girls and boys as homogenous groups.

In the next section we meet the teachers whose lessons in science, design and technology, English and drama were observed over time and consider how they described their subjects as part of the wider context for our later consideration of students' participation. Some of these teachers were reflexively aware of their use of gender and others were troubled by the competing influences of the historical legacies of their subjects and the need to teach that subject to boys or to girls.

Legacies: managing competing demands

Pedagogic discourses project students and knowledge forward in a variety of ways. Teachers explained how they taught boys and girls in single-sex classes. We detected within teachers' accounts traces of anxieties that were circulating in the press at the time when the study was conducted. We explore how teachers reconciled their beliefs about their subject with their images of the future.

Science

In the seventeenth century the discourse about the scientific method mapped versions of masculinity onto cultural representations of scientific ways of knowing and acting that were celebrated by the scientific community (Brawn 2000). These categories included, for example, abstraction, which was associated with masculinity and the mind, and was placed in opposition to holism, which was associated with the 'feminine' concern with the lived world and nature. The characterization of science and masculinity as impersonal and concerned with objects and of femininity with nurturing and care created a distance between women and science.

CURRICULUM STORY 1

> In the nineteenth century science served several purposes but for middle-class girls only the religious and moral aspects of science and the possibilities it provided for enhancing domestic accomplishments were seen as beneficial. Even the 'academic' curriculum that a minority of girls had access to differed from that available for males, relying on examples from the domestic sphere. The curriculum for males was to enable them to take up their roles in the public domain and while it included the physical sciences, it de-emphasized aspects of the biological sciences and excluded the domestic. The polarization between the biological and physical sciences continued in state provision. The labour shortage after the Second World War meant that for the first time in a period of peace, women were urged to take up jobs in industry and engineering, and to participate in science education on an equivalent academic basis to boys. Through the 1960s and 1970s students could, within the school structures made available to them, choose what they studied between the ages of 14 and 16 and their choices and the school option structures reflected the historical gender legacy. The failure of girls to take up the physical sciences emerged in the 1970s as a matter of national economic concern. For example, in England in 1978 23 per cent of boys compared with 6 per cent of girls entered for a physics examination at age 16. This compared with 14 per cent of boys and 7 per cent of girls entering for chemistry and 14 per cent of boys and 25 per cent of girls entering for biology (Sharp 2004: 32). Gender differences in access at secondary level, either through student choices or school option structures, remained until the introduction of the National Curriculum. This combined the separate sciences, which meant both boys and girls studied a broad-based curriculum. However, in some schools, typically selective and independent schools, students continued to have

access to the three separate sciences which remained the most highly valued academic curriculum route. Combined science, the subject taken by the majority of students, with its valuing of the biological sciences and reduction in the physical science component, was regarded by many in the science education community as a diluted version of the academic curriculum which continued to represent knowledge as objective. Critics of the science curriculum described students' experience of science as one where 'common-sense thinking is resisted, quantitative rigour is promoted and feeling and opinions are devalued' (Brawn 2000: 151). Furthermore, the policy of 'science for all' did not have the expected impact on girls' choices post-16. In 2005 in the UK physics was the sixth most popular subject for males at age 18 behind maths, general studies, English, history and biology. For girls, physics was the nineteenth most common choice.

MR WHITE'S BELIEFS ABOUT CHEMISTRY

Mr White, a physics teacher from Monks School, taught a series of lessons on the distillation of crude oil, a chemical process linked to industry and part of the physical science component of the science curriculum. He described some of his aims for the lessons as follows:

> Within the lesson itself it was a highly practical objective related to separating a mixture because different things boil at different temperatures. But the broader and in fact probably the more important aspect is that these materials that we use have to come ultimately from the earth's resources and I would hope they would have an idea, well they should know that the plastic has come from oil and the brighter ones will be able to recount at least some of the steps in getting from the oil to the plastic.

He said that he got 'very upset' when demonstrations did not work. His background was as a research scientist and from his point of view 'scientists must be honest in the work they are doing'. Consequently he resisted fiddling the results as this could undermine his credibility. One way to lose students' interest was to claim to have knowledge that you did not really have, which presented scientists, he said, as 'dishonest'. Mr White's emphasis on the earth's resources and his concern about scientists engendering mistrust suggest that he had absorbed some of the postmodern anxieties about the changing world. This has seen a re-emergence of interest in the organic metaphor where humans are positioned as caretakers rather than controllers of the planet. Mr White expressed his belief in the power of the empiricist method to reveal the inner essence of the natural world and this was apparent in the frustration he experienced when experiments failed. He wanted the discipline to reveal its truths so that students could 'see' these for themselves. Mr White's comments suggest he understood learning as a process of receiving a 'given' meaning rather than the negotiation of meaning. This was revealed further when he described his pedagogic role. He felt he had to break the subject down into bits to prevent students from becoming overwhelmed by its complexity: 'And trying to get them to see that although it initially seems impossibly complicated if you are prepared not to look at the whole thing and think wow, help, but rather to take it in little bits. It's accessible. So, it's partly, it's confidence building, don't be afraid of words.'

A danger was that boys 'lost the thread' and he could not get them back on track: 'I think the most powerful thing is we don't follow what's going on and as soon as you've lost the thread, the children have lost the thread of where we're going and then they switch off and sometimes its very difficult to switch back again.'

His structuring of the 'bits' reflected the metaphor of the teacher as the parent bird feeding the chicks regurgitated food in readily digestible form. He described his role as a leader, even a father figure, taking 'children' along a precarious path towards science. Yet, it became clear that he was imagining himself as a leader of boys rather than girls because he spoke about his surprise at finding the Year 9 girls to be 'confident', willing to 'join in', take risks and sometimes even 'give wrong answers'. In this respect he was taking on board assumptions about the 'feminine' mind which we discussed in Chapter 1 and which were evident in the cultural shift in the discourse about technology, where men were characterized as the doers and the manipulators of nature. Mr White said that the girls did not fit any of the stereotypes he held and they were easier to teach than the boys were because they followed him well. He said that in contrast boys were always 'shouting out', 'getting impatient' or being 'petulant' if he did not respond immediately to their queries. He seemed to imagine that boys required instant gratification and he said that if he got the timing a little wrong and made a boy wait for a response then the boy would experience acute rejection. In the following comment he imagined a boy demanding recognition for him: '... maybe they would petulantly say, oh it doesn't matter now. And *I wanted to talk to you earlier but you didn't want to listen to me and I'm not going to say it again*. Not saying that, but that's the – that's the attitude. That's much more likely with boys than with girls, if it's a science matter that you're talking about' (emphasis added).

This experience of rejection when boys wanted to discuss scientific matters we suggest was due to the fact that they recognized their right to belong and to have that membership legitimized through the teacher's response to their ideas. Mr White's lack of response prevented them from sharing in what matters. He described boys as vulnerable and scared as they waited on the edges of the community of practice of science. This fear of science he related to the inherent complexity of the subject and to the fact that it was aligned with the public world. He mentioned that the children might have negative images of science: 'this is for boffins, I'm too thick to understand that – sort of feeling might be going through their minds'. Losing the thread was to lose the chance to participate and to come to know, which was the boys' right, hence they 'switched off' when this happened. A great deal of his description of pedagogy was about helping boys, and building their confidence.

His surprise at girls' scientific competence provided further evidence of his take-up of the historical gender legacy of the subject. He said that he expected girls to be 'much more timid' than he found them to be. He also associated girls and their concerns with the personal and emotional. This alignment of the girls with subjective knowledge and interiority are gender dichotomies that are used to define what is not science and also locate girls in the private sphere that the contract theorists identified as the place for women. Mr White made it clear that he anticipated their assumption of belonging in this sphere in much the same way as he assumed the boys' right to belong in science. He invoked a classic gender binary in explaining how if a girl came to him with a personal rather than a scientific problem then he would have to treat her with the delicacy that was required in his responses to boys about a scientific query. In this sphere girls would demand recognition of their right to participate and have their contribution taken seriously. Following directly from the previous quotation, he said: 'I think if it was a more personal matter that you were concerned about. A girl had some problems that she'd brought into the lesson with her that she wanted to tell you about then she might well take that attitude, *you wouldn't listen to me when I wanted to talk to you*. The person and the lesson are different I think, there' (emphasis added).

We can see that in some respects Mr White's beliefs about science remained rooted in the past and in other respects related to how he imagined the future. His account revealed tensions between changing discourses about science and between science and femininity. Next we return to design and technology but to another teacher in Monks School who, like Mr Hunt, was teaching resistant materials.

Design and technology

In the earlier discussion we referred to shifting discourses, which sanctioned cultural changes in social actions in the industrial age and how these aligned versions of masculinity and femininity with aspects of technology. To add to this cultural context we consider briefly the curriculum context of design and technology.

CURRICULUM STORY 2

David Layton (1993) describes how the current curriculum drew upon three precursors. The first was the craft subjects that we have already described, taught by teachers often without academic qualifications as the knowledge associated with their practices continued to be associated with manual labour. The second precursor was the teaching of the processes of design, which gave intellectual status to the construction of artefacts and systems, which historically had been denied. The third precursor was engineering, with its emphasis on electronics, structures and systems, and which aligned technology with higher status science. Though this was much contested it nevertheless showed a movement towards a significant shift in the status of the subject. In the 1980s the subject that emerged was craft design technology, which drew on these three strands and raised the status of the subject to that of an essential element of the school curriculum (Department of Education and Science 1985). Thus it had an educational rather than a vocational purpose. Craft design technology emerged at the time when the educational policies of the Thatcher era reflected a view that science and technology would fuel the future economy of the UK. However, traditional asymmetric gender dynamics reasserted themselves within schools. Craft design and technology continued to conjure up images of factories, workshops and machines that signify male territory. This was reflected in the proportions of girls and boys taking examinations at age 16 (7 and 93 per cent respectively) and the low representation of female teachers (2 per cent) (Layton 1993). The curriculum subject design and technology emerged as one of the foundation subjects of the National Curriculum outlined in the Educational Reform Act 1988. Its specification was very broad-based but in its curriculum and examination structures the legacy of the vocational crafts subjects remained in the distinctions between resistant materials, food technology, textiles technology, electronics and systems control, for example. The domination of male teachers meant that in many new integrated technology departments men set the agenda and research has shown that any possibility to develop gender awareness among students was either minimal or non-existent.

MR GREEN'S BELIEFS ABOUT DESIGN AND TECHNOLOGY

Mr Green, in Monks School, presented a contrast between an old and a 'second breed' of design and technology teachers. The old design and technology teachers he associated with craft design and technology, which he described as providing an apprenticeship into crafts that provided skills relating to specific jobs. He made a distinction between the previous role of the subject as a vocational preparation, such as for electrical engineering or joinery, and the National Curriculum subject:

> The craft side is very minimal in the National Curriculum. There was a wide range of people on the course [his teacher training course], people who had, you know, my background is in electrical engineering, control systems etc. although I've worked in engineering environments so I'm familiar with all the processes and everything else. People like myself, people who've been in architectural product design etc. and who hadn't been anywhere near a machine or a tool in their life and we're the second breed who know the National Curriculum and accept the National Curriculum and put it in that context. I think sometimes it's quite difficult for some of the older lot to have changed and accepted that change.

The new version of the subject with which Mr Green identified himself was, he believed, an ideal preparation for a future that would equip students with generic transferable skills, and in particular 'problem-solving' skills. Thus he, unlike Mr Hunt, associated his representation of the subject with its educational purpose rather than its vocational legacy. He described the subject as a survival kit that would help students to become autonomous, self-reliant and flexible. Instead of referring to the world of work his account was dominated by images from the domestic realm, such as: 'decorating your house, doing little jobs around the house themselves, the ability to cut a bit of wood, the ability to join a bit of wood, put up a shelf, hang wallpaper, arrange tiles, fit a carpet, get the dimensions [for the space of a microwave]'.

His description of the National Curriculum subject conjured up a flexible neo-liberal worker equipped with transferable generic skills who created uniquely different solutions to the same problem. He recognized, however, that the subject continued to struggle for acceptance as an academic discipline in spite of its core and statutory status at the time of the study. This reflects the association of practical knowledge with the curriculum of secondary modern schools that we referred to in Chapter 1. He referred to this historical legacy in the following way: 'I think it is a much maligned subject of schools' technology that has low status in comparison with what are deemed as academic subjects, not by staff but by parents and the students, again the various government agencies and people who view English, maths and science as the important subjects.'

In his concern with the status of the subject he referred to the difference in practice between academic and non-academic subjects, particularly in the scope for participation which he saw as central to teaching and learning in his subject. He invoked the notion of academia as the abstract independent movement away from the everyday, the mundane, towards the esoteric, the reified. He challenged this separation of the everyday, the social, from how people both reproduce and create knowledge. Part of his perception of the difference between academic and non-academic subjects was related to the atmosphere he encouraged in the workshop:

> See the interaction you know, they're human beings, and children we're social beings, you know, we define our relationship with other people, that's what differentiates us you know, human beings from the rest of the animal kingdom, we are social beings. Somebody who works in isolation, they're either sort of like deemed an academic eccentric or they're mad!

He compared his role as a teacher with his role as the 'workshop supervisor' when he was an electrical engineer, thus invoking a strong sense of community. At the same time this image tended to align with masculinity rather than femininity. Mr Green justified his pedagogic approach through his vision of the future. His focus on the educational purposes of the subject as a way of relating to, and understanding, the made world and preparing his students for rapid technological change freed him from vocational contexts. This allowed him to look for relevance in the everyday for both boys and girls and meant that he viewed all students as having a right of access to the subject and its practices.

English

In our discussion of English we consider two teachers, Mrs Sharp from Palmers School and Mrs Young from Monks School. First we look at the recent curriculum history of the subject.

CURRICULUM STORY 3

Up until the 1930s English was considered to be a subject 'fit for women, workers and those wishing to impress the natives' (Eagleton 1983: 29). At the heart of English as a school subject is a tension between literacy and literature, and between production and reception (Robinson 2000: 91). Working-class children were educated to spell and to read the Bible but not to write their own texts. If the masses could write, it was argued, they might be tempted to produce texts of their own (Hunt 1972, cited in Robinson 2000). If the masses could not write, the state could at least control the texts that they read. The empowering potential of writing has re-emerged frequently as a concern about social control and can be found as recently as 1992 in a statement by a Department of Education and Science official recorded as saying, 'people must be educated once more to know their place' (Pilger 1992: 29, cited in Robinson 2000: 92). A second important strand in the historical legacy of English is the place and role of the text. The birth of the novel in the eighteenth century opened up the inner world of domesticity, personal relationship and mental interiority. In effect the novel was concerned with women's knowledge and therefore for the first time women were legitimated as writers. However, the first novels were written by men, such as Samuel Richardson and John Fielding, who in the 1740s wrote about women's lives in *Pamela* and *Shamela*. These texts epitomized the struggle in the eighteenth century for control over women's stories and meanings (Jardine 1985: 6). The texts that are studied in English literature go to the heart of debate about what it is to be English or what constitutes tradition (Robinson 2000). Preserving tradition can be achieved by defining and teaching a canon, which Peim (2004) argues has been tightly controlled in the school curriculum. The English instantiated in the National Curriculum (1988) was a new version of the subject made up of four distinct skills: reading, writing, listening and speaking. In effect, this version of English demoted the place of the text and privileged the place of the reader. We can see in this debate the two versions of English: one that privileges a personal, empathetic response and one dominated by grammar that harks back to the trivium. The National Association for Teachers of English (NATE) objected to testing the four aspects of English separately and argued that the national tests for 13–14-year-olds removed secretarial skills from the process of writing within 'meaningful contexts'. The desire to keep analysis and empathetic responses connected represents a bid to retain what arguably had become the feminine core identity carried by school English up until the late 1990s. The English language A level is a new invention that focuses on the structure, syntax and grammar of language as a system. This new A level has further marginalized the place of the feminine text in the assessment process.

MRS SHARP'S BELIEFS ABOUT ENGLISH

We met Mrs Sharp, from Palmers School, in Chapter 2 as she taught a class of average to higher ability boys about creative writing genres. By describing her practice we suggested that she had shaped English specifically to accommodate the needs and interests of the boys. In her interview she spoke about the changes that she had introduced since becoming head of department, aimed at closing the gap between boys' and girls' attainment at GCSE:

> I have reshaped the English course but teaching is better. The emphasis on what's going on in the classroom it has just altered quite dramatically and as a consequence we are getting quite a lot of popular uptake. We are also getting a lot of . . . in the last two years we have had quite a lot of boys taking A level literature, more so than I have ever encountered. In fact both my Year 13 and Year 12 group of this year have had more boys in them than girls.

We asked if she had any idea why this was so:

> No idea. I think they've quite enjoyed it and we've got this year especially extraordinarily bright boys in there, extremely bright, that I should think that 70 per cent of the boys [who] are currently taking (a few figures off the top of my head), I should think 70 per cent boys taking English come out with As. I know and if they fail slightly they may get a B.

With the phrase 'extremely bright' she presented a picture of elite academic masculinity. She told us about a recent visit from an English adviser who suggested that boys have three major problems in English: a low concentration span; they do not write enough; and their inability to break a task down into manageable chunks. These comments reproduced common sense beliefs about masculinity that Mrs Sharpe disagreed with (emphasis added):

> I don't think that is true it depends on what boys are interested in. I look around this group today and at Mark and his mate, OK he was having a fight at one point but they were fighting over the fact that Mark really wanted to get on. He was doing a bit of 'Thunderbirds are go FAB, FAB' and Mark is going shut up I really want to do this because he *had a burning desire to do it*. I think what happens is that you lose sight of the concentration span that boys do have because you become so preoccupied with the child and mainly the boy (nine times out of ten it's a boy) that has lost concentration . . . You have a tendency to forget that there have been 27 children on task in here when three were off task so therefore you have 27 successful boys in comparison to three that aren't. So I think there is a tendency *for*

people to sort of blow things out of proportion and give all boys a bad press.

She drew attention to the kind of behaviours associated with cultural representations of masculinity that usually were salient to her in English lessons. Underpinning these were the historical legacy that we referred to in Chapter 1 that boys are perceived as potentially disruptive and in need of 'firm' control. This influenced Mrs Sharp's practice and her gaze was attracted to the boys who were not on task. She explained her conscious attempts not to react in her usual way and her intention to challenge essentialist representations of masculinity. Previously, her views of the subject had aligned with those that emphasized an empathetic response to texts historically associated with femininity. Within the last few years, however, she had made conscious attempts to imagine boys as legitimate participants in English. She achieved this in a number of ways. She used writing frames, a particular school-based tool, which emphasize the rules and structure of an appropriate response and reduce ambiguity (emphasis added):

> We have actually been using a writing frame for quite some time, whether it be a writing frame with boxes, we have discovered that less able boys (middle to less able boys) love a box. Give them a box and they will fill the box and they will actually shape and extend writing quite dramatically as a result of the box and writing frame. *We have been giving writing frames in an ad hoc way, prompt questions on the board, for example, for years*, I think we have always done it, and boys do respond very well to that sort of stimulus actually.

We asked whether girls respond in a similar way: 'Yes, it doesn't matter whether it is boys or girls. Actually, they all respond well to it. Boys sometimes are very entertaining when they are using it. I have had one guy, you know, he put a finger on the writing frame oh yes and write pages and pages of the stuff.' In her reply she invoked a boy rather than a girl, suggesting that indeed the writing frames were primarily directed at boys.

The introduction of the English Language A level, which similarly emphasized structure, grammar and rules, was another strategy that called upon a historical gender legacy about the role of grammar in disciplining the mind that dissociates the subject from the emotive and subjective forms of knowledge aligned with femininity. These changes, we argue, do not represent ways of modifying participation and opening up practice, but rather alter the representation of the purpose and nature of the subject and what constitutes success in it. This is significant because unlike girls in science and resistant materials the boys were not being extended an identity of incompetence and non-participation. Rather, to ensure male success, Mrs Sharp was prepared to make fundamental changes to the subject domain.

MRS YOUNG'S BELIEFS ABOUT ENGLISH

Mrs Young, from Monks School, unlike Mrs Sharp, did not believe in changing the subject to accommodate boys or girls. The English department in Monks School had created boys' book boxes and girls' book boxes, and taught Year 9 boys *Macbeth* and Year 9 girls *Romeo and Juliet*. This we consider an example of overt gender shaping. Mrs Young disagreed with the strategy because in her view this amounted to a lack of faith in the text. She was worried that students were inadvertently becoming consumers of popular culture that influenced their views of the world. She hoped that English literature would provide them with alternative ways of thinking and the ability to critically evaluate messages from the media. She described how she drew on students' personal cultures as a way to propel them into literary culture:

> I suppose I'm drawing on their knowledge of what they watch on TV, and what they listen to on radio and what they might read around them. And hoping they might recognize that there are different styles and then try to mimic them, you know. So, I suppose I'm drawing on how much awareness they've got of popular type media . . . I think they just stop and listen a bit more when you throw in a sentence about, I don't know Arsenal or . . . like that and I . . . oooh, you, they are just a bit more figured.

Her previous school she described as 'rough and ready' in comparison to the 'white ghetto' of Monks School in which she said she had to 'watch what I say and how I say things'. She was concerned that because she had not been in the area long, she was not yet familiar with the local culture. She hoped to draw on familiar elements of her students' social landscape as a basis for introducing them to the new imaginary characters, alternative social situations and different cultural values in texts. She explained that she wanted to expand students' horizons, just as her many travels abroad had expanded hers. However, her account revealed tensions between class and the role of high and low culture. Although she espoused the view that English should not be changed to accommodate boys or girls, we shall see in Chapter 5 that her pedagogic practice in the boys' and girls' classes respectively varied considerably.

Drama

Mrs Diamond, the head of drama in Monks School, had a very particular view of the nature and purpose of the subject, and we consider this in relation to the recent history of the subject.

CURRICULUM STORY 4

Drama did not become widely established as a school subject until the 1980s. Debates about the educational purpose of drama have been long, contentious and largely unresolved. Drama has its origins in the experimental schools of the 1920s and the progressive pedagogies of the 1960s. Debates about school drama continue to revolve around two diametrically opposed definitions of the subject: theatre studies and self-expression. Theatre studies involves crafts skills such as set-making, lighting and sound. Therefore theatre studies align with a masculine core identity while drama as self-expression carries a feminine core identity. During the 1980s some factions of the drama teaching community maintained that drama was the epitome of active learning. They advocated the teaching of all subjects using drama techniques. Commentators such as Hornbrook (1998) pointed out that a danger with this view was that drama became reduced to a stock of pedagogic techniques and lacked an agreed knowledge base. In a system where knowledge is a commodity to be bartered its absence or ambiguous status reduces the subject's perceived value. Some have argued that this formulation of drama was responsible for it losing its place as an official subject in the National Curriculum. Given drama's unstable subject status it is usual for teachers to attempt to cover areas of the curriculum that teachers of more established subjects are not prepared to prioritize, such as the social, moral and personal aspects of education. Moral control, as we suggested in Chapter 1, has historically aligned with girls and the working classes while autonomy is aligned with elite masculinity.

MRS DIAMOND'S BELIEFS ABOUT DRAMA

Mrs Diamond, in Monks School, described drama as a process that was aimed at increasing students' self-confidence. The subject matter was to arise from students' concerns, understandings and values within role-play, which would become topics for discussion. Such topics might include drugs, HIV/AIDS and truancy. This explicitly locates her view of drama as subjective with no external specification or canon of knowledge to be transmitted to students. Her stated aim was to help students find a sense of belonging within the school and in life more generally, thus giving priority to social justice goals of equality and inclusion. She envisaged drama as an enculturation into citizenry to support students in a world where the moral order was unstable and changing. Mrs Diamond's ideal was that drama could be a subject in which the processes of schooling that hierarchically categorized students could be put aside for a time. She emphasized the diversity of the student population and suggested that this required a sensitive approach to individual needs. The absence of an agreed hierarchy of objectified knowledge supported this approach. This depiction of diversity also revealed the learner as vulnerable and for these reasons she valued participation and the creation of an inclusive community in which everyone had a say and everyone felt they belonged. She valued participation as a means to negotiate meaning. However, she linked 'having a say' to 'belonging' and this gave priority to students who could verbalize creative ideas. Therefore other forms of participation were less visible to her and this meant that she was not aware of some students' creative efforts. These issues distinguished her responses to girls and boys.

She spoke about the different ways that boys and girls undertook the same drama activities. When we showed her clips from the video recordings of parallel boys' and girls' lessons she said:

> ... it was obvious in the clips that you just showed me that the boys, the boys were all talking together and over the top of each other and putting ideas in. Within the girls groups there was clearly a leader and there was less input. They were taking points from the leader and from the character and they were going back and improving things in the clip that you showed. But from the boys it was much more sort of haphazard and there were probably, in both instances, situations where children were not being particularly actively involved in the putting forward of what they were trying to do and I'm conscious of that. I'm conscious as I observe that there are certain children who are not inputting ideas in a very vociferous way. It could be that they're getting just as much out of it by sitting in the sidelines but they're not contributing as much on the ideas front.

Mrs Diamond said that she could leave her Year 8 girls completely alone and they would come up with a role-play because a leader usually emerged who could move the group and sometime the whole class forward. In this respect she anticipated that girls' participation was unproblematic and beyond being given a task required little input from her. In contrast, like Mrs Sharp's use of writing frames and Mr White's sequencing of 'bits' of science knowledge, she felt the need to structure the boys' activities more than those of the girls. She depicted the boys as active and egalitarian and the girls as hierarchically organized and more passive, and in some senses therefore less creative than boys were. She said that the boys were less organized than girls, yet had more ideas. Mrs Diamond's aspirations for equality were in tension with her beliefs about boys and girls. In Chapter 5 we shall see how these tensions played out in her pedagogic discourse and practice.

Reviewing accounts of the knowledge-gender dynamic

We started the chapter by recalling that curriculum subjects have cultural legacies that align knowledge with gender dichotomies: objective-masculine and subjective-feminine; and manual/technical-masculine and aesthetic/non-technical-feminine. We suggested that, through teachers' practices and beliefs, curriculum subjects or aspects of them may extend to students' particular gender identities that reflect these historical alignments. Pedagogic discourses project students forward and therefore teachers have to reconcile historical legacies of the past with the imagined future. Media stories and beliefs about changes in society had presented an image of the future worker as someone who has to be flexible, resilient and entrepreneurial and who has a mixture of hard and soft skills. Teachers recognized therefore that they were preparing their students to live in a changing world. They aspired to provide students with the best their subjects could offer, whether that was the cultural landscape of literature, the reliable world of scientific truths, the transformative power of creative ideas in drama or the generic problem-solving skills represented in design and technology. Yet, the gender alignments of subjects have deep historical roots which anchor subject knowledge in the past and which resist change.

Teachers' interviews revealed a number of tensions between past and present, old and new knowledge, and teaching boys and girls. Having to teach boys and girls separately required teachers to confront either consciously or unconsciously the tensions and alignments between their beliefs about which students legitimately belonged in their subject and the class they faced, either boys or girls. In struggling to account for differences between their approaches to teaching boys and girls, teachers' beliefs about gender came to light. Some teachers suggested that they would not change the subject to accommodate boys or girls and some suggested that they would. We found instances of teachers responding to 'certain signs of identity' (Holland *et al.* 1998) which influenced their interactions with students. Mr White in science maintained a traditional belief in the power of the scientific method to reveal the hidden essence of matter, which aligns with masculinity. This as we noted was in keeping with the practice of science education at the time. He found himself having to account for his pedagogic practice, which excluded girls and aligned science with boys by invoking two domains, the public and the private (see gender story 1 in Chapter 2). Mr Hunt's practice in resistant materials was similarly mediated by this historical belief about the place of boys and girls in relation to his subject. Mr Hunt assumed incompetence on the behalf of the girls. He did not legitimize their membership and extended to them an identity of non-participation (see gender story 2 in Chapter 2). Mr White also made assumptions about girls' incompetence. The girls-only class gave him an opportunity to observe their competence, however, he, like Mr Hunt, lacked the resources to analyse his observations from an understanding of gender knowledge mediation. Consequently he accounted for his observations by labelling girls as 'atypical'.

Mr Green had considerable gender awareness, gained from his personal experiences. His aim was to open up practice to girls and to boys and he saw the single-sex strategy as an opportunity to do this. He had worked in industry for a female boss and was at ease, he said, with women's incursions into traditional male territories. He had re-imagined his subject to align with post-Fordian working patterns and a future in which knowledge would be created in new ways. This was congruent with the National Curriculum aims for the subject. In the following chapter we shall demonstrate how Mr Green's representation of design and technology worked out in his pedagogic practice. We suggest that although he successfully opened up practice to girls there were differences in the ways that he addressed boys and girls, which reflected the core gender identity of the subject.

We have noted how subject alignments can shift through what is emphasized and given value. We saw in the curriculum history of French that the devaluing of fluency and a focus on grammar and rules made it an acceptable subject for boys. Creative writing and novels align with subjective-feminine knowledge while grammar, syntax and structure align with objective-masculine knowledge. Mrs Sharp revealed some awareness of the knowledge-gender dynamic. The boys' use of distancing devices had, however, obscured for Mrs Sharp their willingness and expertise to engage with emotions. In responding to the needs of boys as she perceived them she drew on the objective-masculine relationship and transformed the nature of the subject, not reflecting on how the changes in her practices might impact on individuals. Mrs Diamond claimed no gender issues impinged on her subject, drama, as in her view its goals were to include and to give a central place to learners' concerns. However, she did make assumptions about boys' and girls' characteristics when she spoke about the different ways groups of boys and girls worked. She considered it necessary to open up practice for boys, whereas she assumed girls' participation much in the same way that Mrs Sharp did.

To work with these potential knowledge-gender alignments and to recognize their consequences for students' learning, in the following chapters we consider how students react to the identities extended to them through teachers' practices and their interactions with them. If, as in Mr White's class, scientific knowledge is characterized as objective, fixed and immutable and if the theoretical and methodological knowledge is highly reified, students will be expected to learn the principles, rules and conventions without allowing their subjective opinions to influence their answers. Therefore answers are not interpreted as a reflection of the inner self. The cultural tools of school science mediate between students' inner and the outer worlds. We can imagine that this frees boys from the possibilities of exposing their inner worlds, which they may or may not find empowering. Some girls may face a conundrum in science where the goals and ways of being and knowing that they identify with are either given no value or not recognized or considered 'atypical'. This may make it difficult for them to perceive salience in their science learning, which may undermine their agency and limit their ability to develop competence in the subject. If it is also assumed that girls and boys as groups have equal access to the cultural tools of a subject then we can anticipate that the participation that some students may need in order to negotiate meaning may not be forthcoming, causing further difficulties for them in their learning. If we can contrast how the girls and the boys in Mr Hunt's class were positioned for their next lesson in resistant materials we can perhaps imagine these possibilities more readily. In Chapter 6 we shall investigate how some girls managed these conundrums.

This chapter has acted as a bridge between our historical consideration of curriculum knowledge that we presented in Chapter 1 and descriptions of classroom practice that we shall present in Chapters 4 and 5. We have pointed to some of the dilemmas and difficulties that teachers had to resolve as they mediate knowledge for specific classes. By invoking the notion of a knowledge-gender dynamic we wish to stress and demonstrate that the relationship is not a fixed feature of our cultural inheritance, it is constantly re-imagined, reproduced and reconstructed in classroom practice. Our aim is to suggest to the reader that having the tools to reflexively think about gender and to critically evaluate its influence on representations of knowledge allows teachers to have greater control over how gender emerges in pedagogic practice and discourse.

Chapter/**Four**

Inside the classroom: mathematics, science, and design and technology

In this chapter we go inside mathematics, science and design and technology classrooms to explore how the knowledge-gender dynamic emerged in practice in the interactions between students and their teachers. In the following extracts from classrooms we look closely at how gender emerged in the moment-to-moment enactments of class-room practice and foreground the interpersonal plane of analysis (Rogoff 1995). We view the settings that teachers orchestrate with students as communities that provide the resources, tools and texts that students use to carry out the tasks within the wider activity of the subject that teachers set them. We were interested in finding out how the settings that teachers orchestrated in boys' and girls' classes facilitated or limited students' access to the curriculum subject.

We look first at a mathematics setting, which involved a group of Year 9 boys and their female teacher, Mrs Marshall. We had followed the boys' class across the curriculum and we had seen them sometimes being disruptive and challenging in other lessons. Even although Mrs Marshall was an experienced and skilled teacher we wanted to understand why her lesson worked so well. Mathematics, as we have noted, has a long history as an academic high status subject whose knowledge base is highly reified like science. After the Renaissance (Walkerdine and Lucey 1989) mathematics became increasingly associated with objectivity, dispassionate thinking and analytical classifications. Through its relationship with rationality, intellectual reasoning and the pursuit of disembodied 'truths' it has historically been distanced from females and the working classes. The remnants of this legacy remain as Leonne Burton (1996) points out: 'Mathematics ... stand[s] out as still clinging to an epistemology of "truths" which validates a transmissive educational mode'. That this representation of the subject and its pedagogy can be disrupted by teachers is well documented in research (see e.g. Boaler 1997). However, in the setting we observed there was no such disruption and we suggest this was because in the boys' group this approach was considered appropriate as boys' belonging and competence were assumed and not considered problematic. The teacher's practice had many similarities with those espoused by Mr White in science. Her role was also similar in that she was the authority figure and the holder and giver of knowledge. Thus her task was to hand over the subject's cultural tools and truths to boys, the legitimate inheritors of the domain. We have used the metaphor of 'parent' again here to represent Mrs Marshall's pedagogic approach, though here we talk of a 'mother feeding her children' to capture an important feature of the lesson – namely that this was a woman teacher, passing on a subject that was historically aligned with masculinity to a group of boys.

Mathematics: feeding the boys?

Mrs Marshall was an experienced teacher who was highly regarded by her colleagues and by the students. At the beginning of the lesson she asked the boys to stand while she greeted them with a polite and dignified 'Good morning boys', to which the boys replied, 'Good morning'. Mrs Marshall exerted a firm, gentle and easy authority throughout the lesson which was conducted in a harmonious atmosphere. The boys sat facing the large blackboard in five columns of desks intermittently following illustrations that she drew on the blackboard while explaining a new principle related to 'parallelograms and angles'. The boys worked through exercises in the mathematics text, stopping when Mrs Marshall drew their attention to the board. Near the beginning of the lesson she introduced the terms 'supplementary and auxiliary angles' and told the boys that they needed to become familiar with them. One boy interjected, 'Do we need to write them down?' and she replied saying, 'No, it is just me reminding you of terms before we start the lesson.' Here she made clear her assumption that boys were competent in, and with, the language of the subject and its terminology.

Introducing parallelograms

A few minutes into the lesson Mrs Marshall drew two parallel lines on the board and addressed the boys as follows: 'That is *your* parallel lines, that is *your* transversal, that is *your* ... '(emphasis added).

We noted, as with Mr Hunt, that teachers' discourse can explicitly associate or dissociate students from the subject and its tools. The repeated use of 'your' signalled to the boys that their membership in this community was legitimated and that they were mutually engaged in a joint enterprise: both critical elements of participation. Mrs Marshall was, through her invitation to take up mathematical concepts and terms, assuming their access to the mathematical discourse as she extended the repertoire of the community to the boys. In the following interaction Mrs Marshall pointed to the diagram of two parallel lines crossed by two vertical lines on which she had written the letters 'n', 'm', 'y' and 'x' to indicate angles. The task was to identify corresponding angles. Some of the boys had not worked out what 'corresponding' meant.

Mrs Marshall: X is outside the line. You are looking for correspondence. I'm giving you a clue in me saying angles. Which angle is vertically opposite?
Bob: N.
Mrs Marshall: Yes? Which is vertically opposite?
M, M for mother.

We were struck by the way Mrs Marshall emphasized 'm' by using the term 'mother' and at the time it appeared to have an uncanny significance. Our fieldnotes read: 'this signals that she is their mother, their mathematics mother' which aptly captured the pedagogic relationship between the boys and Mrs Marshall as the following motherly reprimand demonstrates: 'There is no use saying sorry Peter if you don't mean it, if you are going to do it two minutes later.'

Researchers have pointed to the similarities between mothering and teaching that exist within the cultural legacies of the teaching profession, particularly since the Enlightenment (Dyehouse 1981; Walkerdine and Lucey 1989; Widdowson, cited in Walkerdine 1998). Mrs Marshall was dedicated to giving the boys access to a masculine academic domain. At one point in the lesson the boys were murmuring too much and she told them to work in silence. However, she spoke to them in a way that depersonalized the effect of the reprimand, by saying: 'I am tired of [having to] keep telling you to be quiet. I am going to put you on silence.'

By using the phrase 'put you on silence', as one might turn off a radio, she distanced herself and the boys from the reprimand and in effect created a third space that was not them and not her. This technique provided her with a powerful position from which to remain in control while making it seem that she was not the source of the reprimand, which is illustrated in her next comment: 'No, I do not want to hear any excuses. I had to put the class on silence because of the talking; stupid aren't you?'

In a complex way she both spoke to them as a mother by saying, 'No, I do not want to hear any excuses' and invoked a neutral persona by saying, 'I had to put the class on silence.' These techniques allowed her to control the boys while seeming not to directly challenge them. We suspect that the lesson was harmonious because, even when she reprimanded them, Mrs Marshall's pedagogic discourse gave the boys a sense of belonging. The rebuke was a collective one. Mrs Marshall's approach positioned the boys as if they already had mathematical competence and were knowledgeable about the repertoire of the community.

What might we imagine for girls' experiences of mathematics? Research within school mathematics lessons has demonstrated difficulties in recognizing girls' competence in the subject. As Leonne Burton (1986) pointed out, mathematical solutions given by boys tend to be viewed as 'gifted and elegant' while those given by girls tend to be viewed as 'routine and rule-following'. Valerie Walkerdine (1988) found that girls' mathematical competence was recognized by teachers as boring, rule-following and rote learning. Mrs Diamond, the drama teacher, remarked upon girls' lack of imagination and Mr White expressed surprise at girls' willingness to take risks. These views emerge when the historical association of femininity with passivity and civilized behaviour is interpreted as an absence of ideas and flair, which become surrogates in teachers' discourse for ability (Murphy and Elwood 1998). This presents girls with a double bind: first they are expected to behave well and to conform. Therefore to break with the given mathematical procedures goes against social representations of appropriate 'feminine' behaviour that they are confronted with daily. Second, even when girls achieve well in mathematics (as they do increasingly), this is attributed not to ability but rather to diligence in accordance with the cultural myth. We have referred to the way that historical cultural legacies about the legitimacy of who can or cannot enter particular domains re-emerge often at points of challenge for teachers in the 'moment in action'. With Mrs Marshall we can see how historical legacies re-emerge in her practice in a taken-for-granted social order that aligns mathematics with objectivity and masculinity and extends competence to boys even before they walk through the classroom door. We suggest that the boys' lesson was harmonious because the identities that they were offered did not disrupt their shared expectations about 'getting it right' in mathematics as a boy (Davies 2003).

In Chapter 3 we related Mr White's view of science to the scientific method where the hidden essence of the natural world could be brought to light though scientific experiments, which we traced back to Francis Bacon (see gender story 2). He expressed surprise at girls' willingness to engage and to not be fearful in the domain, and to offer answers (i.e. to assume their right to participate in the domain). We suggested his reaction reflected the way women in the seventeenth century were excluded from training in reason at the same time as they were excluded from skilled work. This, as Lloyd (1989: 116–17) points out, left women associated with pre-rational thinking styles which positioned them as 'fancy ridden', intellectually weak and importantly as passive observers of the world. As Evelyn Fox Keller (1985: 175) notes, females doing science confront a critical problem of identity. We noted that in his account of his pedagogic approach Mr White viewed his role as a leader guiding students much as a parent might. In our next gender story we briefly consider the changing role of fathers in society to draw an analogy between the role of male teachers and fathers.

Gender story 3: fathers and male teachers

Carole Pateman (1988) reminds us that according to kinship patriarchy, fathers were guaranteed rights over children based on a biological bond. Within patriarchal structures, men were guaranteed sovereignty over women and hence over the offspring of the union. The state turned to fathers when addressing children and especially their education and their future careers. Within the propertied classes, the eldest son was destined to inherit the father's land. The second son was expected to serve his country as a soldier and the third son was sent to university to study theology and train for the priesthood. However, after the social contract theories of the seventeenth and eighteenth centuries this aspect of the patriarchal structure no longer governed the significant relationship between parent and child. The relationship between the state and men changed because men were no longer defined according to biological bonds. By replacing a biological bond with an emotional bond, the state dispossessed fathers of their rights and responsibilities with respect to their biological children. The breaking of the biological bond between fathers and their offspring has major symbolic ramifications for men. Tensions produced by this social shift have recently re-emerged, for example, in campaigning groups such as 'Justice for Fathers'. In terms of pedagogy, men could no longer rely on authoritarian rule to induce learning and instead had to attain and retain the fraternal bond that was given to them as part of the social contract, yet not as a 'natural' right. Therefore, maintaining the masculine position takes vigilance, effort and social connections. The fraternal bond has to be constantly re-won. Maybe this is why sometimes men collude with boys in reproducing the gender order.

Science: performing the magic

Mr White, like all the teachers in the study, had volunteered to teach three similar lessons to classes of both sexes. The teachers who volunteered to take part in the second stage of the study knew they were going to be video-recorded and that students in their classes would be radio-miked. This demanded a high level of confidence from the teachers. Mr White was a well respected and experienced teacher who had been at Monks School for approximately 20 years. He had confidence in his knowledge of science and his role as a scientist through his prior research position. He had a firm yet gentle manner with both boys and girls. The teachers in the study, although working in a school that saw gender and learning as an issue, received little support to develop their understanding of gender. Therefore, in confronting gender they had to draw on their representations of their subject in relation to it. Part of our thesis is that gender emerges in practice often below the level of conscious awareness and is usually not part of a teacher's intended pedagogy. This we suggest was amply demonstrated in Mr Hunt's lesson with the girls, which is why we refer to the effects as 'unintended'. We suspect this is the case not only with the teachers we observed but with teachers working in single-sex settings in other studies who reported that they did not change their practice to accommodate boys and girls (see Chapter 1). Not only are the effects unintended but they are also unnoticed and because of this are not available for teachers to reflect on to inform their future practice.

Mr White described the conceptual thread running through the lessons: 'where things come from and how we turn them into useful materials. But within that picking out the principles of physical and chemical changes. So that oil experiment was part of a sequence which included on the conceptual side, the idea of separating mixtures according to different boiling points'.

In the first lesson, Mr White discussed where crude oil was found and what it was used for. He also revised and demonstrated the concepts of 'permanent' and 'reversible' change. In the first extract we illustrate how Mr White 'trains' the girls to look at scientific experiments as scientists rather than paying attention to their own subjective perceptions.

Introducing chemical change

In the first lesson in the series Mr White addressed the class from the front, writing on the board and demonstrating a variety of chemical changes through a number of chemical reactions. Mr White's questions guided the girls to recognize chemical transformations through 'look', 'smell' and 'feel':

Mr White:	I have a lot of things to show you today. I don't want to wait for the chatter to stop. I am not going to repeat this. [The demonstration. Mr White sets up the demonstration and puts the lights out as he talks. The performance commences.] So look now. [He sets light to magnesium powder and there is a flash.] Like a sparkler.
Tanya:	Can you do it again?
Mr White:	What did I say earlier? [He does not repeat the demonstration.] Look around, lights. Where has it gone?
Sheryl:	Smoke.
Mr White:	A chemical change, yes or no?
Chloe:	Yes.
Mr White:	It gave off a lot of light and heat energy. It still has a flash on your retina. Why is this appropriate this week? [The day was 2 November, just before Bonfire Night]
Alice:	Fireworks.
Mr White:	Got a metal in it ... why ... someone said it ... the name of the metal? [He picks up on a nearly inaudible response]
Jane:	Magnesium.
Mr White:	Can you give me the name of the chemical, name of that smoke? Magnesium something?
Cathy:	Sulphate.
Mr White:	Not in the air, I hope. Magnesium oxide is what we got – this is chemistry.

Modelling science?

One thing we noticed was how Mr White's pedagogic discourse guided the girls to focus on the significant aspects of the phenomenon from a scientific perspective. His injunctions to, 'look around, lights, where has it gone' drew attention to these. He continued with a range of experiments that allowed him to continually direct the girls' attention to the differences between physical and chemical changes and in particular to how different chemical changes could be brought about through 'heating', through 'adding something else' such as acid, and using electricity. The girls' observations were focused through specific kinds of questions that carefully redescribed sensations such as smell, sight and sound according to scientific categories as indicators of an irreversible change. Through his approach, Mr White trained the 'gaze' and hence the mind. The girls engaged with this and with the conceptual threads he was weaving together using the terms and concepts that he offered in their responses. They also picked up on the performance element of the lesson and demonstrated that they recognized the role that Mr White was playing, as one girl asked, 'Sir, mix some potions again!' The girls recognized their positioning as the passive spectators. Some challenged this. Annabel repeatedly chanted the expected responses and parodied the teacher's emphasis: 'Is *that* a chemical change?' In taking the active role Mr White positioned himself as the most important actor in the laboratory. In exaggerating her reciprocal role Annabel drew attention to the subordinate position that the girls had been offered as spectators. In making her role as spectator obvious Annabel challenged Mr White's authority and signalled her resistance to being positioned without agency. Another girl challenged her positioning in a different way and asked directly, 'Will we get to do an experiment?' Another way we observed that the girls recognized their positioning in the domain was in the way they offered answers. These were often inaudible and typically diffident as though they expected to be incorrect. This behaviour is often interpreted as a lack of confidence, but another way to view it, we suggest, is the girls' recognition of a denial of legitimate membership. When all the signs made available in a setting indicate that an individual lacks the ability and the legitimacy to participate, then to publicly attempt it is a risk. Mr White, in trying to maintain interaction with the girls, typically strove to 'hear' and to create a space for their provisional answers, thus opening up practice in some ways for them.

In another experiment Mr White demonstrated a chemical change using a different method. He passed electricity through a clear solution of potassium iodide and starch. The iodide ions were oxidized to form iodine, which reacted with the starch solution and the colour changed from clear to blue. This colour change was seen as an indication of a chemical change, as Mr White had guided the girls to expect. In no instance were the girls given access to what underlay the phenomenon they were observing – the chemical reaction; to understand *why* a colour change might have taken place, and as such their agency was further undermined. They had to accept what they were told was salient without any understanding of why this should be so. Mr White, in his efforts to focus the girls' gaze even required them to report on the colour they could see even though this was obvious. In a further stage

Mr White added a clear liquid, sodium thiosulphate, which reacted with the iodine and the blue colour disappeared.

> *Mr White:* Science says that chemical changes can not be undone. Watch. [He adds a few drops of clear liquid and the blue colour disappears.] Undone.
> *Annabel:* Is that a chemical change?
> *Sheryl:* Yes.
> *Mr White:* Yes. Two chemical changes.[A girl asked what chemical he had added.]
> *Mr White:* I bet you are glad you asked. [Once again, Annabel interjects.]
> *Annabel:* Was *that* a chemical reaction? [Another girl is heard telling Annabel to stop.]

The girl who asked Annabel to stop was reacting to her challenging Mr White's authority. However, Annabel's question was legitimate in the thread that Mr White had created as the loss of the blue could, if the logic of the lesson was followed, be interpreted as a reversal to a prior form which Mr White implied. The girls had no access to the chemistry behind the two reactions and were not expected to be able to manage this knowledge, which was clear from Mr White's response to the girl who asked for the name of the chemical.

Playing the magician?

We do not have an equivalent section from the boys' lesson to present because we were invited to a slightly different sequence of lessons. However, when we were observing the girls' lesson, Mr White spontaneously referred to a similar incident that had taken place in a previous lesson with boys. It was rare for Mr White to directly address us while he was teaching and therefore his action signalled that the incident was significant.

> *Mr White:* They are quite excited. It's a shame you did not see the boys.
> *Researcher:* What happened, they are a noisy group anyway?
> *Mr White:* When I did that one and it went back to clear, they applauded, quite unnerving really. I think it was quite tongue in cheek. One boy in the front started clapping, they joined in, really, they joined in. Really threw me.

Our interpretation was that Mr White had not quite realized that the boys were drawing attention to his role as the entertainer as some of the girls, including Annabel, had done. It was likely that the boys had been gently mocking him for 'playing the magician'. Mentioning the boys' applause to us may have heightened Mr White's awareness of the students' perception of his role. Following this exchange Mr White handed out worksheets for the girls to complete and as he did so commented: 'OK girls, quiet, you have had your entertainment this lesson, now you need to do some work.'

In the second lesson, the students were engaged in a chemical process called 'fractional distillation' to separate crude oil into its components. This experiment relied on physical reversible changes and so connected to the prior lesson where these were distinguished from chemical changes.

Settings in science

A detailed analysis of transcripts of the interactions in the second lesson revealed no significant differences in the examples Mr White used, the content he covered or the scientific principles he explained between the girls' and the boys' classes. He gave each group the same tasks and the tasks were planned, as Mr White informed us in Chapter 3, to reveal the conceptual thread that defined the topic. There was no question that this thread could be changed to accommodate girls or, separately, boys. This indicates both the values accorded to knowledge in science and also the belief in its objective immutable nature. Scientific endeavour is full of examples of how it has advanced through imaginative creative leaps. From our theoretical perspective the cultural tools of science are tools for thinking which allow us to create meanings that support successful action. As such they, like all reifications, can have their meaning expanded or lose their meaning as other ideas emerge which more adequately enable successful action. We can see this with the changing theoretical accounts of particles, which at each point in their history have taken understanding forward. In such a view, however, the standpoint and the physical and social settings to which the knowledge is related matter, and the subjective element of the domain is recognized. If the dominant practice in science education enshrined in its assessment processes is, however, that knowledge is out there to be revealed and reproduced then teachers quite legitimately do not consider the subjective aspects of the scientific endeavour. We saw this in Mr White's very careful training of what should be 'noticed' and accorded salience. However, while the content of the lesson remained similar, we found that Mr White in his practice treated girls differently to the boys. In the girls' class, he repeatedly told the girls to 'move quietly and safely around the lab' and frequently drew attention to the potential harm they might do, such as dropping hot test tubes or burning themselves. Although he reminded the boys of the same safety precautions, he did not constantly repeat them. What was striking was the difference in what he said and how he said it to the two groups. In the introduction to the girls he said:

> You must clamp your tube carefully right at the top but not actually on the stopper. Make sure that's right at the top but not actually on the stopper and so tip it up a bit. So the flame heats up the oil, without heating all the rubber bits and things at the top. This will catch fire if it gets hot. Now if you have an accident and if it does catch fire, which will happen I am sure for one or two of you, then the key thing is you don't panic, you move the burner well out the way ... and I will come and sort you out.

In response a girl giggled 'Don't panic' as Mr White continued with his final point about safety: '... things are going to get very hot, don't touch anything that even might be possibly hot'. To the boys' group he made no assumptions that they might set up the apparatus incorrectly. His safety instructions also assumed competence on the boys' behalf in dealing with hot objects: '... you will need to pick up a cloth ... this will be hot, be very careful as you transfer into the second test tube. When it reaches 150 ... again with a cloth to protect your hand, carefully move on to the third test tube'.

In introducing the problem of fire Mr White attributed this to the components as opposed to any 'accidents' caused by the students as he did with the girls:

> I have suggested heating the oil with the flame over at this end, and moving the flame away when you transfer from one to the other, then you will not have an accident. Nevertheless there will be problems and it might well be that your apparatus catches fire ... don't panic, you are to move the burner away, draw my attention to the problem please and I will come and help you. It will not be a serious problem ...

Mr White in these exchanges implied a great deal about his views of girls and of boys. The girls were to be protected from themselves, they were assumed to lack the skills and competency with the equipment in much the same way Mr Hunt assumed an inability to deal with three-dimensional sketching. The subject was identified as problematic for girls. Mr White, however, through his instructions and protection, wanted to engage the girls in the practices of the domain. What he seemed unaware of was how he again positioned the girls and reinforced their outsider status. He told both groups not to panic but the discourse within which this injunction was situated conjures images of smelling salts and swoons for the girls and calm authority for the boys. The identity he extended to the girls was resisted as the giggling girl mocked his injunction not to panic. The subtle differences in how he spoke such as 'sorting out' the girls compared with his intention to 'help' the boys defined the different relationships between Mr White and the girls and the boys and where the balance of autonomy lay. Yet what we observed contrasted markedly with Mr White's unconscious assumptions.

At the beginning of the experiment girls assigned each other roles within their groups. These roles included a scribe to record the temperature of a liquid distilled from the crude oil, an experimenter who was in charge of the heating process and others who provided the experimenter with equipment such as the test tubes, matches and cloths. The girls collected equipment in an organized fashion. They discussed what they were doing as they worked and in this way their groups achieved a high level of efficiency and harmony. The boys did not assign roles and there was considerable talk about who would do what without this being resolved. It seemed as if each of them wanted to be the main experimenter. None of the boys wrote anything down during the course of the experiment. They rushed around the room, played with equipment and lit and re-lit the Bunsen burners. In any one group a number of boys indulged in this play despite the presence of the video camera trained on their activities. Some melted plastic pens over flames and one boy burned his arm. In another group the apparatus collapsed.

In spite of these observations Mr White's attention was focused very differently in the boys' and girls' settings. Sophie was the only one in the girls' class to do anything remotely dangerous during the three lessons. She melted a plastic pen over a Bunsen burner. Mr White spotted her immediately. She was severely reprimanded and told to leave the room. Throughout the six science lessons (boys and girls) she was the only person who was asked to leave the laboratory. In interviews in the department, which we have referred to as an arena which mediates individual teachers' practice in a setting, we found beliefs about girls and boys were shared. For example, both male and female teachers judged that girls were passive and failed to engage with equipment unless it was 'plonked on their desk'. This was felt to be particularly the case with low ability girls. The girls were said to be timid 'in case they hurt themselves, they get burnt or whatever' as one female teacher commented. This was explained because 'they didn't know and they didn't understand what to do'. Boys on the other hand were 'very confident in their own ability'. Low ability boys' confidence was considered misplaced but explained in terms of their being excited by science.

While the boys and girls were given the same tasks, we can see that differences emerged in the interactions and the discourse. Mr White controlled the girls' use of space and equipment carefully yet on the other hand the girls seemed spontaneously to work cooperatively and efficiently. Mr White demonstrated a high level of tolerance for the way boys played and moved, and the boys seemed to expect this and assume a high level of autonomy. The consequences of these two different patterns of interaction became apparent in the third lesson.

Testing the limits?

In the third lesson, the fractions that had been collected in the previous lesson were redistributed. The second lesson had gone well in the boys' class according to Mr White but in the girls' class less well. He judged success by the standard of the fractions collected as they were expected to differ in recognizable ways in relation to their smell, colour, viscosity and flammability. In this lesson students were to carry out a series of tests on each of the fractions. Mr White gave out a worksheet with five columns to record results, negotiated with the students at the end of the last lesson. The headings included 'colour', 'thickness', 'smell', 'easy to ignite' and 'flame'. To conduct the flammability test, students were instructed to take a 'pea-sized' piece of cotton wool soaked in the liquid and to set it alight using a lit splint. Mr White instructed the girls to share a Bunsen burner and work collaboratively to produce results. A striking element of the lesson occurred when some girls went to the front to collect fractions. Mr White held out a test tube of substances for the girls to smell. In this way he mediated their access to science, embodied through his extended hand. Again we suggest this was his attempt to control what was salient to the girls and the girls reciprocated by leaning forward over the bench to sniff the test tubes that he remained holding. This act perhaps reflected Mr White's lack of trust in the girls to notice what was important. This kind of interaction would have been impossible in the boys' lessons as we suggest below.

The boys' lesson was the noisiest one we observed in science. Once in the laboratory, the boys jostled to find a Bunsen burner of their own and Mr White did not suggest that they share one or work cooperatively. When the fractions were brought to the front bench the boys rushed forward to collect splints, matches and samples. Mr White had no opportunity to offer the boys test tubes to smell because they disappeared off the front bench too quickly. In the first 20 minutes of the lesson, few boys were engaged in the task because they were building bonfires with splints and cotton wool, setting these alight and melting plastic pens over Bunsen burners. An excessive pyromania had broken out and spread all around the laboratory. Because Mr White was busy moving from bench to bench offering guidance, he could not keep his eyes on everything that was happening. Some boys moved around the laboratory to look at who was melting what over the Bunsen burners. A number of boys burned themselves and did not let on to the teacher. Mr White was aware of some of the activity and on occasion he reprimanded a boy, such as Daniel. However, having been reprimanded, Daniel barely hesitated before continuing to torch his pen with the Bunsen burner. Our fieldnotes read:

> *Mr White:* Daniel this is not what you are meant to do, use a splint to light it. [Daniel throws a handful of splints onto the cotton wool that is on fire.]
> [Daniel has lit (it) with the Bunsen burner. One boy, Richard, has burned his fingers but he does not complain. Our group is now burning a pen. The teacher is not aware of what is going on.]
>
> *Mr White:* Last orders please. [Ben has melted his pen and bent it in two.]
>
> *Joe:* How's you little bonfire? [to another boy, out of earshot of Mr White.]
>
> *Rick:* It's dead.
>
> *Mr White:* You have done very well. [A boy puts three pieces of cotton wool on a tin lid together and tries to light the whole lot.]
> [We see another bonfire going.]
>
> *Mr White:* Well done.

Mr White was only partially aware of what the boys were doing because they were making some efforts to hide their pyromaniac activities. Indeed he was focusing on the scientific experiment and when in interview we probed him about the boys' 'challenging behaviour' he insisted that the important point was that they were 'getting results'.

The class was not out of control and other science teachers spoke about this kind of activity as typical in boys' classes: 'if it sparks or smokes that's a success isn't it?' In general, teachers expected boys to act autonomously in the laboratory and there was a high degree of tolerance for their behaviour. However, the boys' activities were striking when compared to the girls'. In the parallel girls' lessons, no girl occupied the spaces afforded by the laboratory to undertake autonomous play activities and on the one occasion when a girl, Sophie, melted a pen over a Bunsen burner Mr White reacted with strong disapproval. The setting allowed boys control over their agency whereas for the girls their agency was undermined and constrained and several recognized this and tolerated it, while others resisted. For Sophie her actions may have had their source in resistance or she may have just been taking up the space as a person not recognizing that she had transgressed the identity extended to her.

The unintended effects of covert gender shaping in pedagogy

Our observations suggested that the girls did not experience the setting as if they had a legitimate right to be there, and this reflected how they were positioned through Mr White's practice. In contrast, the boys experienced the setting as if they had a right to move around, touch equipment and play. The space was legitimately theirs. Although he insisted on safety precautions Mr White did not repeatedly ask the boys to do exactly what he said, to move with caution or to make sure they did not hurt themselves. The boys acted as legitimate participants in science and Mr White's practice extended this identity to them in the assumptions he made about their competence with the tools of the community and the relationship he assumed between them and himself. The boys were not subordinate but agentive. The girls were passive and when Mr White opened up practices to them he still did not legitimize their membership which unintentionally restricted the girls' agency. We suggest that Mr White's differential treatment of boys and girls can in part be understood in relation to the historical legacy of science education. The girls presented Mr White with a perturbation and he did not know how to offer them science, which was his intention, except through the conduit of his own masculine body, evidenced in the test tube incident. Thus although he had not intended to alter his practice between the girls' and boys' groups Mr White's settings demonstrated how gender emerged nevertheless, but perhaps in more covert ways than in Mr Hunt's setting. We refer to this as 'covert gender shaping'.

The two settings orchestrated by Mr White through the emergence of gender in interaction provided different versions of science and opened up different possibilities for boys and girls to learn. Throughout this section we have highlighted how girls' positioning undermined their agency. However, through Mr White's control and guidance when they handled equipment they remained focused on the scientific purposes for which they were designed. Those girls who could manage the restricted roles they were offered came into contact with scientific concepts more frequently than the boys. This mirrored a general pattern of interaction between the girls and Mr White. In the second lesson, he asked the classes to come up with examples of liquids that could be defined as 'viscous'. In both classes a range of examples was offered, but the girls gave more examples than the boys, and Mr White was able to spend more time exploring these than in the boys' class. However, Mr White remained the gate-keeper to scientific knowledge. This we suggest has a significant impact on girls' ability to identify with the domain and to perceive its salience, which in turn limits their potential to develop expertise through entering more deeply into the practices of the community. We have referred to subject identities as traces of students' experience of agency (Holland *et al.* 1998). We can, if we put ourselves in Annabel's and Sophie's shoes, imagine how they may well, through their awareness of their positioning, choose not to participate in a domain, wherein their agency is denied. This we suggest will depend very much on an individual's sense of competency in a domain and the extent to which that is nourished through their membership in other communities. Other girls may evaluate the trajectory of their agentive experiences and come to a negative view of their self-efficacy in relation to the domain and drop out as a consequence. Needless to say none of these outcomes were what Mr White's practice was directed towards.

At no point have we implied problems for boys' learning and we turn to this now. In the third lesson some boys played with fire for most of the lesson and this prevented them from finishing the tasks set by their teacher. They did not engage with the planned learning objectives or the practices in which they were embedded through their self-selected activities. Consequently they missed opportunities to make new associations between science and objects in the laboratory and instead manipulated them for their own pleasure. By allowing boys autonomy and assuming their competency in the practices of the community Mr White unintentionally both allowed the boys to resist or ignore the scientific purposes of handling equipment and chemicals and did not open up practice to them by guiding and modelling their engagement with these tools. Thus for these boys identification with the domain might in the future be similarly problematic as for some of the girls. To explore this we consider what the boys said about their science lesson.

In interviews many boys referred spontaneously to the influence of peer group culture which reproduces the fraternal bond between males that we referred to in gender story 3. Male peer group culture exerted a significant influence within the matrix of social forces that boys encountered in formal classroom settings and which they described as part of the normal functioning of everyday school life. John, in science, said he was annoyed and frustrated by the high level of noise in the single-sex classes and the ways boys played practical jokes on each other. John described the constant talk about 'football and nothing else' as boring. Dave, who was also in this lesson, admitted that he just liked messing about:

Researcher: Uhuh. Which bit do you like best?
Dave: Probably like lighting the Bunsen burner.

Dave explained that they played with fire in the science laboratory just for a laugh:

Dave: We sometimes just burn things.
Researcher: Umm. Tell me about that.
Dave: We think it's funny to burn paper and everything.

Dave recognized the rituals of burning as collective boys' behaviour. Building fires is attractive because it provides an immediate sense of power. John described how it had started in the science lessons. He said that science came just after the lunch break and the boys were all hyped up from playing football. He described how some boys came to the lesson ready to be bored and so started messing about right from the beginning.

John: Well most people in our class aren't naughty, well none of them are really, but one person talks, another one joins in and it just gradually builds up, the noise, until Sir shushes us down and it happens straight after that again and he gets really annoyed. Nobody likes it. Sir, he doesn't enjoy it. We don't.
Researcher: Yes, does this happen to you as well, you know somebody talks and you carry on or ... ?
John: I think it happens to everyone.
Researcher: Yes.
John: If it was completely silent, I wouldn't say a word because I just, I don't like starting things like that. I'm not one to stop it. I carry on, but I wouldn't start it.
Researcher: Um yes, and are most of them like you?
John: Most of them, if we had everyone like me there wouldn't be any noise so there must be because if nobody ever starts, nobody would carry on because there's nothing to carry on. So there must be a few people, at least three, maybe, in our class that just start noise because they're bored.
Researcher: Is that why it is?
John: Yes, well they just come to every lesson and decide they're going to be bored before they get through the doors.
Researcher: Tell me about that.
John: Well, half the ... it's difficult to get a Bunsen burner that works because gas squirts at all angles, so you just put a splint actually, just somewhere, you know it

shouldn't happen and it sets alight and flares over someone's book and their book goes alight and complete panic! And, you put something near a light and it tends to spit and it gets in . . . it can hurt people, get in their eyes, and on their faces and on their hands. We lose about a test tube every experiment, somebody burns it, heats it too much, but when somebody's done it they never do it again.

Researcher: Um yes.

John: So you have to learn, lose 31 test tubes before it stops.

John described how the mucking about started and spread because no one, including him, was prepared to stop it. He did not blame Mr White for not stopping it either because in line with other boys' accounts, John suggested that this ubiquitous behaviour was an inevitable part of school life. These accounts epitomized the extent to which male peer group culture permeated various school contexts and seeped into all classroom settings. Therefore in order to change behaviours in the laboratory, boys needed some support. They needed the school to provide limits to the fraternal bond. We saw how Mrs Marshall skilfully achieved this through her pedagogic approach as mother and a form of control that invoked a neutral space. We suggest that it is important to recognize that the historical legacies of *some* subjects, particularly mathematics and science, reinforce the fraternal bond more than others. Mr White's interview suggested that there was a tension between his representation of science and the demands to teach girls which became heightened in the single-sex grouping. Like other teachers he needed support to develop more awareness about the science-gender dynamic. In contrast, as we noted in Chapter 3, Mr Green had thought about the historical legacy of design and technology and was committed to making the subject accessible to girls as well as boys.

We have argued that the associations of craft design and technology still mediate how subjects within design and technology are perceived. Resistant materials have a quite different purpose and range of skills and knowledge to the handicrafts of woodwork and metalwork. However, the alignments between functional knowledge and manual labour continue to mediate how it is represented and how girls and boys perceive it as we noted in the sharp divide in uptake of the subject. Girls' classes in resistant materials disrupt this alignment and face teachers with a potential perturbation.

Resistant materials: breaking down boundaries?

In the first of the three lessons, Mr Green gave both the boys and the girls a design brief to design and make a model car that would travel 5 metres carrying a weight of 1 kilogramme. As suggested in Chapter 2, design and technology is a subject in which teachers often encourage a relaxed atmosphere and Mr Green allowed the boys and girls to chat to each other in his lessons. Sometimes, and especially in the girls' class, he joined in this chat. The following extracts are taken from the beginning of the first lesson in the series when Mr Green introduced the design brief and demonstrated the techniques involved in designing and making a model car.

Introducing the design specification: girls' class

Mr Green:	Good afternoon girls, please sit down, take your blazers off, if you want to. You will need your writing-down equipment so please sort your pencils out. Right, we've got . . . Someone is playing music out front . . .
Raya:	Is it going to be interesting?
Mr Green:	We'll see how interesting we can make it. We seem to have a few missing, let's see who is here. Do we have a few on French exchange?
	[A girl drags a chair round to my place.]
Mr Green:	Oh . . . pick it up, don't drag it. [Mr Green takes the register, then as he goes through the names he overhears girls talking.]
Mr Green:	Congratulations on getting engaged again Kylie.
Girls:	Oh.
Mr Green:	Thank you, take it off, or I will . . . tell everyone it is Tom Croft. [A boy in Year 9.]
	[Mr Green introduces the practical.]
Mr Green:	I also have had a problem with continuous monitoring. I want to be able to write something nice about your work. Keep all your work in your folders, try to be cooperative and keep your writing in your folder. Could you quietly go through there. [To the workshop.]
	[Mr Green starts the demonstration by saying . . .]
Mr Green:	Sleeves up job.
	[He demonstrates the stages of making the car using

	models of cars while talking about the specification. Some girls chat.]
Mr Green:	Can you be quiet so we can hear the conversation . . . Is it private?
Raya:	Yes.
Mr Green:	Well, you will need to be quiet or the whole school will know about it.
Mr Green:	I will try to get the technician down here to cut up wood for you. Do you think that would be a good idea?
Jane:	Yes.

In the following extract we turn to the boys' introductory lesson that started with Mr Green taking the register and explaining the design brief. We pick up the lesson five minutes in.

Introducing the design specification: boys' class

Mr Green:	Then put together a parts list, material you need. It's no good saying next week, 'I need a piece of wood', so we don't have to waste valuable time next week. Plan it out. I am determined to get in there to get on with the practical as soon as we can.
	[A boy has been tapping on the desk.]
Mr Green:	Oh we've got a drummer boy. Can I ask you to go into the workshop.
	[The boys get up and go through to the workshop. As they walk in Mr Green says . . .]
Mr Green:	Turn round, get your paws off . . . right on your desk is a red plastic . . . Gentlemen, we have at least one person who has his eyes in his ear-hole . . . turn round. When we were doing our design work last week people were very concerned with how it looked. Unlike in art we don't just draw pictures, we actually design . . . if you don't get over . . . draw – you need that skill. No Ferarri testosteroso or something like that, I worry about that. No go faster stripes, fluffy dice. It needs to travel a distance of 5 metres and carry a weight at the same time. With that in mind I want you to consider the framework, chassis. Wheels, it does not matter about the size. Wood dowelling comes in lengths of about two metres and in diameter . . . not thickness or width . . . this is a 6mm dowel. You can see the size of it.

Jason: What's that black thing sir?
Mr Green: I'll come on to that.

Settings in design and technology

Mr Green enjoyed exchanging banter with the girls and boys. He joined in the girls' chat when they talked about boyfriends and he joked with them about their 'romantic' secrets. The girls moved round the classroom freely: they got up to carry on a conversation with a girl in a different place, they touched the model cars in the display cases and they searched in cupboards for pencils and rules. Mr Green lent one girl what he called 'My Japanese-designed ruler'. Later in the lesson the girls discussed the price of a perm and Kylie told the other girls how much hers had cost and where to find the best hairdressers in town. Towards the end of the lesson, Kylie combed her hair in full view of the class and although aware of what was happening, Mr Green permitted it to continue. Mr Green and Kylie enjoyed an easy repartee. Yet Kylie was also one of the girls who answered technical questions that he posed about the design of the chassis and materials. He talked to individual girls about drawing the chassis and wheels. He advised on which materials to use, yet said that in the end the choice was theirs. One girl asked a question (which we could not hear) and he replied: 'Well I would advise against it. I've given myself a bad manicure on a sanding machine.'

In the workshop, Mr Green demonstrated: how the car had to be powered, either with an elastic band to catapult it or by pushing it; the various materials that could be used to make the car such as metal, wood and vacuum-formed plastic; and the requirements for a chassis frame, the wheels and a base. Throughout the demonstration girls interjected with questions that he took seriously and answered fully. For example, in response to a girl's question he described how the vacuum form was made from a clay mould. When they returned to the classroom from the workshop, Mr Green explained the design brief to the girls again. At no point in the introductory lesson did he raise the subject of how the car should look in an aesthetic sense.

In exchanges with the boys Mr Green used witty comments that were meant to appeal to their sense of the absurd such as, 'one person who has his eyes in his ear-hole'. He disciplined boys in an easy-going manner by using phrases such as 'shut it' and 'belt up'. There are similarities here with how Mrs Sharp in Palmers School (Chapter 2) spoke with the boys and used humour and forms of language that they themselves would use with each other. By comparing the lessons we found that Mr Green controlled the boys' movements more than those of the girls, especially in the workshop where he steered them away from touching materials and machines. As with the girls, he asked the boys to be quiet and listen, yet when the boys asked spontaneous questions he did not follow them through as he had with the girls. When one boy asked about the 'black thing' he said he would return to that later. He stressed that the design drawing was not the same as an artistic interpretation, it was a modelling tool. The aim of the drawing was to generate, explore and manifest ideas. He tended to emphasize the functional aspects of the design and referred to aspects of the production process, while downplaying the aesthetic considerations with the boys. In his comments he anticipated that the task of designing a car would generate fantasy images of sports cars etc. which has been found to typify boys' designs in research (Murphy 2006). Mr Green spent a considerable amount of time addressing technical aspects such as forces and gravity with the boys. He told them that a 'bit of team work would not go amiss' and that he did not mind them working in pairs, suggesting that he was aware of the tendency of boys not to collaborate.

The differences between the ways Mr Green addressed the boys and the girls relate to concerns we raised in previous descriptions when Mr White did not curtail the boys' pyromania in the science laboratory. Mr Green, in comparison, restricted boys' movements in the workshop, censored their questions and steered their attention to focus on issues, concepts and machines that he prioritized. In effect, his comments mocked the boys' potential interest in aesthetics by referring to 'Ferarri testosteroso', 'go-faster stripes' and 'fluffy dice'. Therefore, he narrowed the legitimate practices that boys could undertake to create a successful car by discouraging their interest in style other than in technical terms. In his discourse Mr Green separated the subjective, emotional and aesthetic aspects of the car from the objective, technical features and in so doing he aligned the boys with practices associated with masculinity. While he appeared to be more willing to control the boys than Mr White, on the other hand he allowed the girls to occupy the workshop in a similar way to the way the boys had occupied the science laboratory. This we suggest was one of the ways he made explicit to the girls that the workshop space was a place for them, thus extending to them an identity of belonging and legitimating their membership of the community. With the boys we suggest that their sense of belonging was considered unproblematic, as in the maths and science settings, reflecting the historical gender legacy of the subject. Mr Green's control was a way of maintaining the boys' attention on the learning objectives and he set parameters about what was and was not legitimate to do, excluding aspects of the boys' assumed agenda (e.g. fantasy cars).

Further evidence of Mr Green legitimating girls' membership was the way in which he opened up practice to them and extended their access to, and use of, the tools of the community. Over the series of three lessons we observed how girls used the potentially dangerous sanding, sawing and drilling machines, manipulated pieces of wood and freely collected tools such as hammers. In this way they displayed similar behaviours to the boys in Mr White's lesson. Some made holes in pieces of wood in the wrong places, threw them away and started again. This freedom to fail is important for novices who have to 'catch up' with practice and they need teachers to recognize this by modifying practices so that participation is prioritized as students learn about the tools of the culture. By using equipment freely, making mistakes and trying out techniques, the girls learned to become competent in the techniques associated with design and technology. The identity extended to the girls as legitimate peripheral participants (Lave and Wenger 1991) was recognized by the girls in the same way their 'outsider' status was recognized in Mr White's class. One girl commented about the purpose of the activity that it was about learning how things work 'even if you don't get it right'.

To achieve this experience of belonging for girls Mr Green had to overcome a historical legacy that aligns masculinity and not femininity with a subject like resistant materials. Mr Hunt and Mr White held an image of girls that reflected the historical positioning of women as weak, both physically and intellectually, passive and in need of protection. Mr Green on the other hand was committed to single-sex classes because he had watched girls gain mastery of materials and techniques, the repertoire of the community, in ways that contrasted with how girls functioned in the mixed classes he had previously taught. He also had experience of competent women in industry. Having a personal awareness of gender is well established in the literature as essential if single-sex organization is to be effective in enhancing access and learning (e.g. Berge with Ve 2000). Mr Green had experience of successfully opening up practice to girls in the masculine territory of design and technology. Let us now look more closely at his approach with the boys.

So far we have seen that he was willing to control the boys' behaviour in a male territory. In this respect his pedagogic practice we suggest interrupted the fraternal bond and helped the boys to remain focused on the learning objectives of the lesson. In so doing he altered the emphasis of the subject values in much the same way that Mrs Sharp did in her strategies to support boys. The boys were in danger of experiencing resistant materials as a technical subject devoid of any personally meaningful investment, that is, in which their subjective interest had to be suppressed in favour of objective, rational and depersonalized criteria. This is quite contrary to the intention of the subject where design is understood as a manifestation of creative ideas in which aesthetics and the social are valued alongside the technical. Mr Green, like Mr White, ensured a similar task but unintentionally orchestrated settings in which different versions of the subject were made available. To investigate whether or not these settings had any ramifications for the ways boys and girls experienced the subject we turn next to interviews with students.

Experiences of the setting

Developmental trajectories can be imagined as routes towards norms of masculinity and femininity and this places resistant materials as a staging post that boys and not girls were expected to pass through. Therefore, before boys even touched a machine, expectations about their competence already existed as part of the cultural legacies of the subject.

In Chapter 3 we described how objects, spaces and artefacts, the tools or repertoire of the community, reify something of the practice of the community and are marked with signification that accords with the values, practices and conventions carried by curriculum subject cultures. We described these reifications as 'projected meanings'. However, the meanings attached to objects such as sanding machines are carried through ubiquitous culture and so exceed any one person's meaning and are open to multiple interpretations. We have argued that they act as a focus for negotiating meaning in participation in practice (Wenger 1998). Therefore we have to look at how individuals used and spoke about such objects to work out what significance they had on the personal plane of analysis (Rogoff 1995). We have suggested that handling machines that were replicas of industrial machines empowered girls because it gave them access to the cultural tools of a community denied to them in the past. We will focus on two symbolic elements from the cultural reservoir of design and technology: machines and 'design ideas'.

ENGAGING WITH THE MACHINES

Both boys and girls were very aware of the dangers of using electrical machines. Some students were comfortable about using them while others were not. Brian commented, 'I think some of them [the boys] are scared to use the machines.' Two boys spoke about their anxiety concerning using the machines. Trev said they were dangerous and

said, 'If you slip or take a chunk out of your finger or something . . .'
James shared this concern:

James: I just don't feel confident in front of the machines.
Researcher: Oh. So tell me about the machines. What's particularly hard about it?
James: Well I'm just afraid of hurting myself really.
Researcher: Are any of the machines you know are more dangerous than others?
James: It might be the sander. Because my mate the other week he was going round and he took four layers of skin off where he just slipped.

All the girls we interviewed spoke about machines as frightening. Julie said, 'Some girls don't enjoy it, they're just kind of scared to use the machines or make out that they're scared.'

However Kylie spoke about gaining confidence using the machines: 'I like using the machines. I think it's really fun, well not fun but I like it. And I feel a bit older by using them, in Year 7 you didn't use them a lot but you still used them. And I just like using them because I don't normally do that sort of thing at home and when I was younger.'

Kylie spoke explicitly about how using the machines made her feel older. Other girls made similar comments about 'knowing how to work it [the machine]' and that 'It's nice to be trusted to use the machine.' Both boys and girls suggested that the autonomy, freedom of movement and informal chat enjoyed in the workshop was based on trust and that if they took risks with the machines their practical lessons would cease. The experience of trust aligns with the notion central to participation, of being involved in what matters in the community. The significance of mastering the machines was, however, different for girls and boys. Boys were expected to be competent with the machines as part of their identity of being a boy and their anxieties were concerned with being found out, or not being good enough, according to historical precedents about masculinity. Mr Green was either unaware of this or in his control of boys' potentially disruptive play disallowed the participation with the machines that these boys needed. Also for boys the representation of the subject that extended an identity of competency did not allow for an understanding of activities where the emphasis is on learning the processes and which accepts failure or 'not getting things right' as a route to this learning. For the boys the emphasis for their learning appeared to be on the product, which caused them further anxieties in contrast to the girls. To protect themselves these boys planned to 'leave' the subject as their participation was not an empowering experience. For girls these anxieties did not exist, except perhaps in that competency in any domain that is not aligned with femininity can be perceived as transgressive. We shall demonstrate that success in design and technology was not unproblematic for girls because they had to contend with conflicts between displaying a socially acceptable feminine identity and 'masculine' competence.

These different aspects of girls' and boys' competency were reflected in the way they spoke about the finished product. Mr Green's discourse about the relationship between technology and the domestic realm disrupted the assumption that boys' identities were bound up with their relationship to the physical world and labour. This latter perspective presumes that boys value the opportunity to take home the product of their physical labours. Consequently the role of individual products in enabling the home-school boundary crossing was only supportive for boys with an identity as technologically competent. One boy said it was important to him to show his parents what he had achieved. This boy considered himself to be 'very competent ... I always get high marks'. Another boy described how he policed what he took home as he anticipated negative feedback. He saw himself as not very good at technology, an identity he was not comfortable with, and an individual product made visible his inadequacies. Girls looked forward to taking their products home and said they were confident that whatever kind of car they took home their parents would be proud of them. The knowledge-gender dynamic of the subject offered boys and girls different trajectories forward and their success or failure had different social consequences. We turn now to an issue that boys spoke about a great deal in interview; the role of their 'ideas' in the design and making of the car.

Perceptions of salience

Boys spoke about the need to create a car that was technically excellent. For some boys this was paramount: 'it's the capability of the designs that's the key'. In interviews most of the boys stated that they were confident that their car would fulfil the technical requirements, whereas each of the girls expressed doubts about this. This placed boys in a position in which they were likely to get high marks in design and technology. For girls, the design and its aesthetic aspects were more significant than the technical 'making' aspects and this threatened the achievement of the brief and therefore the potential for gaining high marks. The technical requirements of the specification were more salient to the boys than the girls and this we suggest was reflected in the differential emphasis Mr Green gave to the technical aspects and his explicit requirement for the boys to suppress the aesthetic. Two boys we interviewed had tested their car before it was finished to check that it could carry the 1 kilogramme of weight. The boys said that the look of the car was a secondary issue, however they did give value to creativity and the product for them represented the expression of their ideas. They found collaboration difficult because it could undermine the 'visibility' of their personal creativity and they also had to take time to work out other boys' thinking, as Josh explained:

> Yes, if you've got your own idea then you don't need to worry about what anyone else is doing. And if it's someone else's idea that you've got then you're not going to be all that sure on how to make it, and how to do different bits with it. But if you've got your own idea then you're going to know how it works and how you made it. And if there are any problems then you can go straight to the problem rather than asking your friend, you took their idea off.

The look of the car marked out boys' personal investments in the making phase. All the girls we interviewed spoke about their investment in the aesthetic element of the task yet did not speak about these personal and distinctive aspects of the design in the competitive way that boys did. However, as we shall explore in Chapter 6, this may have been because of historical legacies of femininity. These make it difficult for girls to talk about competition and discord or indeed to take up a role as a creative person in technology, given the historical legacy that denied women the role of inventor.

Next we present some individual accounts to consider students' experiences of participation.

DARREN

Darren, in his descriptions of the task, made clear how he had entered into the practices of the community. When asked about whether or not there was to be creativity in the design of the task, he emphasized the importance of the brief given by the teacher: 'Um, well he gives you things you have to have, you have to have on the car and the things it has to be able to do and then you just build your design around that.'

He spoke at length about the practices of the subject, referring to rules, equipment and materials of the workshop. He spoke about the technical needs of the brief for the car to be lightweight yet strong and to run smoothly without the wheels rubbing. He described the processes of sanding, carving and hollowing out and using the big and small electric saws for different purposes. He worked alone and paid great attention to the instructions and the functions that his car had to demonstrate. He proclaimed with confidence that his car was going to win. There were no extraneous distractions either to create a good-looking car or in wishing to have girls in the workshop to talk to. He gave a sense of having a clear focus and being involved in purposeful activity.

MIKE

Mike understood the task and what success in it involved. He had an elaborate and extended technical language and was able to talk as well as, if not better than, Darren about the specific challenges of making the car in terms of materials, functions and capabilities. Unlike Darren however, he spoke of the problems that he was encountering with constructing aspects of the car. He was not as confident as Darren that he would produce a 'winning' car. He also spoke of his problems relating to the other boys in his class. He said that they would not 'tell the truth', had a limited range of topics to talk about and refused to discuss what was 'really going on': 'All they talk about is football, football, football. Even though I like it, it gets boring when you just don't stop talking about it.'

Although he recognized that aesthetic appearance was not an important aspect of the brief in terms of assessment criteria, he described the importance of a personal creative response in the design: 'Well it's not that important but it looks better when you've got a different one to everybody else. And you can just take more pride in it rather than just saying well I copied your idea. But you can say I just made that up myself.'

Although Mike had a strong grasp of design and technology, its specialist language and the technical requirements for success, he distanced himself from the subject. We suggest that this was because he struggled to associate himself with the masculine identity extended through Mr Green's practice and his own experience of the all-boys' setting.

JULIE

Julie said that resistant materials was her favourite subject and that her parents recognized that she was good at it. She explained that she had decided to make the model car in the shape of a sheep: 'Because I'm making the base and then you put the wheels, I made the base and I made the wheels and then I'm just making like the sort of sheep cutouts to put on the sides.'

The sheep image represented a personal and aesthetic investment in the object. Together with other girls Julie spoke about the importance of designing a car that would be interesting and nice to look at. However, she recognized that the vehicle would be too heavy to travel the 5 metres required in the specification. So we asked if the sheep design was interfering with getting the car to work. She replied, 'You do think about that but I'm just hoping that the design mark is really good and it will make the 5 metres. In the end you just take it home. The design was really good um, but it kept falling apart. The elastic bands kept breaking.'

She was hoping that the design of the vehicle would be good enough to get her marks even if the vehicle did not meet the other criteria. Her investment in creating the sheep design was so great that she seemed prepared to live with the possibility of failing to fulfil the design brief. However, assessment was not the most important outcome for her, because she anticipated taking the sheep-car home where she was confident that her parents would validate her work: 'Yes, because after a long time at school designing, making, thinking and, and to take it home to show your mum and dad. If it's really good, it boosts your confidence.'

If students are to manage in a subject they have to be aware of what is required to succeed in order to exercise their agency, taking account of the risks and benefits in particular resolutions. For Julie, her competency in the subject, essential to her participation, was derived as much from her membership in her family as in the school community of the subject, if not more. Her parents' perceptions of what constituted a good product were her source of validation and their criteria were the ones she gave value to more than those of the teacher. Julie's investment in the personal, individual and aesthetic aspects of the product looked as if it would cost her marks and cause her to miss opportunities to learn about the technical aspects of the subject. It was most likely that she would therefore be disadvantaged in dealing with the technical requirements of the subject when she moved to the examination class.

AMANDA

Like many girls, Amanda spoke about the problems she was having in constructing the car and hoped that marks awarded for effort would compensate for a lack of technical competence:

> I mean they do go well but mine don't always go that well, but the wheels on my one they won't go round, I'm not sure why. They're too big I think. In my projects when I've made them they don't always look like what I've designed them to be but the teachers won't understand that you can't make it exactly so. They grade you a lot on your effort because if you've just done something it's like OK but if you've put a lot of effort into it and it's not like really

good but if you've really tried then they give you good marks for that.

Part of her concern about not meeting the criteria specified was because she recognized a misalignment between the drawing created at the design phase and the material object she was constructing in the workshop. She realized that the most important issue was to get the car to work and therefore to meet the brief. She explained that teachers often did not understand that the finished product could not replicate the drawn design exactly. This is an issue of authenticity which is recognized as a significant problem in design and technology, as what students can achieve given their resources and those of the school is often very constrained. Hence the students know that their products lack authenticity in a subject which gives priority to it. For some, as we have seen, this tension is overcome by taking the risk of challenging the teacher's criteria and establishing their own as Julie did. For others, like the boys, the task is often reformulated and competition for the 'best' car or the most creative way of meeting the brief overrides authenticity. For Amanda, not being able to do either and needing to comply with the teacher's task and representation of the subject, in line with a feminine identity of good behaviour, presented her with a considerable tension. This tension was between holding these two aspects of the task, the design and the material manifestation of the design, and hence of herself, together. Amanda tried to reconcile her need to produce an authentic car and one that would fulfil the technical requirements of the task. This may well be an unsatisfactory resolution for Amanda and as she reflects on her experiences and the constraints on her agency may influence her decision about whether to continue to study the subject.

Managing the task

Mr Green tolerated the girls' interest in aesthetic features of the car, however, the assessment criteria in design and technology ensured that it was the technical and functional aspects of the activity and not the aesthetic aspects that were rewarded. Girls often speak of the need for their artefacts to be authentic and to have functional use in the real world (Murphy 1999). It was difficult for some girls, like Amanda, to create artefacts that were crude yet fulfilled the design brief because it violated aspects of the cultural legacy of femininity. Kylie was the one girl who we interviewed who managed to retain her feminine identity and demonstrate technical competence in design and technology, and we shall return to her account in Chapter 6. Most of the girls in contrast to most of the boys spoke about the importance of being able to take their products home to show their parents because it provided tangible evidence of their creativity, competency and effort. They hoped that the teacher would value their effort and originality and that this would compensate when and if their car failed to meet the brief. Mr Green tolerated the girls' interest in style in their classroom banter yet he did not make a connection between the girls' investment in aesthetics, style and fashion and how they drew upon those very same symbolic resources to create their designs. These aspects of girls' personal investment in the task were *invisible* to Mr Green and were not valued in the assessment process. Mr Green considered that the task was authentic as the skills acquired through the design and making of artefacts such as a model car had an obvious relevance to life. Thus measurement in relation to where to drill the holes for the model car axles was linked by him to the context of putting up a shelf and buying a microwave to fit a given space. Creating joins was another feature of the activity and for the teacher this knowledge would enable students to 'do those little jobs around the house'. We can see that legacies of common sense ideas about femininity did filter into Mr Green's pedagogic practice, because he allowed the girls to 'act like girls'. His practice however left the girls to achieve in the resolution of their designs a precarious balance between masculine/objective and feminine/subjective features of the task.

In contrast, Mr Green's pedagogical discourse focused boys on the functional and technical elements of the design and steered them away from producing cars that would look good. Boys were more prepared to interpret the task within the confines of the technical requirements, emphasizing the making over the designing of the car. Their ability to see their creativity expressed in personalized response was, however, a tension that made them resist Mr Green's requirements for them to think about teamwork or to work in pairs. Mike's comments revealed that resistant materials was experienced as a narrow reproduction of masculinity by some boys. Mike wished to opt out of the community rather than give up his personal interest in making, creating and engaging with things that mattered to him and in ways that he valued.

Masculine identities: pedagogy and learning

Mathematics, science, and design and technology are curriculum subjects that are aligned historically with masculine identities. This we suggest is why no attempts were made to subvert the subjects: when they were presented to boys and to girls the tasks were identical. However, across the subjects we observed different *versions* were enacted for boys and for girls. This means that before students entered these classrooms historical legacies had already set up expectations that extended identities of competence to boys and not to girls. These subjects also reinforce the fraternal bond that historically has been associated with masculinity and which set up precedents about boys' legitimacy, autonomy and participation. Aspects of the historical legacies of masculinity that are revitalized in boys' peer groups are difficult for teachers to counteract because they belong to our shared common sense culture. To be able to resist these influences we need to recognize this aspect of the knowledge-gender dynamic.

Our analysis of classroom interaction revealed how Mrs Marshall's, Mr White's and Mr Green's practice extended identities of subject competence to the boys. Mr White allowed the boys a great deal of autonomy in science as an expected aspect of normal boys' behaviour, which made it difficult for him to notice the behavioural consequences of this autonomy and to curtail them. John's interview revealed how the 'mucking about' interfered with the process of learning science. Without actively addressing and curtailing the informal practices of male peer group culture, boys are left to constantly push the boundaries. John and Mike suggested that boys wanted teachers to make the limits explicit yet spoke with resignation about the possibility of that happening. For them, as for Mr White and Mr Green, the fraternal bond was part of their common sense understandings of life. The consequences of this assumption are that for some boys the opportunities to learn about a subject are constrained. Therefore such behaviours need to be challenged rather than accepted as inevitable even if historical legacies make it difficult to recognize that such behaviour is unacceptable.

We were struck by the way the boys' pyromania was not salient to Mr White although Sophie's minor infringement of the laboratory rules attracted his immediate attention. We have suggested that Sophie crossed an invisible boundary when she not only participated in the masculine territory of science but went one step further and acted like a boy. In his interview Mr White said that he had reprimanded Sophie in order to give the girls a message that the 'funny business' must not spread. We can draw an analogy between the funny business and out-of-place femininity. For girls in science the intention to extend practice to them was clear, however, assumptions about their incompetence coupled with a transmission approach to learning as the reproduction of knowledge frequently denied them agency and made them an instrument of the teacher's agency. There continue to be not only limits to tolerance of femininity in science but a lack of awareness of appropriate pedagogy that opens up practice and enables girls to identify with the domain.

We noted that Mr Green demonstrated a confidence to curtail the influence of the male fraternity and this may have been because of his awareness of gender gained through personal experience and reflection. He, as with Mrs Marshall, legitimated boys' membership of the subject communities while offering them structures to limit the influence of male peer group culture in the classroom. We have hinted that Mr Green had further steps to travel in gaining awareness of how the gender-knowledge dynamic was imperceptibly emerging in his practice.

Teachers can extend learning opportunities for students if the kinds of control they exert and the pedagogic strategies they employ open up practice in ways that enable girls' and boys' participation and their successful boundary crossings into subject territories historically dissociated from them. Here we consider what our observations and analysis suggest may facilitate this. First we have made explicit the historical legacies that align mathematics, science, and design and technology with masculinity. We suggest that teachers can draw on an awareness of these to consider in their settings the relational identities of girls and of boys in terms of the identities extended to them and the identities that students might anticipate. This requires reflection on teachers' discourse and practices.

We have demonstrated how the male peer culture permeated settings and this was heightened in the single-sex settings according to many of the boys. We saw how Mrs Marshall skilfully controlled the boys in mathematics by finding an indirect means for reprimanding them that avoided any personal confrontation. This is a useful technique to curtail the influence of the fraternal bond. We saw too how gender legacies set up expectations about girls as more fragile, weak and timid than boys. Our observations and interviews with boys and girls in science laboratories and design and technology workshops challenge this cultural legacy. Boys were as concerned as girls about using machines, some were as interested as girls in design and style, although possibly for different reasons, and some boys were actively frustrated by the macho behaviour of their peers. The ways that boys and girls experienced and spoke about tasks showed that they did not personally align themselves with historical legacies of masculinity and femininity, even though they often recognized the influences of these on behaviour. Therefore teachers also do not have to align boys with common beliefs about masculinity and girls with common beliefs about femininity. Our observations suggest that, in assuming these alignments, practice and hence learning is closed down for some students. Mr Green's way of extending practice to girls provided an example of how increasing opportunities for participation and placing an emphasis on 'catching up' with practice could be achieved. His approach allowed the possibility of learning through trial and error and consequently things going wrong became as valued a source for learning as success.

Finally, we wish to highlight the considerable variation between boys and girls in their interest and investment in the same task, such as building a model car. This variation further indicates the limitations of imposing essentialist assumptions about students' gender. It gives teachers a legitimate place from which to encourage students to do things in classrooms in ways that do not align with traditional beliefs about gender. As we saw from the girls' resistance to Mr Hunt's pedagogic approach in Chapter 3, and Annabel's mocking of Mr White in this chapter, girls come to school with expectations about having access to male domains and of being treated as autonomous, even when, like boys, they may not yet be competent in all areas. The students expressed their commitments to tasks and linked these to commitments outside school. These commitments influence how they reformulate tasks. It would therefore be an important step forward in working with gender if, as part of formative assessments, students were invited to discuss their perceptions of what was planned for their learning and how it, and the tasks selected to achieve this learning, linked with their experiences of the world.

We have seen how the subjective and creative engagement with tasks was closed down in the science settings and in design and technology in the boys' setting. We also speculated about the potential risk girls took in prioritizing aesthetics in design. If there is a commitment to work with gender then creative engagement with tasks needs to be encouraged both for boys and for girls and implicit definitions of what counts as valued knowledge in their subject domain need to be broadened both in the curriculum and its assessment. It is most likely that the younger generation has already moved beyond the gender norms and beliefs that their teachers were brought up with and this opens up a gap for social, personal and pedagogic change, if teachers wish to go there.

Chapter/ **Five**

Inside the classroom: English, drama and art

In Chapter 3 we suggested that subject arenas are cultural streams which interact differently with gender legacies. In this chapter we outline the dynamic interactions in classrooms where subject knowledge carries a core feminine identity. In the first section we focus on the way Mrs Young deliberately changed a feature of the boys' lessons and consider the consequences of this action. When we enter the drama studio we shall examine Mrs Diamond's pedagogic discourse and practice in depth, while the example from the art class focuses on one incident.

English: changing the subject

In Chapter 3 we found out that Mrs Young was rather critical of the English department in Monks School for providing book boxes and separate texts for boys and girls. This strategy contravened her belief that good literature would take students beyond their immediate expectations and launch them into other cultural worlds:

> That's just in the department. I prefer to teach the boys *Romeo and Juliet* to be honest, because of the innuendoes and the sword fights. And you know they think Romeo is a big girl's blouse and you know, you can have them chanting things and they quite like it. And the boys feel I suppose in this day when they can be a bit more open about their feelings. In a mixed class it's gone down really well, and I don't see why an all boys group wouldn't enjoy *Romeo and Juliet*.

From her interview we could tell that she was committed to giving boys and girls access to the same kinds of text and in this respect she did not align with ideas that boys and girls have different ways of learning.

We observed three consecutive lessons in which students were instructed to produce three pieces of work: a script for a radio report that they audio-recorded, a TV report which they video-recorded and a newspaper report giving accounts of one incident. Mrs Young told us how she had tried to draw on students' personal culture (Valsiner 1998) to help them to explore issues raised in the text *Buddy* that both the boys' and the girls' classes were studying. In the first lesson with the girls she gradually filled the board with features of genres that she derived from the answers given by the students to her questions. She said that her aim was to help students to understand that different writing styles achieve different purposes. Once they had composed a written version of the report, groups took it in turns to audio record the script as if presenting a news slot on the radio. In effect, she wanted them to gain the analytical tools to read and interpret reports and media messages and to understand how the world is constructed by texts. The activity also fitted with the emphasis on the child as the producer of text and not only the reader of others' texts. This reflected the more progressive models of English in which literature and language were integrated. In the second and third lessons groups of approximately four students worked together to write a radio commentary.

Removing the text

In the second lesson in the girls' class Mrs Young told the girls to pay attention to the events in Chapter 9 of *Buddy* in which the main character discovers a burglary in a neighbour's house. The girls went through the text to work out how events had unfolded and which characters to include in the radio commentary. In this way the text provided resources that they drew on to compose the radio reports. Through discussion girls' groups chose characters and incidents from *Buddy* to write the radio script. During the third lesson Mrs Young played the tape and the girls looked bashful, amused and sometimes embarrassed as they heard their voices played back in front of the class.

The first lesson in the boys' class was similar to the first lesson in the girls' class in which Mrs Young introduced features of three genres – the radio, TV and newspaper reports respectively – using the same question, answer and validation as in the girls' class. However, when it came to the second lesson where the boys had to work in groups to create the text, she did something that initially surprised us. She removed the text, *Buddy*, from the activity and instead instructed the boys to create a radio commentary of a football match. This was not a planned aspect of her pedagogic approach with the boys and seemed to us to arise spontaneously during the lesson. We asked her why she had changed the activity for the boys and she told us that complications such as having to teach the boys in two different rooms, and trying to help the boys to remember what they were doing from one lesson to the next, had influenced her decision: 'Because my experience of that group has been that if I would have given them the chapter like I gave the girls; one, their reading isn't that strong so they wouldn't be able to skim the bits of the chapter they wanted necessarily, and two, they would copy them.'

This quote points to her differential expectations of boys' and girls' abilities to handle such a task of reading and writing. By directing the girls towards Chapter 9 of *Buddy* and then by removing the text in the boys' class she also orchestrated two different versions of the subject in the settings, the consequences of which we analyse next.

Girls' and boys' experiences of the setting

Students receive clues about what they can legitimately write according to the instructions that teachers give them in the classroom. The girls understood the activity as one in which they were expected to reconstruct the plot in Chapter 9 of *Buddy* in three different genres and therefore they referred back to the text to achieve this. The text provided a source from which they reminded themselves of plot, characters and atmosphere and proceeded to use this information as the basis from which to compose the radio script. The text also provided a common reference that anchored the negotiations and choices that group members made about what exactly to include, how to create a sequence and what to emphasize or leave out. In interviews the girls spoke about the way everyone shared ideas during group discussions. Having a copy of *Buddy* to refer to allowed them to achieve a high level of intersubjectivity, as Molly explained: 'Um, well we discussed it as a group and then we was writing it out like roughly and then we done a final copy and done it so that Francesca had a line and then I had a line and then just kind of, I had a paragraph where the beast comes. When you have to – I mean I was doing it panicky so it come out.'

Molly used the technique of a 'panicky' voice to create her character. The girls themselves said that the task had been interesting. The girls' interviews demonstrated that they believed they were using their imaginations in creating radio scripts. Some of their scripts were very funny. Some not so good and there was a range of successful and less successful performances. Nicole was very enthusiastic about the radio script activity and said, 'It was fun. It was wicked.' Laura described how one group had started the radio commentary with a jingle:

Laura: I think they sung at the start of it.
Researcher: Yes. And what did you think of them?
Laura: I think it was good. Like a real radio ... It was funny.

In interview other girls referred to this as the best radio script produced in the girls' class. Without a text to refer to the boys had to call on their experiences of football and offer these ideas to the group as the basis for negotiations about how to write the radio script. The ideas had to come from the boys and not a text. One boys' group had a great deal of difficulty in creating a script and some boys remained quiet throughout most of the writing phase. Some boys told us in interview that they had never been to a live football match. Two of the other boys in the group were too concerned about the quality of their ideas to offer them to the group. Jeremy expressed concern about letting the group down, and refused to read out any part of the script for the oral recording: 'I didn't like want to make a mistake in it so I didn't want to let them down so ...'

Robert reported how boys with few ideas and a lack of confidence in oral work were teased by other boys: 'But – and there were some that weren't so good and you felt sorry because half the class took the mickey out of them and it was a bit out of order.'

Seth contributed most of the ideas in his group. He was the only member who was able to maintain his identity as 'good at English' and his status in the male peer group. We shall explore how Seth managed his social identity as 'good at English' in Chapter 6. Because one member contributed most of the ideas a hierarchy emerged in this group, yet for understandable reasons. Joe justified Seth's dominant contribution by saying that his ideas were funnier that the other boys:

Joe: Er one person's ideas got used quite a bit because they were quite funny but it was like shared quite a bit between us all.
Researcher: Ahah, OK. So why did ... tell me why you wanted to put in funny ideas.
Joe: It ... we thought it might capture attention of the crowd who's listening?
Researcher: And when you were thinking about the people who were listening, who were you most aware of?
Joe: We were thinking of the classroom and thinking what they'd like, what we'd quite like ourselves.

Joe's comments, as with Steven's in Chapter 2, made it clear that the public to whom the boys addressed their work was a self-referential group of boys. One of the techniques that they felt was appropriate in male peer groups was the use of humour. Because boys believed that they were addressing other boys they restricted their writing to what they thought were appropriate forms for their male peers. One of the boys in this group spoke enthusiastically about the group product:

Robert: We put a bit of comedy in it to make it funny. And well we did get down to the point. We would sometimes go into detail in a match, but then would mention how great the atmosphere was and fans supporting their team. And the way like the teams, like they looked determined. Not just like, oh that team's scored one goal. Or that one's just got a penalty.

Seth, the principal author, did not share Robert's enthusiasm about the final script. He felt his ideas had been exploited when they were reworked in the group and became somewhat debased. His solution was to refuse to read out the script when it was to be audio-recorded, so that his voice was not heard by the class. He managed to distance himself from the group and disown the ideas that were presented in the semi-public space of the classroom. There were costs involved in disowning ideas as we shall see later in Chapter 6. He said that football was an uninspiring topic to write about:

Researcher: Have you been to a football match?
Seth: Yes, but.
Researcher: Yes. Was it – just as a matter of interest was it possible to bring in anything ...
Seth: Yes, well I mean you pretty much know what it's like at a football match. From like watching it on the TV. It's, you know, people were shouting, there's not much more to it than that.

When we asked Seth what kind of things it was important to write about, he spoke about people's parents splitting up and other life events experienced by students of his age.

Mrs Young's views of the boys' and girls' work

When we asked Mrs Young if she was pleased with the scripts that had been produced she said that she was encouraged by what the boys produced, 'they rose to the occasion'. On the other hand she said that the girls had used the text to reproduce ideas that were already there. She described the text as a safety net and this was compatible with her notion that the girls had produced less imaginative and interesting scripts than the boys:

> They [girls] liked, you know, safety in something that's there, that they can look at. I think they like to be exact. When they were talking about the boy, about Buddy going to, you know, trying to make it like it's a radio commentary. But they wanted to make sure they had their facts straight. Whereas the boys are quite happy for their imagination to perhaps you know ... They probably would have Buddy with a machine-gun or something, coming round the corner. In a way I wouldn't put it past them!

Having told the girls in the lesson to use the text as the basis of the radio commentary Mrs Young then criticized them for using it to form their sequence of events in the radio script. Instead of viewing the text as a resource for creative writing Mrs Young demoted it to the status of a prop that she believed the girls used to bolster their self-confidence and 'to get the facts straight'. In contrast, we viewed this as a successful realization of the instructions that the girls had received. At another point in the interview Mrs Young said, 'I gave them the text because the girls asked for it'. We interpreted this as a reasonable request for the tools to do the job. She assumed that the boys and not the girls would take liberties with the text and embellish it with extreme fantasies such as giving Buddy a machine-gun. Yet, the humour, wit and imagination that Molly and Laura had used, and which the other girls recognized in each other's radio scripts, were not salient to Mrs Young.

Beliefs, intentions and consequences

In Chapter 3 we suggested that English carries a core feminine identity and that the subject privileges subjective meanings. In interview Mrs Young suggested that texts could be used to expand students' experiences beyond their personal culture, dominated by the media and common sense ideas. We showed how the girls used the text to provide characters and incidents from literary culture, here signified by the text *Buddy*, and combined these with their own ideas to write a radio script. In the boys class she removed the text – why?

She described her decision as a spontaneous enactment that arose when she was worried that the activity might be too complicated for the boys. It may also have been prompted by our presence in the class, making her wish to 'play it safe' with the boys. Yet, this moment-to-moment enactment demonstrated that she did not trust *Buddy* to speak to boys' interests. Instead of them having a text to call upon as a cultural resource she forced the boys to rely on their personal culture (Valsiner 1998), namely their assumed knowledge of football, to find ideas for writing. Instead of freeing up the boys Mrs Young's pedagogic practice placed them in a situation where they were in danger of being exposed for not knowing enough about football. An unintended consequence of this was that it prevented some boys from participating at all in the writing activity and helped to create a hierarchy in Seth's group based on the contribution of one boy who felt confident enough to put forward his ideas.

Creative writing requires that students find ideas from their personal culture and align them according to the conventions of writing. The girls' setting provided a literary text as a further cultural resource while the boys setting did not. Once a student offers an idea to a group it enters into a semi-public space in which it becomes open to judgements such as praise, blame or 'not being good enough'. The historical legacy of English, which privileges subjectivity, ensures that ideas are viewed as a manifestation of the person outward. Therefore the judgement attached to the idea acts back on the student leaving him or her to face the social consequences (Ivinson 2004, 2005; Zittoun *et al.* 2003). Thus the ideas offered in the boys' class carried the potential to expose them in front of their peers as not having the 'right kind' of knowledge about football. The text would have provided the boys with resources such as fictional characters that they could have used to mediate their inner and outer world.

The brief history of English presented in Chapter 3 suggested that the novel epitomizes a feminine form of writing. We can see aspects of this cultural legacy emerging in Mrs Young's pedagogic practice. By removing *Buddy* and replacing it with the topic of football she attempted to undermine the feminine alignment of the task. However, the consequences of removing the text from the boys' class was to limit their participation in group work and deprive them of the very resources that would have allowed them to contribute ideas and negotiate in a more equal way. Similarly, Mrs Young's implicit belief about femininity prevented her from recognizing the witty and funny aspects of the girls' performance. Her pedagogic practice thus inadvertently reproduced legacies of masculinity and femininity and revealed an opposition between text, fact and compliance on the one hand and imagination let loose, interesting work and risk-taking on the other.

We have shown that what happened in the boys' and girls' classes was a direct result of the settings orchestrated by Mrs Young which provided boys and girls with different possibilities and resources for achieving the task and for learning. It was in her moment-to-moment enactments that Mrs Young brought gender legacies into the classroom and this helped to influence her decision to remove the text from the boys' class. None of this hidden knowledge-gender dynamic was visible to Mrs Young. Before we turn to Mrs Diamond and the single-sex drama classes in Monks School, we speculate here about the role of women within institutions such as schools by turning to another gender story.

Gender story 4: the bourgeois mother and women teachers

The social expectation of teachers has been to produce the citizens of the next generation and historically who counts as a citizen has been deeply gendered. Women's roles in nurturing and caring have often been imagined as 'natural' and much has been written about the mother-child bond as instinctual. The idealized relationship between mother and child, which is imagined to be fine-tuned (Walkerdine and Lucey 1989: 64) can never properly be emulated by the nursery or primary school teacher. The notion that the woman teacher is expected to develop just the right kind of sensitivity towards the learner underpinned much of the child-centred ideology epitomized by the Plowden Report (1969). Ideas of liberation in progressive pedagogies emanated from a radical bourgeoisie in modern demo-cratic societies. Pedagogy in which self-expression is valued such as child-centred approaches places the teacher in a position where she nurtures rather than uses an authoritative position to bring about learning. Teachers in primary schools, mainly women, were ruled by the bourgeois masters' regimes that 'reflected the soft benevolence of the bourgeois mother' (Walkerdine 1988). The labour of female teachers makes the liberation of the 'normal child possible'. However, the girl, the black student or working-class boy do not conform to the 'idealized' child. The 'nurturance trap' (Walkerdine 1986, cited in Burge with Ve 2000: 30–1) places a duty on women to care for and therefore produce the idealized male child. Girls' education has historically prepared girls to undertake a nurturing role even if they aspire to professional careers.

Drama: freedom and moral control

Mrs Diamond, the head of drama, introduced girls and then, in a later lesson, boys to a series of role-play exercises about a fictional character called Harry Roberts. The aim of the lessons was to explore the moral problem of truancy. Mrs Diamond hoped that by getting students to role-play characters in Harry's life they would learn that truanting from school was counterproductive. In interview Mrs Diamond expressed a belief that drama came to life in classrooms when 'children' made contributions and listened to each other in discussion. According to this understanding of drama, knowledge did not come from the teacher, but instead the teacher provided the structure that allowed ideas to emerge from the students. In the following sections we explore the settings orchestrated in boys' and girls' classes and students' experiences of these.

In drama lessons teachers set up an imaginative space and then invited students to enter it. The creation of fictional worlds, whether in drama or any other subject, relies on teachers maintaining them throughout the lesson. Mrs Diamond used body postures and gestures such as sweeping the air with her arms to signal the creation of an imaginary place, which also placed a boundary between the fictional world that was being conjured into existence and ordinary classroom life. Mrs Diamond anchored the fictional scenario in drama settings by varying the tone and pitch of her voice, by her posture, facial expression and head movements as well as her instructional talk.

Settings in drama

The extracts below are from the third lesson of the series about Harry Roberts, a school truant that Mrs Diamond had adapted from a play of that name. During the previous lesson, groups had been introduced to a fact sheet providing information on the various characters in Harry's life such as his mother, teacher, headteacher, boss at the market where he worked part-time, and his friends. In groups students discussed in role the cause of Harry's truanting problem. During the third lesson Mrs Diamond used a cultural tool, a mock photo album, to remind students of the text and guide their role-play activities.

Mrs Diamond explained to the class that they were about to meet Harry for the first time. Using a technique called 'hot-seating' a student played Harry and other students 'in role' as friends, teachers etc. asked questions about his life. The hot-seating session was to flesh out Harry's biography and try to work out why he was truanting. Students sat in a wide horse-shoe shape and had been instructed to take off their shoes in preparation for practical work. Mrs Diamond introduced the fictional scenario by reminding students of the work undertaken in the previous lesson. We are going to compare how she introduced the 'hot-seating' activity in the girls' and boys' classes. Both classes took the lesson seriously and fully entered into the fictional scenarios that Mrs Diamond set up for them.

Girls' drama lesson

At the start of lesson, Mrs Diamond addressed the girls' class as follows:

> *Mrs Diamond:* We were dealing in the last lesson with the case of a truant, Harry Roberts. We never actually met Harry Roberts we just had opinions about him expressed by various people in his life. For example, his mother, there was his school friend, there was the boss of his casual job, and there was his teacher and there was his head of year and those people all had an impression of Harry, because Harry was not attending school, he was a truant. So there were two things to discover in this ... number one, what was the problem with Harry, what was his problem, why wasn't he at school and the other thing was what can we do to get him into school, because it is the law that everyone has to be educated. And how are we going to conduct the meeting to make a plan to get Harry back to school? At the end of your case conference each group gave a report about what your plan was for Harry. Okay now a bit of time to think, what your group said for me to tell to Harry. [She moves on after a brief pause.]
>
> Okay now, this is the next bit, I want you to think of the character you played last week. Which role did you play and in that role I would like you to think of what you would want to know from Harry if you were to meet him, because the next stage of events is to call Harry in, to tell him what we decided. Ask him what is going on, we haven't even met him yet. So what did your character want to ask Harry? Okay I want to think back to all that information on the sheet.
>
> Now this is the next bit. I would like someone who can remember some of the details of Harry's life to offer themselves to the next piece of drama. [pause] Is there anyone here who can remember ...
>
> [Hands go up, Mrs Diamond looks around and chooses a girl for the role of Harry.]
>
> Okay now, Georgina. Yes, Georgina, Harry.
>
> [Mrs Diamond points/gestures to a chair at the front. She stands up and drags her chair to the left,

leaving the chair at the front for Georgina to come
and sit in. Georgina sits in the chair at the front
centre.]
Right, Harry has come to this meeting.
[She sweeps the air with her outstretched arm in a
wide arch to signify the space as the place of the
meeting.] We want to record questions about his life
and then we might get on to what we ... OK.
[She turns to talk to Georgina.]
Now Harry, you are in charge. People who have got
questions can put their hands up and you can take a
selection of those questions. Over to you.

Mrs Diamond first explicitly reminded the girls of the fictional
scenario introduced in the previous lesson in which they had enacted a
case study to consider Harry's truanting problem. In order to invoke
the memory of the last lesson she referred to the roles they had played
in the fictional case study scene. She reminded the girls about a fact
sheet that contained information about Harry's life. We turn now to
the parallel section of the boys' lesson.

Boys' drama lesson

At the start of lesson Mrs Diamond addressed the boys' class as
follows:

Mrs Diamond: Now we had this case conference and each group
came up with a plan ... what that group was going
to do to help Harry, what Harry's problem actually
was. I'm asking you to spend one quiet moment
[pause] one quiet moment thinking about what your
group said about Harry.
[Silent pause.]
One quiet moment, everyone is thinking about what
their group said would be the best thing for Harry.
[Silent pause.]
I would also like you to think which role, which
person you were playing in that case conference and
what *your* point of view was about Harry *as you saw
it,* remember some of the things that *you* said about
Harry, what were his problems in life as *you saw it.*
[Silent pause. Mrs Diamond now speaks quietly.]
Very important that you remember ... right ask

Harry a few questions about his life ... he was not asked. This is your opportunity that we did not have last week, that is the opportunity to ask Harry a few questions about his life. He was the one person who was not represented at that meeting last week. *If you think you could put Harry's point of view across* would you like to put your hand up?
[She looks around the room to choose a boy.]
Right.
[She points to Sam. He comes forward and she moves her chair to the left and sits down again.]
Right, would you like to come and sit in the seat here, thank you.
[She pats a chair at the front. Sam takes up a position centre front and sits down.]
Now then Harry has come to our meeting. This is the next part of the case conference.
[She sweeps the air with her outstretched arm in a wide arch to signify the space as the case conference setting.]
This is the next part of the case conference. Right this is the next part of the case conference. You are going to take on the same role as last week. OK. So, you're his boss, you're the friend, you're the parent, you're the teacher. You have got the opportunity of asking Harry whatever you would like to know about his life, about his views about life.
[She turns to face Sam as if coaching him in how to play his role.]
And you are going to answer them. OK, it might be things we already know about Harry or it might be things that you *imagine* that Harry might say in answer to that. So in other words, it might not be things that we know about him already but what you *imagine*. OK can you think of a question for Harry and we'll let Harry be in control. Harry can select the people.
[Harry points to a boy.]

(Emphasis added)

The hot-seating exercises were supposed to steer students to discuss the moral and legal imperatives to attend school. By comparing the two lesson openings, it became clear that in the two settings that emerged girls and boys were provided with different clues, resources and sociocultural tools for realizing a role-play. Mrs Diamond built the atmosphere in the girls' and boys' classes differently. She had two main intonations, an everyday voice of instruction and a slightly higher and quieter pitch that she used when sharing a fictional scenario with students. In the boys' class, she whispered when she asked the boys to think back to the previous lesson invoking a hushed silence to facilitate thinking and remembering. She repeated the request to retain 'one quiet moment' in the boys' class, and not in the girls' class. She varied the intonation less in the girls' class and stayed longer in the everyday voice of instruction than in the boys' class. By maintaining the hushed pitch longer in the boys' class she signalled that she valued the fictional world that the boys were bringing to mind and in comparison did not give the girls' as much time to recollect and draw on that imaginative world.

Mrs Diamond encouraged the boys to focus on their personal views and placed the emphasis in the girls' class on recalling facts about Harry from the fact sheet. The criteria for playing Harry varied; in the boys' class she encouraged the boys to use their imaginations and not to worry about her instructions or the fact sheet. In the girls' class she asked for a volunteer to play Harry who could 'recall' the facts about Harry. When she tutored Sam about how to play Harry, she said, 'So in other words, it might not be things that we know about him already but what you *imagine*.' She did not suggest that Georgina call upon her imagination.

She encouraged the girls far less to use their imagination and instead steered them towards addressing the problem of truancy in the 'real' world of education and the law. In this way she reminded the girls of the moral intention of the role-play activity. In contrast in the boys' class she encouraged them to use *their* ideas and *their* imagination irrespective of the text, the fact sheet or the requirement of the law.

In the next activity students were instructed to work in groups and prepare a role-play to depict a 'day in the life of Harry Roberts' which Mrs Diamond told both classes they would perform at the end of the lesson. In order to create a role-play that could be performed in front of the class, groups had to assign each member a character and agree and work out a storyline that led to a moral end point. Finding the moral end point to the role-play was crucial for planning a coherent series of scenes in Harry's day that would give a message.

In the boys' class Mrs Diamond made sure there was time for each group to perform their role-play in front of the class. After each presentation she gave the boys positive feedback. In the girls' lesson only two of the five groups presented their role-play because Mrs Diamond decided to spend a considerable part of the end of the lesson discussing an issue with the girls and therefore left no time for three groups to present the role-play they had been working on for the majority of the lesson. When we asked why she had allowed all the boys' groups to present their play yet only two of the girls' groups Mrs Diamond said she had had a 'gut reaction' to do so:

> Umm it would be different for different lessons I think, I think it's a kind of *gut reaction* on my part to see what's the main aim here you know. I think that's, I think the boys' group there was quite umm I don't know that was *quite a pressing need for them*, it was a need for them to feel that it *was fair*, that everybody had, you know, had their opportunity. Whereas, I mean this is my perception, it could be wrong who knows, but the *girls had brought up issues* that you know, that were ones that were perhaps a bit I don't know, a bit too . . . ? But they'd expressed them in a *verbal way* so I suppose I went with that.
>
> (Emphasis added)

She said she had a 'gut reaction' that it was important to the boys to show their plays because they expected to be treated fairly. In the girls' class she said that discussing issues was more important than performing. In interview some of the boys emphasized that performing in front of their peers was important but if they had not presented in the lesson it would have been annoying but not crucial. They spoke about the chance to perform as a pragmatic issue of time.

In both English and drama lessons we encountered cases where boys chose not to present in front of the class. For example, Seth had refused to perform in front of his peers in English because he believed that the group's radio script was not good enough while Jeremy had been too shy. In drama we found that not all of the boys were comfortable with performing while some of the girls would have been and therefore were disappointed about being denied the opportunity. Yet, when Mrs Diamond justified her differential treatment of the girls it became clear that performance was not an issue that she believed girls valued. This assumption reflects traditional beliefs about gender and public space. In the next section we compare experiences in a boys' and girls' group respectively who undertook the role-play activity.

Girls' and boys' experiences of the setting

Students had to find a role from the subject's cultural repertoire such as the 'naughty boy', the 'authoritarian teacher' or the 'caring mother'. This allowed students to find a role to play. For example the role of the 'authoritarian class teacher' provided a well-defined script because it was familiar and pertinent to students' immediate concerns, as Dave from Year 8 explained: 'It was fairly easy because you know roughly how to act like them because they teach you everyday.'

In contrast, Lynne struggled to reconcile the cultural script of the 'authoritarian teacher' with her knowledge of *real* teachers who had feelings and emotions the same as she had. She explained:

I think it was quite difficult because when you're not a teacher it can be quite like, you're trying to sort of think now what is it like but they're probably not really sure about how you see them. So you're trying to figure it out, how to sort it out ... You can't really *act* a teacher unless you *are* a teacher I think because I mean people will say oh this is what it's like to be a teacher when they're not a teacher and the teacher will say it's nothing like that, it can be enjoyable, but it can also be awful.

Lynne's need for authenticity prevented her from playing a type. Her comment typified a recurring pattern that we identified between boys' and girls' accounts of the role-play activity. The girls spoke at great length in interviews about the importance of finding a plausible reason for Harry's truanting:

Debby:	Um, I think in that I was actually the bully and taking money and things like that, just being horrible to him and his friend.
Emma:	That people cannot want to go to school for many different reasons like bullying, or they just don't want to go to school, nothing interests them so they may want a change of school or they're just not happy and might need to be taught at home.
Lynne:	Then eventually there's a meeting, to try and sort out with the parents and the parents are all very, oh no there's nothing wrong with my child. So I think we were just trying to work out the way things were going.
Beth:	Yes because I sort of thought about his mum spoiling him a bit too much.

Their accounts expressed a need for psychological credibility and resonated with Mrs Diamond's instruction that they find out 'what was the problem with Harry'. The girls' group we observed did not manage to resolve these competing explanations of Harry's truanting and therefore did not find an agreed end point for the drama to work towards.

Three out of the four girls in the group described the role-play activity as an exercise in compromise. Learning to compromise meant recognizing that others in the group had different ideas to their own and as Lynne said, 'you have to accept that' and realize that 'maybe mine isn't so true'. Because the girls failed to achieve a consensus the moral end point of the role-play did not come into view and the girls spoke about having to act out roles that they did not feel confident about, not knowing what to say next and being confused about the plot. In the end Karen won the prize role of Harry which allowed her to dominate the action and imposed her moral end point on the others. Yet even Karen spoke about the need to compromise: 'We worked quite well, but when we were discussing it, some people wanted their ideas in it and some people didn't like those ideas so we had to compromise a lot.'

Lynne described the chaos in the group:

> Because people were running around saying what am I? What am I? So thinking we weren't quite sure what we were doing, work out the scenes. Because we're all like running from place to place and you're like sitting there in the middle of the kitchen when you're meant to be in a school classroom, so it could be a bit more organized.

Beth said that Karen and Lynne had dominated discussions. Her account demonstrated how the girls with the most ideas had dominated and this echoed what had happened in the boys' group in English when Seth provided ideas for the radio script. Hierarchical ways of working were not consistent features of boys' or girls' groups, as teachers often maintain; they developed when groups had difficulty in achieving a shared reference to anchor discussion and debate. In the English lessons the girls had used the text, *Buddy,* as the focal point for deciding which characters and events to include in the radio script. In drama it was the boys' group who found shared references in the form of props and well-defined roles. This allowed them to achieve more intersubjectivity than the girls.

In the hot-seating activity Sam had created a Harry who was a 'cocky' young entrepreneur who was going to make his fortune by taking over the market stall from his boss and expanding his empire by acquiring further stalls. According to Sam because Harry was making money in his part-time job, school was a waste of time. The boys did not talk a great deal about how their group functioned. They spoke about being satisfied that they had all contributed ideas and had produced a good performance. There was no debate in the group about why Harry might be truanting. They took the moral end point of the play literally from what Mrs Diamond had told them – that children have to go to school – and used this to guide the plot. In general the boys described Harry as a typical 'naughty boy':

Paul: She wanted us to find out that it is better to go to school than not go to school.

Ryan: He was selfish and just wanted everything.

Alec: A cocky boy that wants it all for himself. I think because of him working at the market and his mum gave him quite a lot of money as well and quite lazy I think, because he'd be lazy to get up for school but he'd be OK to get up for working on the stall.

The moral 'to go to school' worked as a device for creating the drama and the boys did not connect Harry's problems with their own lives. Alec managed to get the role of playing Harry. He told us how he had drawn on his personal experience, just as Mrs Diamond had encouraged him to do to create his character: 'I just thought of the market-place and thought of ideas, because I live near Forestown market and all the kids grew up down there. And I got some ideas from that. All the men shouting out.'

Alec brought his experience of the local market in Forestown to elaborate the familiar 'naughty boy' script. Given that the boys had unanimously accepted this version of events they turned their attention to theatrical devices such as the use of funny voices and creating props. Don and Alec explained how the group came to use a blazer and chairs as props:

Don: We said like for the blanket we use a blazer and everyone just said that and we all thought that was a good idea.

Alec: The way we put some accents on and where we put all the chairs and tables into like a stall and we were talking quite well.

Objects such as these were appropriated and used to mark out physical spaces. Therefore props, accents and cultural scripts became available as visible and symbolic resources for the group. These, plus the agreed moral end point, provided a high level of shared meaning to anchor the fantasy scenario they were creating.

When we asked how different ideas were resolved within group work, Paul pointed out that the resolution came in the performance. The observational data demonstrated that boys had at least as many conflicts, if not more, than the girls, yet the boys did not talk about them in interview. Even when presented with an example of conflict in a video clip, Ryan dismissed it as 'nit picking'. Instead in interviews the boys spoke about finding a strong role, using props and their voices. The differences between what the boys and girls chose to talk about in interviews were so striking that it led us once again to suspect the influence of gender legacies. We speculated that the boys refused to talk about the conflicts, difficulties and negotiations in their group because 'getting it right' involved placing an emphasis on pragmatic issues of action and achieving a 'performance'.

The girls did not achieve shared meanings as securely as the boys. The biggest obstacle for the girls was finding an agreed end point. Finding authentic roles and thinking about the moral problem of truancy became matters of debate and personal reflection for the girls.

The text, the law and public space

Mrs Diamond's classroom practice and instructional discourse allowed different versions of the subject to emerge in the boys' and girls' classes. She insisted that the girls pay attention to the information provided in the text and work out what was really wrong with Harry. In this way she signalled to the girls that they should consider others in accord with their future roles as carers of children, husbands and boys. She invoked the law in the girls' and not in the boys' class. These instructions meant that some girls' role-play failed to fully get off the 'real' ground into imaginative realms. Yet in one group girls created Harry's mother as an outrageous flirt who tried to seduce the headteacher when called in to account for her son's truancy. This entertaining aspect of the role-play was not salient to Mrs Diamond. Historical legacies of femininity do not make it easy to think that girls have lively and subversive imaginations. Instead femininity is associated with security, safety and constraint. This makes it easier for teachers to say things like girls need 'safety blankets' and 'facts'. Yet, in both the English and drama settings we saw girls being playful and witty. The imaginative and creative aspects of girls' work are rarely encouraged.

Mrs Diamond did not believe it was essential for the girls to perform their plays at the end of the lesson. The consequence of this was that some groups of girls left the lesson with no feedback at all about their group work. We have noticed this pattern in other lessons. Without regular feedback girls had to find ways to make sense of the subject and this forced them to search a wider landscape to work out what the teacher was looking for. Girls accessed a different qualitative range of clues from boys. Without clear feedback girls draw upon their traditional roles as carers, and this led Lynne to say that in the end the group had to produce a role-play so as not to hurt the teacher. Hurting the teacher was not something boys spoke about in interviews.

In the boys' class Mrs Diamond had stressed the legitimacy of boys' ideas, personal views and use of imagination. She did not insist that they pay attention to the background information provided in the text or that they needed to work out what was really wrong with Harry. The setting in the boys' class allowed the performance of fictional characters without the need to think in any depth about the moral imperative for, and psychological authenticity of, Harry's truancy. The boys understood drama as a subject in which the performance itself was the aim and their job was to develop theatrical techniques to portray a message. They said that the teacher wanted them to act out a fairly obvious and uncontroversial moral imperative that students have to go to school. Mrs Diamond removed obstacles such as the text that might have interrupted the boys' creative self-expression. Therefore, as in Mrs Young's English setting, she removed the subject cultural tools such as the text and moral controls that historically have a feminine value.

We showed that in the boys' setting there was an alignment between the demands of drama, the school rules (the law says that students must attend school) and the social norms of masculinity. Creating a role-play for performance was compatible with a western cultural legacy that boys will become men who perform within the public realm (see gender story 1 in Chapter 2). Mrs Diamond colluded with this by ensuring that each of the boys' groups had the opportunity to perform. Therefore, working out what was required within drama was a relatively easy task for the boys. Mrs Diamond's classroom practice thus reproduced conventional gender legacies because she colluded with the demands and expectations of the boys rather than trying to direct them more firmly to investigate the moral dilemmas associated with truancy.

Let us consider the effects of the more straightforward feedback the boys received. First, Mrs Diamond praised each and every group for their performance. In interview the boys said that the teacher thought the role-play had been good because 'she said so'. This is a pattern of practice that we have noticed across a range of single-sex boys' classes. Boys hear teachers telling them explicitly that what they have produced is good and they take this at face value. Why should they not? Second, almost invariably teachers tell us in interviews that boys' work is immature, superficial or concrete, especially in English and drama. Yet, we have shown how both Mrs Young and Mrs Diamond removed the cultural tools that would have helped the boys to move more deeply into the practices of the subject. If the boys had had to pay attention to the text they would have encountered alternative sources of ideas and these would most likely have interrupted the reproduction of ideas that the boys drew on from familiar culture. Without insisting that the boys use the text and without giving feedback that their work was lacking in depth, the boys were denied the resources they needed to produce work of a high standard. If the boys had been encouraged to consider the moral dilemmas faced by Harry instead of creating funny voices then they might have started to work out how to think and write about emotions, empathetic feelings and complex ethical issues in their own lives as well as in those of others. Yet the reasons why teachers shy aware from challenging boys' 'preferred ways of working' relate to the difficulty in working against the flow of deeply entrenched gender legacies.

We can begin to see that the boys' and girls' accounts were infused with cultural legacies of gender. It is not socially legitimate for boys to focus on the process so much as the product, or for girls to ignore the concerns and feelings of others. Boys and girls drew upon the cultural legacies of gender that belonged to their near culture to create characters, action and plot. This familiar culture is itself imbued with cultural legacies. In orchestrating the settings differently in the boys' and girls' classes Mrs Diamond did not interrupt these historical legacies. It was the combination of Mrs Diamond's differential classroom practice and the way boys and girls drew on gender from their near culture that together created two different versions of drama. Mrs Diamond was not aware of having orchestrated two different versions of the subject. Gender was working implicitly in practice, below the radar of conscious awareness. In the next example we focus on one incident in an art classroom to demonstrate what happened when boys mobilized gender as a defence.

Art: reforming threatened identities

We observed a Year 9 boys' class in an art lesson in which the activity was to paint a scene from a jazz café. Mr Fellows, the art teacher, was in his 30s and regularly organized football trips with the boys. In this lesson he had shown the boys copies of an artist's work to demonstrate how to restrict colours to yellow, grey and black and to work on the flesh-coloured tones of the jazz players. We observed Mr Fellows teach the same lesson to a parallel Year 9 girls' class. The girls' lesson was relaxed and the students chatted with Mr Fellows throughout. From the minute the boys entered the art room we sensed tensions. Mr Fellows started the boys' lesson using the same informal approach adopted with the girls. However, the boys were more reluctant than the girls to collect brushes, paint pots and paper. One boy managed to occupy himself by walking round the classroom, going to the sink and avoiding sitting at a table for almost half the lesson before eventually starting to paint. When we compared the boys' entry into the art studio and their entry into the science laboratory it became clear that the material culture of the art room did not invoke masculinity and the boys' reluctant behaviour signalled that they were uncomfortable with the environment.

As they painted, fewer boys than girls obeyed the basic rule about colour. The boys used more primary colours than the girls including bright orange, green and red. Mr Fellows had a continuous problem keeping the boys focused on the task. As the boys worked they chatted and the main topic of conversation was football. At one point a boy asked how to mix flesh-coloured paint. Mr Fellows carefully explained to him that he needed to mix red and yellow to produce the colour pink. As he gave these instructions, the underlying peer group discourse shifted from football as a few boys started accusing other boys of being 'queer'. From that moment onwards a homophobic discourse spread across the class as more and more boys joined in the banter, taunting each other with half-joking, half-serious accusations of homosexuality. To change the subject, Mr Fellows took this opportunity to remind the boys of the football trip that he had recently organized and we can read this as a bid to move the chat back to a safe male topic.

On inspecting the boys' paintings after the lesson we noticed that hardly any boys had used pink colours for flesh and instead had chosen black or dark brown. Mr Fellows told us at the end of the lesson that he had realized that the activity was not good for the boys. He said that the boys had put less effort into their paintings than the girls and that next time he would substitute a different exercise for the boys to do. Painting pink flesh had not been a salient issue for the girls and they had produced some good pictures. Pink is a symbolic resource that is overwhelmingly linked to femininity. It seems that the presence of pink in the boys' art class tipped them into a defensive response in which they tried to contain the emergent femininity within the label 'queer' which each boy projected outside himself and onto another boy (Kenway *et al.* 1998). As the accusation 'queer' was received by one boy he seemed to feel the need to pass it onto another boy and so the homosexual banter spread furiously around the classroom as boys passed the 'insult' of being 'queer' from one to the other like a contagion (Jodelet 1991; Joffe 1999). Mixing 'pink paint' had introduced a ubiquitous femininity into a classroom setting that was already marked as feminine due to the historical legacy of art. The boys would also have recognized pink as an indicator of homosexuality. The introduction of such a visible manifestation of femininity into an already compromised male space provided the boys and Mr Fellows with an almost intolerable threat. The boys' name-calling and accusations can be seen as a bid to expel femininity based on a collective fear that it would pollute an already precarious masculinity. In our discussions with Mr Fellows after the lesson it became clear that he also shared the boys' fear and experienced the threat. By invoking football he attempted to dissipate the problem. Mr Fellows told us that next time he would change the activity in the boys' class, thereby abandoning one of the principles of art – mixing flesh-coloured paint – in a bid to make the lesson more acceptable to boys. In the following section we shall explore the role of peer group culture as a vehicle for the relay of beliefs about gender.

Stemming the flow?

Research in schools suggests that hegemonic masculinity (Connell 1995) is powerfully reconstructed within male peer group culture. In line with ethnographic work carried out in secondary schools we identified the resources that boys deployed to recognize, police and maintain peer group membership (Mac an Ghaill 1994; Epstein and Johnson 1998; Francis 2000). Girls' peer group culture operates differently as we shall demonstrate in the following chapter (Gulbransen 2003; Ringrose 2006). Peer group cultures tend to be carriers of conservative legacies of gender and provide powerful markers of masculinity and femininity. Students acquire beliefs about gender from cultural resources such as magazines, TV, film and video games (Walkerdine 2007). The range of resources available to boys to reconstruct masculinity is narrower than those accessible to girls to reconstruct femininity. This is because masculinity has higher status than femininity and therefore boys have more to lose than girls when expressing themselves using cultural resources that are marked as feminine (de Beauvoir 1972; Pateman 1988; Lloyd 1989; Walkerdine 1989; Duveen and Lloyd 1990; Lloyd and Duveen 1992).

While boys in our study spoke at length about the influence of male peer group culture and how they restricted their behaviour to that which they believed was acceptable to other boys, they often spoke about this with regret. Many boys' accounts showed that they were ambivalent about their own participation in male peer group culture. Seth's comments above demonstrated that although he recognized that producing a funny script in English was a 'crowd pleaser', as Steven in Palmers School had done, he did not personally value the script. He distanced himself from it by refusing to read it out in class. In many respects boys wanted teachers to limit the influence of peer group culture. In the passage below Joe describes peer group culture and explains how 'funny' can shift to 'rowdy', which can then become 'boring', 'stupid' and a 'waste' of school time.

Joe:	I think it gets a bit rowdy sometimes when it's all boys because if one starts they all try joining in so it gets a bit rowdy I think sometimes.
Researcher:	Um what do you think about it?
Joe:	I think sometimes it gets a bit beyond a joke and they just carry it on and try to be funny when they're not like, try to interrupt the class.
	I think it's a bit boring after a while. I think it's . . . the teachers think it's the boy's attitude
Researcher:	Um and why does she have that attitude do you think?
Joe:	I'm not too sure.
Researcher:	And what is the attitude do you think?
Joe:	Bit cocky, like answering back, bit too big headed.
Researcher:	Um and so why, why do you think he's doing it?
Joe:	Well it's, to get attention.
Researcher:	Um and what do you think of that?
Joe:	I think it's stupid in some way, like you come to school for five or six hours a day, I mean if you're going to be here for that long, you might as well learn something, I think, out of it instead of just mucking about. I think it's stupid.

Joe suggested that the reason why teachers let boys get away with 'funny' and then 'rowdy' behaviour was because 'they think it's the boy's attitude'. His comments signalled an alliance between teachers' expectations about boys and common sense notions about masculinity. He expressed his regret that school life was dominated by the stupidity of 'mucking about'. In effect he wanted teachers to stop the flow of hegemonic masculinity.

Part of the reason why we were working in Monks School was because the behaviour of the Year 9 boys was deteriorating. Sixth-form girls were being wolf whistled in corridors and had reported levels of sexual harassment from Year 9 boys that had not existed before the intervention of single-sex classes. At times we observed and experienced intimidating and violent forms of behaviour from some of the Year 9 boys. Some boys had become skilled at mobilizing the class through extreme masculine resources of chanting, homophobic name-calling and physical expressions such as banging on desks. The single-sex grouping allowed these practices to spread rapidly among the boys. Some boys seemed to have become stuck in a position in which they were expected by other boys to use extreme forms of macho expression.

It is commonly believed that boys need to prove their masculinity to girls and that this issue is heightened in mixed-sex classes where girls are present (e.g. Hannon 1997; Hawkes 2001; Gurian 2001). Our observations suggest something different. We found that boys together created the need for them to constantly prove and defend masculine credentials in front of other boys. This is why we believe the homosexual banter spread rapidly among the boys in the art class. Our research suggests that the presence of girls makes sex difference visible and clear and therefore reduces the need for boys to prove that they are getting it 'right as a boy'(Walkerdine, personal correspondence).

Feminine identities: pedagogy and learning

There are many cultural streams that come together in classroom practice and discourse. On a broad sociocultural plane there are gender cultures and subject cultures that historically have fused and aligned in complex ways. In Chapter 3 we outlined knowledge-gender alignments that included objective/masculine to a subjective/femininity alignment. In tracing the history of subjects we have suggested that English, drama and art are associated with identities that align with femininity. We showed that teachers' accounts of their pedagogic practice were fraught with tensions and in this chapter we have demonstrated how these worked out in practice. The tensions that we pointed to in Chapter 3 between historical legacies of knowledge and gender became palpable when we observed teachers' practice. We found that despite their stated beliefs about gender, teachers' pedagogic practice tended to accommodate masculinity rather than hold boys to the conventions and principles of English, drama and art. Girls and not boys were expected to use cultural tools such as texts and follow the rules. We suggested that moment-to-moment enactments effectively removed impediments that might have been obstacles blocking the expression of normalized masculinity. Teachers changed the subject, the activity and the cultural tools to make tasks more compatible with masculinity as they imagined it. In contrast, girls were continuously caught between two worlds: the fictional world of drama or creative writing and the authentic realm of emotions and social relationships. This provided girls with a different conundrum than boys which we shall explore in more detail in the following chapter. By bringing historical legacies of subject cultures to light we suggest that common sense beliefs about gender can and should be challenged. Beliefs about gender are neither fixed nor do they enhance learning when they emerge in practice in unreflexive ways.

We are all embedded within our cultural (Schutz 1962) environments and cannot act without calling upon the symbolic materials that culture makes available. Like all practices, pedagogic practices are imbued with historical legacies of gender. Under pressure, Mrs Young encouraged the boys to reproduce common sense masculinity even when she specifically told us that she hoped to propel students beyond their personal cultures into literary culture. Mrs Diamond also allowed the boys to call on their personal views and imagination in place of the text and the fact sheet that contained information about Harry's life. Mr Fellows said he would remove the need to paint pink flesh from the boys' classes in the future. In effect, teachers removed the text and with it aspects of the curriculum subject principles, the law (to go to school) and the social constraints that remained in place in the girls' lessons. The settings that arose in boys' classes were compounded by the boys' anxieties about the need to appear as a 'good enough' boy to their peer group. Therefore, when teachers did not give strong instructions which clearly told them that they were expected to undertake activities such as reading a text for ideas, or discussing ethical issues, the boys were left scanning their familiar culture for resources and ideas to complete tasks. By drawing on their near culture, boys re-created in their role-play and texts stereotypes such as the 'naughty boy', which reproduced common sense masculinity (Lloyd and Duveen 1992; Francis 2000; Skelton 2001). Boys did not learn to expand their cultural landscape and instead learned that common sense masculinity provided a legitimate social role to act out and write about in drama and in English. Why was masculinity allowed to overpower the aims, principles and cultural resources of these subjects? Cultural legacies tie teachers, and especially women teachers, to the social project given to the 'bourgeois mother' to nurture masculinity (see gender story 3 in Chapter 4 and gender story 4 in this chapter). The public space was historically a masculine space made up of male ideas, rules and conventions, and each teacher removed obstacles that might have prevented boys from expressing themselves within the public realm.

However, boys do not identify themselves with narrow versions of masculinity and some boys expressed regret that teachers were not 'stemming the flow' of common sense masculinity. As Joe said, 'funny' leads to 'rowdy', and that leads to 'bullying'. When asked why teachers let the boys get away with it Joe invoked a form of masculinity similar to that which Sam had invoked in the drama when he played Harry. Joe suggested that teachers imagined all boys to be like Harry 'the lad'. In effect, Joe was saying that teachers did not try to bring 'the lad' under control and gave up teaching boys the rules of legitimate subject practice as well as failing to insist on compliance with the law and submission to social mores. Seth and other boys in the study wanted there to be limits to the flow of ideas that reproduced narrow beliefs about masculinity because although it might get a laugh from the other boys it was not a worthy subject for writing about and did not allow them to engage in really important personal and social issues. Boys and girls need spaces in the curriculum to talk about the pressing social and personal issues of life, albeit in mediated ways.

So how can teachers stem the flow of common sense beliefs about masculinity or femininity? Let us return to the issue of texts. The historical legacy of the curriculum subject English is bound up with values attached to texts. With the invention of the novel in the mid-eighteenth century the texts associated with English were those that opened up the inner world of intimacy, emotion and relationships. Therefore texts such as novels have the potential to offer boys and girls resources such as imaginary characters, alternative social settings and ideas about action that they can use instead of drawing on what they already know from their near culture. Texts can indeed expand students' imaginary worlds, as Mrs Young suggested in her interview. Texts help boys and girls to find vehicles through which to express emotion and knowledge of relationships. They allow students to explore psychological authenticity without the danger of being exposed in front of their peers. *Romeo and Juliet* is as accessible to boys as to girls and hopefully Mrs Young was right in saying that these days boys can be 'a bit more open about their feelings'.

English is a subject that has become recognizably feminine (Gee 1990; Lankshear and McLaren 1993; Alloway and Gilbert 1997; Alloway *et al.* 2003). We have suggested that English texts could have acted as mediational means (Wertsch 1991) for boys and provide them with ideas and resources for creative writing. Shakespeare explored emotions through male characters and such texts expose boys to a broad repertoire of cultural resources relating to masculinity. By recognizing the dynamic between gender and subject knowledge teachers may think about opening up subject domains rather than closing them down. Students reproduce hegemonic masculinity or femininity in their classroom practices either as defences or because they do not have other imaginative possibilities to draw upon. Stemming the flow of common sense beliefs about masculinity and femininity involves changing the curriculum subject by making it safe and legitimate for students to express a *wider* range of ideas. To achieve this we need to work against the historical legacy such as the public-private divide which associates masculinity with features that are opposite to those of femininity. We shall return to this problem in Chapter 7. In the next chapter we listen to four students who told us how they managed the conundrums produced in the classroom settings described in this chapter and Chapter 4 while retaining 'good enough' identities as boys and girls.

Chapter/ **Six**

Students' gendered experiences

This chapter focuses on the individual plane of analysis and investigates how four students, Kylie in design and technology, Seth in English, and Alec and Lynne in drama improvised solutions to the tasks set by their teachers. Chapters 3 to 5 explored classrooms from across the curriculum and identified systematic patterns of practice that distinguished boys' and girls' settings. We examined how cultural legacies of knowledge and gender became active in moment-to-moment enactments and how teachers' pedagogic practices orchestrated the setting within which students had to work. In Chapters 4 and 5 we focused on curriculum subjects that align with masculine and feminine identities respectively. We found that for boys' and girls', classroom settings made available different versions of the curriculum subject, cultural resources and learning opportunities. Here we explore how these four individuals navigated pathways through settings to achieve performances, texts and artefacts while trying to 'get it right' as a boy or girl (Davies 2003).

In the first account we return to Mr Green's design and technology resistant materials lessons to explore how Kylie managed the uneasy balance between the functional-masculine requirements of the task, which were to make a car that could carry a 1 kilogramme weight 5 metres, and retain her feminine social identity. In the second account we consider how Seth, who we met in Chapter 5, managed to undertake a creative writing task which is associated historically with the feminine legacy of English and retain his credentials as a 'good enough' boy within the male peer group culture of his classmates. Although these students negotiated crossings into alien gender territory it required considerable effort to manage these precarious positions. One of our general aims is to make visible the gap between teachers' beliefs about gender and students' experiences of the knowledge-gender dynamic in subject-based classroom settings. By opening up this gap we challenge directives which advise teachers to change their pedagogic strategies in line with common sense beliefs about gender. In providing accounts from students within the personal plane of analysis (Rogoff 1995) we wish to show that classroom life is more complex (c.f. Younger *et al.* 2005) than these directives suggest and does not provide straightforward solutions to boys' or indeed girls' perceived underachievement.

Boundary crossings recounted

In Chapter 4 we suggested that the conundrum that girls had to face was to produce a car that was successful in terms of the technical requirements of the design specification without suppressing their personal investment in the objects they were creating. We presented Julie's account which demonstrated how her personal investment in the task had led her to design the sides of the car in the shape of a sheep. This altered the task significantly for Julie and her reconciliation of the tensions she experienced in the setting undermined the possibilities for her to achieve the expected outcome, the brief, and to experience herself as competent. We pointed to two general tendencies that have been identified in girls' practice in design and technology. The first was their investment in the aesthetic and the design aspects of the task over and above the making aspects; and the second was their concern for cultural authenticity (Murphy 1999). We suggested that historical legacies of femininity make it difficult for girls to produce artefacts that are messy, dirty or ugly and not 'fit for purpose'. Kylie was a girl who, in contrast to Julie, managed the masculine/feminine conundrum successfully. She made it clear that her purpose was to meet the brief and meet it well. She gave value to both the design and the making. We look now at how she achieved this.

Kylie's 'girlie' identity in design and technology

Kylie's looks, hair and ability to flirt with Mr Green created an image that was unassailably feminine. She was a central participant in female peer group culture in which symbolic resources that signify contemporary versions of femininity were discussed, disputed and exchanged (Holland *et al.* 1998; Gulbrandsen 2003). Not only did she have one of the most fashionable hairstyles, she also led the discussion about the price of perms and hairdressers, as we described in Chapter 4. Kylie appropriated the cultural resources of femininity to create a position from which it was safe to demonstrate design and technology competence in much the same way that Steven did in his performance of his text. She was known to be good at design and technology. The work she undertook to maintain her central position within the girls' peer group culture prevented other girls from judging the objects that she produced as a reflection of her not 'getting it right' as a girl (Davies 2003). Kylie recognized that design and technology was a masculine as opposed to a feminine domain:

Researcher: The first thing is off the top of your head tell me what design and technology is all about.

Kylie: It's about learning how to do things by yourself. Girls don't normally do things like that, do they, when they get older.

She gave a strong description of design and technology as a place where she was able to gain a sense of forward movement in the world. Using the machines and tools made her feel older she said:

I like using machines. I think it's really fun, well not fun but I like it. And I feel a bit older by using them because in school and that and in Year 7 you didn't use them a lot but you still used them. And I just like using them because I don't normally do that sort of thing at home and when I was younger.

The machines marked a threshold into a more adult world. For girls, gaining access to design and technology resistant materials had different associations than for boys because it was not a taken-for-granted aspect of their gender identity. Their sense of achievement in design and technology rather than in other subjects acquired extra significance. The imaginary world of design and technology came into view for Kylie as a disruption to a traditional feminine trajectory:

Researcher: And the point you started to make at the beginning was that girls are not supposed to do these sorts of things, so tell me a bit more about that.

Kylie: Well, normally when you grow up, they're just beauticians or working on computers and all things like that. And when something goes wrong, like my mum, she can never do it, and my dad's got to get someone out or the car's gone wrong and she's got to call someone out. When I get older I just want to be able to do it all myself instead of relying on everyone else. I just want to be able to do it all myself.

In her account Kylie identified the historical positioning of males and females in relation to technology that we referred to in Chapter 3, associating the male world with autonomy and the female world with dependency as she explained in the next comment about her mum:

> *Researcher:* And when did you start to kind of know that about yourself?
>
> *Kylie:* I think I always have. Because my mum, she would never do anything on her own, she always needs someone to help her, like my dad and stuff, and I think I don't want to be like that, I want to do it all by myself and when I get older I'll be on my own.

It may be that Kylie recognized that the machines that belonged to men's work had higher status than the machines that no doubt her mother used at home such as washing and sewing machines that belonged to the domestic realm. The denial of female involvement with technology in the face of women's overt daily engagement with it has a long history, as David Layton (1993) notes. This tends to render invisible or non-technological the artefacts and machines deployed in work in the domestic and private sphere that is associated with women. Kylie positioned her mother as 'outside' technology and hence presented her as dependent on her father, and stated a preference for accessing the machines associated with the public/male realm. For Kylie, entry into design and technology represented the chance to learn to be independent and to create an alternative future in which she did not need to rely on others. Design and technology signified a repudiation of her mother and her mother's world that was related to another aspect of her biography. In every sense Kylie was asserting an identity of competence in the domain counter to its gender legacy. We wondered what experiences enabled her to identify so strongly with the subject and to imagine connections across history and the social landscape in which she could locate herself. In her interview Kylie revealed that her father was a builder and from an early age she said that she had been helping him to make things in the garage.

> *Kylie:* I like it [design and technology] and I'll probably take it while I'm in school as a sort of school hobby and then because my dad's a builder and he's got them sort of things at home as well and I always go out to the garage and play with them and build things. I used to build little aeroplanes and things.
>
> *Researcher:* You used to build what?
>
> *Kylie:* Little aeroplanes and things but I'm making a dolls' house at the moment, a big one and I normally go out there and play with that, so I'll probably have it as a hobby.

Researcher: I mean do you think that a lot of your interest in design and technology might have come from your dad?

Kylie: Yes because when I was little I used to watch him making things and when he does things around the house I used to always do that and want to help and stuff and make it with him.

The garage was a place that she associated with her dad and having watched and helped him she had gained the capacity to play there and to make objects such as a dolls' house for herself. The garage was a space that she shared with her dad and was therefore associated with him and not her mother. We pursued the topic of independence with her:

Researcher: And do you think that idea of doing it all on your own and knowing how to do it is that hard?

Kylie: No, I think he [Mr Green] wants you to go and help each other and learn how to use it all. I don't want to go like completely on my own, I want to be with everyone else but I just want to know what to do. So I know if I'm doing it right all by myself because if I ask someone else what to do I'll probably get it all wrong and be doing it all wrong and I just want to learn myself.

Researcher: So you don't think that part of a design and technology teacher's job is to try and get people to do things sort of independently?

Kylie: Yes I think it is when you get older, that they know how to do it their self, as you say, independently. I think, because if we didn't have design and technology we wouldn't be able to do that when we get older.

Kylie entered the workshop with an identity of participation and membership that her dad had legitimated. Through her play and her legitimate peripheral participation in the 'garage' she moved more deeply into the practice of the community, creating her own artefacts, and developed expertise and competence in using the tools of the subject. Mr Green, in extending the workshop space to the girls and opening up practice further for them through participation with the machinery, further extended Kylie's agency and identification, and her identity as a competent member of a 'masculine' domain. Both Mr Green and Kylie's father had given her access to spaces, tools and know-how that allowed her to develop a sense of her own competence. She associated this competence with growing up and she had not had to sacrifice her femininity, represented by her interest in hair and in making the dolls' house. However, she did not intend pursuing design and technology as a career and said she wanted to become a vet. Her access to, and experimentation within, these male domains did not constitute a rejection of femininity but rather an extension of possible femininities because she had used these experiences to expand her vision of the future. Consequently she was not restricted to typical female careers such as becoming a beautician or working in an office and instead envisaged pursuing a male-dominated profession. Design and technology had given Kylie an expanded view of the world and she had found a way to think about being independent *and* being a woman.

By achieving well in design and technology Kylie had gained a strong sense of competency and therefore autonomy and came to associate this with access to male domains such as the garage and the workshop. She retained a strong sense of her femininity yet separated those elements of cultural constructions of femininity that she recognized to have traditionally kept girls in subordinate roles and a narrow range of jobs. Kylie had a achieved a complex perspective (Penuel and Wertsch 1995) because, we would argue, she was able to occupy simultaneously and be competent in at least two knowledge communities, as Steven was: the peer group culture where the symbolic resources of femininity were traded and displayed, and in the community of design and technology dominated by technical subject expertise.

However, there is a caveat. Even though Kylie managed the masculine/feminine conundrum with success it needs to be pointed out that she could not see herself developing a technological career, which fits with similar patterns in mathematics and science career choices. Indeed Kylie referred to her participation in design and technology as a 'school hobby'. This we suggest is because although Kylie took up the space offered to her it nevertheless remained for her one associated with masculinity. Being a vet is to engage in a caring profession associated with the body and biological sciences, areas which historically were associated with femininity. When girls do well in masculine subjects in school, this success often does not follow through to careers and positions in public office (Murphy and Whiteleg 2006; EOC 2007). Kylie's story suggests that tensions that have been indicated before, between social expectations of femininity and academic success (Walkerdine and Lucey 1989) are still being experienced by girls in the twenty-first century. We turn next to Seth, who managed to write a radio script in English. His story provides an example of a boy crossing into alien female territory.

Seth's 'weird' identity in English

Seth was the boy we encountered in Chapter 5 who refused to read out the radio script in the boys' English class. In general Seth's male peer group did not value writing, suggesting that they had some awareness of the association between creative writing and femininity carried by the historical legacy of English. We look at what was at stake for Seth in retaining his personal investment as a writer and the effort required to maintain this position as a boy in the boys' class.

Seth liked English and was considered by his peers to be good at it. He told us that the other boys, who described English as boring, considered him to be 'weird'. He spontaneously described himself this way and so we can assume that he was comfortable with the label that had been ascribed to him. As he spoke it became apparent that he had cultivated the 'weird' identity from a range of symbolic resources drawn from the cultures of music, film and writing. He let the other boys know that he listened to alternative music (see MacDonald *et al.* 2002) that was not part of the contemporary popular music scene. He used his knowledge of retro bands to mark out a space of difference. Being recognized as 'weird' provided him with a distinct image that deflected the norms of masculinity and gave him a position which allowed him to be recognized as a boy who was good at English. However, the weird identity came at some cost because he had to constantly maintain it in front of the other boys. We can draw a parallel between the ultra-feminine identity created and maintained by Kylie and Seth's 'weird' identity.

In Chapter 5 we reported that Ben and Joe both said that Seth's ideas had been used for the radio script because they were the funniest. When Seth explained why he had flatly refused to read out the script in class, even though he had written most of it, he talked about the embarrassment he would have felt:

Seth: I don't know. Probably because it's embarrassing. But
                 . . .
Researcher: Okay. For all of them in that situation?
Seth: Yeah.
Researcher: Okay, but just tell me why. Just talk to me about why it is embarrassing.
Seth: Well if someone else is going to watch it, it makes you stand out more and people are like looking at you. If you're just like standing there like a bystander, you know they – the attention isn't drawn to you. So if you do something, like stupid, then you know.

When asked what the perceived danger was, Seth explained it as 'the whole popularity thing':

Seth: Well if it's like lousy then you know it's the whole popularity thing, you know what I mean? If you're not like funny or cool then they won't like you. And then you've got no friends and you know. Whereas the teacher, it doesn't really matter.

I was just waiting for someone to go you know, 'what the hell is this?' Because if it isn't funny. Because I was like sinking in my chair a bit.

Seth felt that he had lost control of the writing process by having to work in a group and feared that the script was not funny or good enough to sustain his reputation. There was a double risk in having his work exposed in front of the class. Because he had constructed a social identity that incorporated 'writing' and having good ideas, an incompetent performance in front of his peers first risked having his writing criticized and second having his social identity of 'weird' being ridiculed instead of admired. The English activity had put at risk his 'reputation', his image and his personal investment in the symbolic world of English. He defended himself in a number of ways. He blamed the teacher for devising a 'lousy lesson' thus externalizing the task. He refused to read the script in front of the class, thereby eliminating the risk of whole class exposure. He seemed to have set this condition quite early on in the group work, demonstrating his awareness of the need for extreme vigilance in protecting his identity from the scrutiny of the male peer group.

When listening to Seth's account of his 'weird' identity we became aware of the competing demands that boys and girls face when producing texts and artefacts in subject settings that align with 'oppositional' gender identities to the ones they are trying to maintain. We can see that, given a hostile male peer culture and the threat of being stigmatized as 'other' or 'queer', the strategy that Seth adopted was to deliberately become 'other'. His taste in 'alternative music' set him apart from his peers in a positive way and the writing that he produced could also be associated with the 'romantic world' of the arts, painting and films. However, Seth had to constantly prove his skill in language and produce alternative, clever and witty writing in English to fend off attacks from his male peer group. Contributing to the radio script placed him in a critical situation. We can see how vulnerable his position was from his comment, 'I was like sinking in my chair a bit'. Maintaining a reputation required considerable improvisation (Holland *et al.* 1998) as well as much effort. In the following section we shall elaborate the relationship between social identity and learning from a sociocultural perspective.

Social identities and setting

The social gender identities created by Kylie and Seth were dynamic in that they had to be constantly re-won and we have pointed to the effort and the symbolic resources that were required to achieve this. In a sociocultural approach identities are not fixed attributes of a person; they are always linked to specific settings or social contexts. The identities produced by Kylie and Seth were responses to curriculum settings in which the historical legacies of design and technology and English extended identities to them that conflicted with the gender identities they had to maintain with their peer groups. In other social contexts the demands and the historical legacies that frame settings, which in Chapter 2 we referred to as arenas, will be different. In less demanding or less constraining social contexts (Lave 1988; McDermott 1996) Kylie's exaggerated 'girlie' identity and Seth's exaggerated 'weird' identity would not have been so obvious or necessary.

We can consider the micro-dynamics of how the danger of being judged as 'other' (Paechter 1998) or not 'getting it right' as a boy or girl (Davies 2003) work. In classrooms, students produce artefacts and texts such as model cars or radio scripts as improvised responses to teachers' instructions. As we pointed out earlier, the objects that emerge from students' hands do not enter into a neutral social space. Historical legacies and institutional practices set up the possibility that objects will be judged in certain ways and one of the problems for students is that their peers may read and interpret their artefacts and texts as having the wrong gender value. The danger for Seth was that a piece of creative writing would be interpreted as a feminine expression and jeopardize the need to be recognized as a 'good enough' boy. We gave an example of this in Chapter 5 when we described what happened when one boy asked the teacher how to mix flesh (pink) colours. The historical legacies attached to curriculum subjects such as design and technology ensure that objects such as model cars, once produced, become anchored within the field of masculinity. We have demonstrated how Kylie and Seth created exaggerated identities to offset the dangers of being recognized as gender transgressive because of the texts and objects that they produced in lessons.

When they produce artefacts, responses or texts, students sometimes find themselves instantaneously repositioned within social networks of peers, teachers, and even parents and siblings. Students have to undertake symbolic work to either reject or appropriate labels such as 'the one who is scared of machines', 'the one who likes pink paint', 'the one who has all the ideas'. The meanings that become attached to artefacts, texts and responses by peers or teachers are complex, sometimes incompatible and incomplete, and students have to navigate a hybrid multiplicity of signification in order to locate themselves within subject cultures. During the fieldwork we were struck by the range of reactions which students experienced based on what they wrote, said or created. Boys spoke about losing or hiding model cars that were not good enough to take home to show. Yet boys and girls also told us positive stories such as how a role-play, a cake or a pillow case, created in school, had been highly praised by parents, teachers or siblings. These acted as 'good objects' (Benson 2001) that could sometimes remind students of their competence and anchor their identity in that curriculum field long after the object had been produced.

The expression of social gender identity is revealed through the work that an individual has to undertake in order to retrieve or maintain a position that they can live with within a subject territory – what Wenger (1998) refers to as 'reconciliation' and Holland *et al.* (1998) refer to as 'improvisation'. Kylie imagined that being seen to be 'good' at design and technology might have threatened her identity as a 'girlie' girl. She enjoyed her position as a 'girlie' girl because she was able to flirt with Mr Green and be admired by the other girls for her perm and fashion knowledge. The work she undertook to maintain this position was to scour the landscape and constantly come up with fashion knowledge, tips and know-how to pass on to other girls (Gulbrandsen 2003). Her ability to trade this knowledge within the girls' peer group gave her an unassailable feminine identity that allowed her to focus on the technical specification as well as the aesthetic elements that the other girls such as Julie and Amanda prioritized in their cars.

Identity and practice always involve interplay between local demands and their socially and culturally embedded features. Although none of the boys would have explicitly identified creative writing as feminine they recognized enough of this historical legacy to call writing 'boring'. 'Boring' here means 'not something that I, as a boy, wish to be associated with'. We described the manoeuvres Seth made to create an alternative position within the male peer group by appropriating symbolic resources that related to the Romantic tradition. Social identities arose due to the demands and constraints of classroom settings that carried knowledge-gender legacies into the present so that texts, artefacts and responses came with values already attached to them as part of our shared ubiquitous culture. We have shown how students used symbolic resources from within the curriculum subject cultures and from outside school to improvise responses to tasks and to create, maintain and repair social identities. Social [identities] play a pivotal role in learning (Duveen and Lloyd 1990; Lloyd and Duveen 1992; Abreu 1995; Duveen 2001) and in these two examples we have demonstrated how a 'girlie' and a 'weird' identity allowed Kylie and Seth to cross into alien knowledge-gender territory. We showed the reconciliation work that was required by Kylie and Seth to maintain their reputations within these two settings that involved what Penuel and Wertsch (1995: 87) call a 'complex perspective coordination'. These identities allowed them to become central participants within communities of practice and thereby facilitated their learning. In the following section we show how two students, Alec and Lynne, created social identities from what was made available to them in drama settings that interfered with their learning and prevented them from becoming central participants according to the conventions of drama, defined by their teacher.

Performing for whom?

In Chapter 5 we suggested that Mrs Diamond orchestrated a setting in drama in which girls were given a more complex task than boys. The aim of the role-play was to get students to explore the moral dilemmas involved in the truanting behaviour of a fictional character 'Harry Roberts' so that students would reflect on their own attitudes towards school. Girls had to navigate two sets of demands: those of the subject discipline that required them to produce an imaginary scenario and those that lingered from a historical legacy of femininity broadly captured by the term 'caring for others'. We showed that Mrs Diamond reinforced the historical legacy of femininity through her pedagogic practice. In contrast we found that she removed cultural tools that were marked as feminine in the boys' class so as to allow masculine behaviours and identities to be fully expressed. Alec was successful and epitomizes one end of the range of solutions given by the boys. Lynne's account alerted us to the opposite extreme because she was unable to resolve the conflicts between the two competing demands of the task set up in the girls' class.

Alec 'performs' in drama

Alec was lucky enough to win the prize role to play 'Harry Roberts'. He described how a good performance became a social resource within his male peer group because boys continued to talk to each other about the performances days and even weeks after the drama lesson. Alec explained the role of the other boys:

Alec:	If everyone sees you do something good they're all going to like praise you but if you do something bad they're all going to have a go at you. But if it's just your mates or when it's your mates looking at you then they're all going to say after, oh, I remember in drama last week when we done that Harry thing, they're all going to remember it and then have a laugh about it.
Researcher:	I mean do they do that, I mean do they remember it?
Alec:	Yes, they remember it.
Researcher:	A week later or so?
Alec:	Yes. And like straight after some of the lessons we say, say someone was Harry, we go up to them and go, 'Alright Harry', like that and they just laugh and they say oh how about that bit when they were and they just think of the memories.

Playing Harry had provided Alec with a fictional identity that followed him around after the drama lesson. He said that the roles boys played in drama became part of the symbolic material that was traded in male peer groups. A good role would be praised by other boys while a bad one would invite teasing and ridicule. The continuous negotiation of positions within peer group culture was achieved through accessing new symbolic material. Alec was able to capitalize on the role of Harry Roberts, the archetypal 'naughty boy', to express himself in a way that the other boys were impressed by.

However, taking up this script and acting out the 'naughty boy' role did not help Alec to consider in any depth why Harry was truanting. Therefore, in being allowed to align himself with a role that reproduced a typical form of masculinity, he learned that he could be successful in drama without having any access to what Mrs Diamond was actually looking for according to her lesson aims. We saw in Chapter 5 that Mrs Diamond did not disabuse the boys of the idea that they had done very well in the role-play exercise. The 'naughty boy' script that Alec was given in the boys' setting reinforced the amusing and high status masculine identity that opposed interiority, authenticity and caring. The role prevented Alec from thinking reflexively about truanting. Lynne faced an almost opposite problem: she could not stop reflecting about the role she was given to play.

Lynne 'compromises' in drama

Lynne described the considerable effort required to understand emotions, moods and motives, not only of the characters in the role-play but also her own and those of the other girls. In Chapter 5 we showed that all four girls we interviewed described the role-play activity 'A day in the Life of Harry Roberts' as an exercise in compromise. Learning to compromise meant recognizing that others in the group had different ideas to their own, which Lynne described in the following way:

> I think she [Mrs Diamond] was hoping we'd learn that it's not your choice, there's not just your version and everybody else is wrong. There are other versions to the story and you have to accept that and then try and think well, this is what they think and they think something else and there's three different versions of it, well maybe mine isn't so true and maybe theirs is true in their eyes. Because people see things in different ways and you have to work it out. So I think she was hoping that we would learn that you have to sort things out yourself. And you can't always say well I didn't do it and walk off, you have to sort things out. And with Harry if you're bullying somebody you don't do what he was doing, trying to either bully or whatever, he had to sort it out. He had to talk to somebody, whether it was his or whatever and rather than just not do anything. Talk to somebody about it instead of getting told off all the time.

Lynne made connections between Harry's predicament at school and her own. She empathized with Harry's truancy through her own desire to 'walk off' when the group was not listening to her point of view. She reflexively engaged with the topic of truanting. Lynne spoke about having to put ideas forward even if they were rejected by the group. At other times she said she had to compromise her views to accommodate others 'without going off in a strop'. She spoke more than once in the interview about having 'no choice', 'having to get on with it' and 'having to overcome her nervousness' in relation to performing. The effort of compromise was considerable.

For Lynne, therefore, the point of the drama was to recognize that there were many points of view in a situation and part of this involved realizing that people have motives that are not immediately obvious from their behaviour. Lynne elaborated this further by making a connection between Harry's truancy and a baby crying. The class had role-played families with young babies in the first of the sequence of three lessons we observed. Lynne put it like this:

I think she [Mrs Diamond] wanted us to be able to know you aren't just; there are different sides to a story. So say if you're being bullied. I am being bullied, you might think of a way and do something else to show that you're angry, like a baby. They can't walk up to someone and say, 'Oh I need my nappy changed', or something, they will cry as another way of doing it. So I think the idea was to see different perspectives of things and to understand that your way isn't always the right way. There are always other people in the situation that will have different views to you.

Lynne suggested in this passage that the baby crying stood in for 'I need my nappy changed'. The act of crying reflected a hidden motive just as Harry's truancy did. Understanding that people have motives that are not directly accessible and which are different to one's own was the work of compromise. Lynne understood drama as a subject in which students were expected to learn about people and life, including the psychology of emotions and behaviour. Her experience of drama aligned with wider cultural legacies about the caring and containing role of women in society. She spoke about her fear of performing publicly which she tried to rationalize by telling herself that she was not on her own: 'just don't think you're just singing or whatever on your own'. She spoke about the need to take Mrs Diamond's position into account in realizing a performance. She explained: 'And you've got to think of the teacher's benefit. You can't just go up and do what you want. You have to think well I've got to stick to the subject and include what the other classmates would do and think.'

Her account portrayed the messiness of producing a performance and the disorganization of the group that was linked to the problem of finding a clear moral message. In Chapter 5 we suggested that girls worried more than boys about psychological authenticity. A consequence of this is that an end point in a role-play is less easy to imagine and, in the case of Harry, the girls failed to create a consensus about what his 'real' problem was. Lynne did not feel that she had produced a good performance, yet she did not blame the teacher. Instead she identified with the teacher's predicament and tried to achieve a performance even though she felt exposed, unprepared and even scared. In the end Lynne got on with the drama as a kind of moral duty. Lynne's account showed that the requirements to enter into an imaginative realm and retain a focus on 'what was *really* wrong with Harry' provided her with incompatible, if not contradictory, requirements. Lynne had reflected so much on Harry's problem that she could not lift herself into an imaginary role to create a shared fantasy: a role-play scenario, with the other girls. Learning to compromise resulted in her fulfilling neither set of requirements.

Compromised learning

Above, we suggested that social identities play a pivotal role in the dynamic of learning. Here we show how learning was compromised rather than enhanced through the settings orchestrated by Mrs Diamond. The resources provided by these settings forced students back onto their personal cultures to fulfil the task. In the drama settings during role-play, Alec and Lynne created social identities that did not help them to learn enough about the moral problem of truanting. In these two cases neither Alec nor Lynne managed to achieve the 'complex perspective coordination' (Penuel and Wertsch 1995) required to navigate peer group culture and learn in drama according to Mrs Diamond's lesson aims. Alec gained a high status reputation within his peer group culture by playing Harry, yet this very performance prevented him from engaging with the moral complexity of truanting. The 'naughty boy' role pushed him further into peer group culture and away from the skills required to engage with a moral dilemma.

Lynne met with almost an opposite problem: she became so involved with the moral dilemma that she could not see the wood for the trees, as it were, and she was unable to find an imaginative role from which to successfully enter into the role-play. In the previous section we focused on the gender identities associated with different curriculum subjects, such as English and design and technology, and suggested that these legacies set up different kinds of constraints and affordances (Gibson 1979; Rogoff 1990) for students. In this section we focus on the way teachers' practices compounded or interrupted identities extended within a curriculum subject culture, such as drama, and how students managed this aspect of the setting.

Mrs Diamond changed the activity in the boys' class by removing the text. Alec's account demonstrated that in doing this, Mrs Diamond orchestrated a setting which allowed Alec to reproduce a narrow version of masculinity through the 'naughty boy' script. We would argue that in terms of the subject criteria of drama, Alec learned nothing. In the girls' setting Mrs Diamond reinforced the historical legacy of femininity by insisting that the girls work out what was 'really wrong with Harry'. We saw that Lynne came to the lesson already primed to worry about Harry because the message to 'care for others' belongs to a strong yet ubiquitous cultural legacy of femininity that is reinforced through numerous media and forms part of girls' personal cultures before they even arrive in school. As a result of Mrs Diamond giving the girls two competing messages and little explicit feedback about their success, Lynne resorted to searching a broad landscape to piece together an understanding of what her teacher expected. In doing so she resorted to scouring the ubiquitous cultural legacies of femininity. Lynne could not escape the social expectation to care for others and therefore failed to find a focus, a distinctive imaginative role and concrete props, that would have helped the girls to enter into an imaginative space together. The cultural legacies of masculinity and femininity dominated the social identities that Alec and Lynne found in drama and in different ways prevented them from accessing the conventions that ought to belong to drama as a community of practice. In Chapter 3 we suggested that part of the problem lay with the history of drama as a curriculum subject that has not yet achieved a clear consensus among practitioners about what the subject conventions are. Without access to clear drama principles, Lynne called on the historical legacy of femininity and Alec that of masculinity to provide the symbolic resources they needed to improvise solutions to the task. In doing so Lynne learned to compromise and Alec learned to show off.

The cultural legacies of masculinity and femininity are carried through peer group cultures even more strongly than through curriculum subject cultures and it is to this that we turn next. Before we do so we pause for a gender story that refers to Beverly Skeggs' (2004) notion of 'passing' and Alice Jardine's (1985) account of women's 'secret wisdom'.

Gender story 5: passing as a lady

Alice Jardine (1985) reminds us that in the Victorian era conventions, manners and rules obsessively regulated femininity and masculinity. In the eighteenth century gender was determined by birth into a class and then proclaimed, examined and defined in texts, manuals and papers – both scientific and fictional. Gender became tied to social hierarchies based on economic wealth. The struggle to demonstrate masculinity and femininity required a social display of the right kind of manners, dress and speech. A woman was constantly in fear of being found out, of betraying herself or of not 'passing' (Skeggs 2004) as a proper lady. Not wearing the right hat, not stepping from a coach in the required manner and not addressing servants in specific ways could give a woman away. Finding the right symbolic resources to display the appropriate signs of femininity required access to the right people. Only by being or becoming a lady could women get access to bourgeois society. The body became the key signifier of class and gender. As Jardine tells us, women have historically borne the responsibility to awaken men's desire by presenting their bodies adorned according to social and cultural codes of beauty. She refers to Baudrillard's (1997) modern conduct for young ladies which echoes 'a traditional form of maternal discourses, that constituted a "secret wisdom" that mothers shared with their daughters: how they must awaken the desire of men, but never respond to or initiate it' (cited in Jardine 1985: 67–8).

Peer group culture: surveillance and silence

As we have seen from Seth's and Alec's accounts above, the peer group was the primary audience that the boys invoked when telling us about how they managed tasks. Girls did not present their peer groups as the primary audience to whom their solutions were addressed and instead Lynne and Kylie invoked teachers and Julie in Chapter 4 invoked her parents as the groups who would validate their artefacts and texts. We feel that this has implications for the way social gender identities mediate students' access to knowledge and therefore we shall explore peer culture and sub group hierarchies in more depth. We start by using what seemed like a curious incident that we observed in a geography lesson in the first phase of the study in Monks School.

Boys' peer group culture: 'being the "best"'

In one geography lesson that we observed the boys came into the room and rearranged the desks. It was a big room and the teacher did not object to a slight rearranging of the furniture. It was not a practical lesson and the boys were expected to do a considerable amount of writing. We had been told that this was a subject that the boys enjoyed and our observations demonstrated that the teacher had less trouble with classroom management than teachers in other lessons. In interviews the boys spoke to us about why they rearranged the furniture. They described how they arranged themselves into their 'own groups' so that the seating arrangements in the geography class matched the groups within their peer group culture. These groups were similar to the 'Macho Lads', the 'Academic Achievers', the 'New Entrepreneurs' and the 'Real Englishmen' identified in Mac an Ghaill's (1994) study of masculinity in secondary schools. Once they had done this they mainly worked individually, yet they felt comfortable and relaxed. Being able to sit in their self-made groups gave them a sense of security. By rearranging the furniture the boys gave the hidden group typology concrete form. This visible manifestation of the hierarchical groups within their peer culture appeared to reassure them and offset any need to dispute and bargain over social positions.

It may be worth bearing this in mind when teachers rearrange classes into, for example, gendered seating or ability groups, such a strategy removes control from students and could increase feelings of insecurity. Earlier we drew attention to the likely significance of the visible presence of girls in classes and suggested that this also may act to reassure boys about the clear distinctions among hierarchies. This visible manifestation of sex difference may offset some of the teasing and testing out of gender identities that, for example, we described in the art classroom in Chapter 5. Recognizing clear distinctions and categories was something that boys spoke about in relation to other aspects of school life, such as ideas.

In Chapter 4 we suggested that boys spoke about ideas as if they were personal possessions of some worth that had to be guarded from others. Mike, for example, in design and technology, suggested that having ideas helped him to maintain a distinct and autonomous identity of 'being different' from the other boys. Boys also spoke about the need to declare to others that their ideas were good, or the best. Some boys explained that they wanted to take pride in their ideas and they compared this to 'just copying off someone else'. They gave us an insight that ideas represented a form of capital that set up an exchange system between boys. Good and original ideas acted like money that could be used to secure their reputations, achieve acclaim and gain recognition from other boys. They spoke about rivalry and competition in terms of the danger that others might steal their ideas. The way boys spoke about the production and display of ideas through texts, artefacts and responses aligned with features of masculine culture such as individuality, separateness and autonomy. For these boys, the production of ideas relating to subject knowledge provided important symbolic elements in the armoury of resources they used to create and maintain masculine identities.

We suggested in Chapter 2 that the potential cost to a boy's reputation within the peer group culture of producing a piece of writing that could be judged as feminine, such as a piece of romance, created a need for vigilance. Boys' comments demonstrated how certain practices were not considered as legitimate. The greatest fear that boys spoke about was that other boys would interpret their texts as representations of their inner worlds and this made them feel vulnerable, as Lawrence, who was in a single-sex boys' class at the co-educational Palmers School explained:

> If you write something that is not good, like a romantic novel, and it is pretty bad, and the girls think it is bad, then they are going to think that he did not have any clue at all about relationships and the boys are going to crack up at him and they are just going to really, really embarrass him.

Lawrence pinpointed the element of authenticity as the problematic area; a point reiterated frequently by boys. James, also from the single-sex class in Palmers School, spoke about the vulnerability that boys would feel if they revealed personal concerns through their writing:

> It would make you feel like vulnerable because if people were taking the mickey out of that, there would, its like they would be taking the mickey out of *you* as a person, but if you wrote something that was just fantasy then if they took the mickey out of that, it does not really matter.

James suggested that boys could not write about authentic relationships because the other boys and girls would interpret what was written as an expression of 'you as a person'. So, to avoid becoming vulnerable, being exposed, or letting anyone know what you were really like it was better to write 'fantasy', as we suggested in Chapter 2 when discussing Steven's creative writing about the deformed banana. In their writing, boys employed fictional devices, such as writing as an alien, setting the story on a different planet, in the future or in a war zone and using characters that were not fully human (Ivinson and Murphy 2003; Murphy and Ivinson 2004). Interviews revealed that boys were deliberately using these devices to avoid expressing feelings and experiences directly in their writing. The boys explained that they resisted writing directly about feelings for a number of reasons: to avoid being ridiculed within male peer groups; to mask their personal knowledge of relationships with girls (which girls and boys might judge to be inadequate); and to prevent their inner thoughts being exposed to the outside world. Fantasy also provided an escape from mundane life and 'real' situations relating to school and the domestic world. We can speculate that boys used fantasy to distance themselves from the private, feminine domain.

In Chapter 1 we explored the way different kinds of knowledge such as science and English construct the social world in different ways. We described a major shift that took place with the Enlightenment and the invention of the scientific method. This marked a shift in the conception of knowledge from old to new. In the medieval era knowledge was believed to reside in ancient and sacred books and could be distilled through interpretation using deductive logic. Science involved the exploration of the material world through inductive analysis and the creation of new hypotheses. We described the way the monk had to repress temptations of the flesh to attain spiritual knowledge and become closer to God through the movement away from the body, while the scientist had to suppress passion, sensuality and emotion in order to attain objective knowledge, similarly separating mind and body in the process of coming to know. When the boys described masking their emotions by using alien characters and fantastical settings they too were using a form of suppression. When boys censored each other about what could be written, spoken and created in lessons they were doing more than expressing masculine identities. By hiding or excluding aspects of their texts that historically align with femininity they were actively shaping knowledge. In this way they were also contributing to the construction of knowledge associated with the objective-masculine, knowledge-gender alignment introduced in Chapter 3.

We can imagine boys' peer group culture as a recontextualized version of the public domain (Pateman 1988) in which boys were continuously and vigilantly aware of how other boys would judge them and how they were expected to judge other boys. Peer group culture exerted a strong influence within the matrix of social forces on the kinds of knowledge that boys were prepared to display. It may well be that in Year 9, peer group culture is a dominant social force and that in other years it exerts less influence. Boys spoke vividly about the contortions they had to go through to maintain masculine identities while, for example, writing fictional stories in English. We suspect that male peer group culture acted as a filter that influenced boys' reconstructions of knowledge across all subjects of the curriculum. When boys spoke about the suppression that they were undertaking in English they were implicitly confronting the feminine identity associated with it. Even though students described the suppression required within a subject setting, evidenced, for example, in Lynne's account of drama and Seth's account in English, they would also have been required to conceal aspects of their personal understandings in science and design and technology.

The more a specialist discourse such as science expels humanity the greater the pressure to resist. We provided an example of this in Chapter 4 when we described the way boys entered the science laboratory, turned their backs on Mr White and exerted their own autonomy by 'playing with fire'. Their actions could be interpreted as a resistance to the suppression required in scientific writing. Initiatives that have successfully extended girls' agency, engagement and achievement in science (Hildebrand 1996; Murphy and Whitelegg 2006) have simultaneously extended boys' agency and achievement though it has to be said not for all girls or all boys. The historical legacies of masculinity carried by boys' peer group culture reinforced the need to expel subjectivity, interiority and empathy in all curriculum subjects and not just in those that are associated with masculine identities. Interrupting historical legacies of masculinity by controlling and containing the influence of peer group culture in subject classrooms would provide an important step in legitimating boys' interests in a broader range of topics than those permitted by boys. Our interviews with boys such as Mike, Seth and Joe revealed clearly that boys are interested in aesthetics, relationships and moral dilemmas. Next we consider the effect of girls' peer group culture on their learning.

When reviewing the cohorts of interviews from boys and girls we were struck by a recurring feature. Boys spontaneously told us about the pressure they experienced from male peer group culture. Girls did not speak like this about their peer group culture. We wish to argue that the dynamic between girls' peer group culture and knowledge worked differently. In gender story 5, above, we drew attention to the way gender identities have to be constantly re-won. Jardine (1985) described how a slip at any moment could bring the danger of social condemnation and showed how surveillance worked as a general social gaze. The same process can be seen at work in boys' and girls' peer group cultures within schools.

Girls' peer group culture: 'silences and omissions'

Even when we probed girls about how they operated in group work activities they repeatedly told us that they got on well together, were collaborative and shared ideas. Some girls told us that they could try out ideas with other girls in their group in science before presenting them to the teacher. Yet, our observations suggested that the girls had conflicts while working in groups and that not all the solutions they achieved jointly were through harmonious discussions. Indeed, Lynne's interview alerted us to the disharmony of group work and the way ideas were compromised, lost and went unrecognized. This was not an easy situation for some girls as Lynne made clear. We suspected that girls appropriated the dominant discourses of femininity in their interviews with us and that this made it illegitimate to actively talk about conflict and rivalry. We know that girls do harbour aggressive fantasies (Austin 2005). Girls only revealed their frustrations and anxieties when they were talking about solving academic problems and not when they were talking about other girls. When asked directly how girls worked together, they repeatedly talked about cooperation and collaboration. However, the problem appeared to be broader than this, and we came to suspect that the knowledge-gender dynamic was mediated differently by boys' and girls' peer cultures. It seemed that the audiences to whom girls imaginatively addressed their work were different to those of boys and so were the forms of vigilance required. Boys imagined that other boys were aggressive and competitive and girls imagined that other girls were not. We would like to characterize this as an asymmetry not only in how girls and boys spoke about group work but also in the publics to whom they addressed their academic solutions. Girls seemed to overlook other girls and directed their work at representatives of the institution such as teachers, while boys directed their work at other boys.

Mediating public and private identities

We have shown how social identities arose in settings due to the constraints and functional necessities to produce texts and artefacts. According to a sociocultural approach, identities emerge in settings which 'edit' ubiquitous cultural streams in specific ways. Subjects with masculine core identities edit out feminine symbolic resources and make it difficult for girls to access these curriculum subjects without giving up their personal investments in style, aesthetics and authenticity. Subjects that carry feminine identities edit out masculine symbolic resources and make it difficult for boys to display knowledge without risking judgements from other boys about their masculinity. In Chapters 4 and 5 we demonstrated how these cultural legacies re-emerged in everyday classroom practice and provided different versions of subjects in boys' and girls' classes. In the first part of this chapter we described how Kylie and Seth managed the demands of their classroom settings by drawing on symbolic resources from their personal cultures to achieve protected positions within peer groups. Their accounts revealed that winning and retaining social gender identities in subject settings is an ongoing and dynamic process that requires effort, complex perspective-taking and know-how. We showed how Kylie and Seth displayed this and how they were able to create identities that protected them from peer group judgements so that they could express gender transgressive knowledge. Yet these performances came at a cost and they had to continuously guard their social gender identities and reputations as 'good at' design and technology or English.

We showed how in other situations maintaining a good enough gender identity closed down students' access to knowledge, as when Alec performed the 'naughty boy' script in drama. We suspect that the dynamic of peer cultures mediates subject knowledge in different ways for boys and girls. Having to maintain masculine identities in the face of other boys provided greater restrictions for boys than girls about what could be produced, displayed and written. As other researchers have pointed out, the pathways towards knowledge were narrower for boys than for girls (Lloyd and Duveen 1992; Skelton 2001). We have shown that this is exacerbated when the curriculum subject is associated with feminine rather than a masculine identity. To complicate the picture,

1. Teacher should stem and control of male
peer group culture
2. Expand subject territories to include
masculine + feminine element

Students' gendered experiences **167**

however, we found that teachers were more likely to remove cultural tools carried by feminine subject cultures in boys' classes.

Boys spoke about displaying knowledge only via the scrutiny of the generalized male gaze of the peer group while girls did not invoke a generalized feminine gaze when they spoke about producing texts, artefacts and responses. Instead they invoked the generalized *institutional* gaze which historically has aligned with the patriarchal gaze. It may well be that the patriarchal gaze has taken on a new form for this generation of girls because they did not invoke an authoritarian figure who was the judge of their work. We suspect that girls *do* challenge, judge and scrutinize each others' work, yet historical legacies of femininity make it difficult for them to speak about this explicitly. If the pressure of girls' peer culture was absent, why would Kylie have gone to such lengths to create and maintain her 'girlie' identity in design and technology?

In conclusion we would like to make two suggestions. The first is to reiterate what we said at the end of Chapter 5: that if teachers wish to provide boys with extra structures and rules, these ought to be aimed at stemming and controlling the effects of male peer group culture. Anything that can be done to reduce its influence will open up a broader range of symbolic resources that boys can use to write texts, perform roles and express their knowledge of relationships. We have shown how boys suppressed their emotions and their interest in aesthetics because they feared the gaze of other boys. In interviews the boys made it clear that they have this knowledge, yet they expressed the need to mask it or face the ridicule of being judged as not a proper boy by their male peers. Seth's need to create a weird identity made visible the contortions that boys were undertaking. Second, we suggest that instead of removing cultural tools such as texts, we should do the reverse. Many of the symbolic resources that Seth had found in his personal culture of music to create his 'weird' identity can be found in literature. The tradition of Romantic literature, including the writings of Coleridge, Wordsworth and Keats, has been used by many English teachers for years to subvert gender norms. Expanding subject territories to include both masculine and feminine elements can provide students with a wider range of symbolic resources with which to piece together subject-gender identities in classroom settings, and may reduce the need to provide protection by adopting exaggerated or weird identities. Teachers can often find the resources they require to open up knowledge-gender territories to boys and girls within the cultural reservoirs of their own curriculum subjects, as we showed in Mr Hunt's design and technology lesson in Chapter 3. However, we suggest that teachers use these ample stocks of resources for gender trangressive purposes and as a way to increase learning and expand students' future trajectories. In this respect Mr Green had gone a long way to opening up design and technology for Kylie. We need to resist the pressure to close down subjects. In the final chapter we pull together the tools that we hope will assist in this process.

Chapter/ **Seven**

Renegotiating the knowledge-gender dynamic

Throughout the empirical chapters we have looked at how gender emerges in the everyday settings of classrooms. Our sociocultural approach placed activity at the centre of the research design. We alternated our analytical lens between historical legacies and teachers' and students' personal accounts of classroom activities. A moment in time can be seen as a point in a historical trajectory. An activity can also be viewed as process that is situated one context rather than another. We have suggested that the significance of a moment-to-moment action is revealed when we bring multiple analytical lenses with these different temporal and spatial perspectives to bear on that action. Barbara Rogoff (2003) described this as if we are looking down a microscope at a slide while changing the strength of the lens to zoom in and out. What we placed on the slide was a moment-to-moment interaction from a classroom, workshop or laboratory. By changing the magnitude of the lens we showed that a teacher's view of an activity was different to a student's individual experience of it and that it looked different again when we as researchers viewed it, for example, from a long historical perspective or from an institutional one. As researchers we have used the analytical language of sociocultural theory to reveal the gender values of activities.

In this last chapter we point to some tendencies or patterns of practice that, once made visible, might enable practitioners to exercise some further choice over their moment-to-moment actions in class-rooms. We have been concerned to make the knowledge-gender dynamic visible in order to suggest that alternative actions could open up knowledge territories for boys and girls and allow them greater participation within subject domains. In the moment-by-moment enactments of classroom practice students often find themselves repositioned as either peripheral or central participants within communities of practice that relate to curriculum knowledge. It matters, therefore what teachers make available to students in settings through instructions, texts and material culture. The moment-in-action takes place within social contexts, so that while an action has significance and social consequences for the actor involved it can also be viewed as a semi-public affair that others interpret. Further and imperceptible to the social actors involved, it can also reproduce or interrupt cultural legacies of gender and disciplinary knowledge.

This chapter has three sections. We elaborate the conceptual issues that make up the sociocultural toolkit that offers one way to view the relationship between knowledge and gender and we use this to highlight the patterns of practice that emerged from the empirical work. The final section suggests how teachers can work with gender in their classroom practice to open up new learning territories for boys and girls.

The invisible made visible

We focused on the moment-in-action in subject classrooms, that is, the point at which a teacher or a student has to make a move, give a response or write something that relates to, for example, science, design and technology, English or drama. This is a moment when agency is exerted, yet in quite specific ways. We paid attention to the improvised nature of such moves in which teachers and students searched their personal culture to find the resources needed to speak, to write or to act. Crucial to this is what was available or became available to the person *at that moment.*

Teachers and students are differently positioned within schools, communities and society and therefore what they bring with them into classrooms reflects their different priorities, concerns and anxieties. Both teachers and students are exposed in the moment-in-action, yet the consequences for them are not equal. Thus, by focusing on the personal plane of analysis, the moment-in-action can be viewed as an ongoing process of managing social identities in settings where reputations, authority and public images are at stake. We suggested that in these moments of micro-transition 'things happen'. Both student and teacher can find themselves instantaneously repositioned within groups of peers or colleagues. At such moments, reputations based on the need to demonstrate authority or popularity may be enhanced, diminished or threatened. This crucial interaction between teachers and students may result in moments of synchronicity, conflict or ambiguity. At these moments students may be able to imagine themselves moving forward in the subject community of practice or they may feel blocked and disassociated from it. The possibility of finding a forward movement and therefore being able to participate, make sense within and feel connected to a subject community is how learning is understood in a sociocultural approach. Our aim has been to unpack the social influences that come to bear in these moments of action. We have stressed that in interactions between teachers and students, what teachers make available to students and what students bring with them create settings. In the following sections we describe what was at stake for teachers and for students in these moments. To do this we have to draw on the full panoply of contexts, settings, arenas, subject communities and historical legacies in which a moment-in-action is situated. In order to make the knowledge-gender dynamic visible we need to rehearse the conceptual tools that we introduced in Chapter 2.

The sociocultural toolkit revisited

In Chapter 2 we used the example of Mrs Sharp's English class in Palmers School to demonstrate how the planes of analysis interconnect so that one moment-in-action, such as reading out a creative writing text, needed to be understood within several planes. We start by considering the social influences that prevailed at the time when the study took place between 1999 and 2001. As we noted earlier, an arena 'is outside of, yet encompasses the individual' (Lave 1988). Influences that help constitute a teaching arena include:

- historical legacies of knowledge and gender;
- professional teacher training in a curriculum subject;
- contemporary education policies;
- media representation of gender as fixed, innate and dichotomous;
- institutional pressures: 'The Year of the Boy' and the strategy of single-sex classes.

We suggested in Chapter 2 that the standards debate, which was exacerbated by performance data recorded by sex group, had heightened the salience of gender in schools. Headteachers in both schools had directed staff to address boys' underachievement. In Palmers School, Mrs Sharp had created single-sex classes for the successful boys. Monks School had introduced single-sex classes in the lower school. When teachers enter school they have already been educated in a knowledge domain and through experience they acquire professional identities as subject specialists. Therefore the reservoir of symbolic elements that they draw upon as they teach single-sex classes reflects the historical legacies of their subject. Through the history of schooling and curriculum, in Chapter 1, and the brief descriptions of curriculum subjects in Chapter 3, we pointed to the way constructions of knowledge are intertwined with *gender legacies*. We characterized curriculum subjects as part of knowledge-gender dynamics that can be imagined along a continuum with fixed and objective knowledge at one end and creative knowledge derived from subjective meanings at the other. Moreover, we suggest that *identities* associated with subjects reflect their historical legacies along gender lines. For example, a creative writing task comes already marked with a feminine gender value, due to the historical legacies of English that include the invention of the novel. Constructing a model car comes already marked as masculine due to the historical alignment between design and technology and apprenticeships in industry. Together, all these aspects provide the sociocultural and temporal context of the school arena because they exist outside and yet encompass an individual. In comparison to an arena, a setting draws attention to dynamic processes that unfold in moment-to-moment enactments.

Settings emerge in practice and refer to the transient and dynamic aspects of classroom life as immediate experiences which then disappear. Yet, while the action disappears a *trace* of it remains and we suggested that students' *identities* in subject classrooms can be imagined as a trace of their participation in the setting. In Chapter 6 we gave accounts of students' experiences of tasks set for them in science, design and technology, English and drama. We demonstrated that Seth adopted a 'weird' identity in English to provide him with a strategic position from which to undertake creative writing and Kyle developed a 'girlie' identity to overtly express femininity while she constructed a model car. We suggested that sometimes a highly valued masculine identity interfered with boys' participation in a curriculum subject, distanced them from it and thus prevented them from gaining the competences needed to become a central participant. An example would be Alec who played the 'naughty boy' role in drama. We pointed to the symbolic work needed to both 'get it right' as a boy or girl and participate in the subject community.

We used Wenger's (1998) notion of a *community of practice* to suggest how the interaction between arena and setting, that is, between sociocultural legacies and immediate practices in subject communities, facilitated or impeded students' learning. For example, we showed that Mrs Diamond in drama and Mrs Young in English removed the text in the boys' classes. On the one hand this encouraged boys to use their own ideas to achieve the task, and yet on the other it removed some of the very resources that would have given them access to a wide range of ideas. So, although they were encouraged to be autonomous and make meanings of their own, they ended up drawing on a *common sense stock of ideas* from their personal culture instead of the stock of ideas carried by the cultural resources of the subject. Boys tended to use common sense ideas about masculinity in this situation because it was safer for them to do so, given their fears about how other boys would judge them. We suggested that the communities of practice that arise in classrooms and which then provide the norms, conventions and principles that guide action, are not insulated from everyday culture. For example, boys' peer group culture was ever-present in boys' classroom settings, kept alive because boys imagined that their comments, texts and artefacts would be scrutinized by other boys.

We showed that boys' peer groups actively reconstruct historical legacies of masculinity. Therefore we need to recognize that communities of practice in subject classrooms are already made up of a mixture of formal subject knowledge and everyday common sense beliefs. *If teachers remove the cultural tools that belong to curriculum subjects, such as texts, specialist vocabularies and machines, they simply open up more space for the common sense ideas of students' personal cultures and peer groups to enter classrooms.* Learning about the subject in these situations is highly compromised.

Learning involves a change in *social identity*, that is, a movement forward from a peripheral to a more central position in the community of practice. This movement implies an active engagement with the tools, resources and specialist language of the curriculum subject. When students use the tools of the curriculum subject as *forms of competence* they undergo a change in identity. We stress again that according to sociocultural approaches identities are not fixed and instead are *situated*, that is, they emerge through the constraints and openings afforded by specific subject settings. Learning involves participation of a particular kind. It does not arise from the participation that we described in the boys' science classes when they turned their backs on Mr White and played with fire. In this setting, boys expressed their autonomy, yet it was an active engagement that fulfilled only their own desires but did not involve *forms of competence* associated with science. They actively made meanings but these meanings related to their fantasies about science. These fantasies in turn demonstrated their implicit awareness of their positions as the legitimate inheritors of science. The alignment between the historical legacy of science and masculinity meant that the boys' off-task behaviour was not salient to Mr White. He, like many teachers, tolerated it as an example of 'boys will be boys'. Girls were not given the chance to express this level of autonomy in the laboratory and, as a consequence, most of their activities were purposeful and directed at learning the principles and practices of science. This allowed the girls to develop forms of competence and to exercise *agentive mastery*. Yet, the other message girls were likely to be receiving was a more ubiquitous one that told them that they were *not* the legitimate inheritors of science.

Findings, reflections and implications for learning

In this section we are going to draw on insights from our study to suggest some of the pitfalls that we as practitioners are liable to stumble into in our own practice. Throughout the study we used our sociocultural concepts to make aspects of the knowledge-gender dynamic visible. Here we wish to highlight three interdependencies:

- the influence of gender identities associated with curriculum subjects;
- the imperceptibility of gender emerging in classroom practice;
- typical gendered patterns of practice.

In Chapter 3 we outlined the gender identities associated with the historical legacies of the subjects in the study: science, design and technology, English and drama. We shall rehearse some implications of this for teachers and students, but let us start with students.

The ways boys and girls interpreted instructions and made sense of their tasks remained invisible to teachers and it is by making some of these individual re-enactments evident that we can reveal some of the unintended consequences of pedagogic practice. In Chapter 6 we described how individual students managed the intended and unintended effects of pedagogic practice. Classroom settings provided differential spaces in which individual students improvised, innovated and attempted to 'get it right' as a boy or girl. We need to stress, however, that there is no one-to-one mapping between the spaces that are opened up in classroom settings and the practices of individual students. Instead, classroom settings provide *possibilities* for action, resources and opportunities that each student will experience differently. It is only by recognizing what is at stake for students that teachers can mobilize gender as a resource to open up further possibilities for students' participation.

The cultural legacy of a subject provides a particular kind of analytical lens through which to view phenomena. The masculine identity of science gives boys legitimacy, autonomy and thus agency, even before they enter a laboratory. Therefore when they acted in ways described as 'boys will be boys' their behaviour was not salient to teachers. We saw this agency extended to boys also in Mrs Marshall's pedagogic approach in the mathematics lesson referred to at the beginning of Chapter 4. According to the historical legacies of science, girls were not expected to become scientists so, even before they walked into the laboratory, their actions were 'suspect'. Indeed, we saw that Mr White controlled their movements carefully and worried about them burning themselves. When Sophie acted like a boy, her behaviour almost jumped out at Mr White and in a sense confirmed his worst fears that girls should not really be in the laboratory. This is an exaggerated account, yet we use it to make a point. The historical legacies of subjects, which will have been reinforced through training and professional practice, are likely to influence a teacher's gaze and ensure that some aspects of behaviour will stand out and others will appear as 'natural' according to the cultural legacy of the subject. Who undertakes which kinds of actions in a setting is significant because, as we suggested in Chapters 1 and 3, curriculum subjects can be associated with masculine or feminine identities.

When girls acted like boys in male territory they moved beyond what some teachers were able to tolerate. We observed similar problems in classes in which boys experimented, for example, with the romance genre in English (Ivinson and Murphy 2003). Through their moment-to-moment actions these students crossed an invisible barrier into knowledge-gender territories that were previously out of bounds for them. These gender crossings were tolerated up to a point because equal opportunities discourses, instantiated in the National Curriculum, give boys and girls a legal entitlement to all curriculum subjects. However, in relation to the long historical trajectories of curriculum subjects, this entitlement is relatively new, as we indicated in Chapter 1. The development of entitlement to all subjects and the related discourses of equality have set up tensions within some subject communities of practice. Muddling up the gender categories, such as allowing girls to stray into male subject domains, was particularly threatening at the time of the study, we would argue, because media stories and educational directives had given teachers the responsibility to solve the problems of masculinity and underachievement. Teachers were expected to do this by readjusting the school environment to make it less feminine. In effect, teachers were being asked to create clear and unambiguous gender demarcations to prevent masculinity from being contaminated by femininity.

Teachers bring the cultural legacies of their curriculum subjects into the present simply through the process of teaching. To instruct students, teachers have to draw on the cultural tools that belong to their curriculum subject and this reinvigorates the subject culture through pedagogic use. Thus, teachers can reproduce, reinforce or transform the cultural legacy of the subject through their practice. *Without an awareness of how gender legacies are tied up with cultural legacies of curriculum subjects it is likely that the core gender identity, carried by the subject, will be reproduced in pedagogic practice.* This is especially the case in boys' classes because masculinity carries (still) more social value than femininity. These processes usually operate below the level of conscious awareness as we shall reiterate by returning to Mr Hunt's lesson on joins.

Throughout the book we have inserted gender stories to remind ourselves of the way dominant metaphors of specific eras are implicated in the social construction of knowledge. The purpose of reminding ourselves of gender legacies is to recognize how these deep historical influences re-emerge in everyday practice. Gender story 2 pointed to a shift in the dominant metaphors of nature related to changing social conditions, such as the opening up of trade in the medieval era and industrialization arising after the Enlightenment. With the Enlightenment, metaphors repositioned man in relation to nature from steward to master. The metaphor of man dominating nature in order to improve it carried a gender inflection in which man the scientist had to 'correct' and 'improve' a recalcitrant or unfinished femininity ('Mother Nature').

Mr Hunt drew on the historical legacy of design and technology when he instructed the boys about joins. When he addressed the boys as builders, explorers and navigators, he reinvigorated the agentive role of masculinity, depicted by the heroic figure who conquered, tamed and mastered nature. Inadvertently he also reinvigorated the association between femininity and passivity. This was apparent throughout his instruction in the girls' class. Although he had good intentions and tried to open up design and technology to girls, his practice kept sliding back into the deep cultural channels of the knowledge-gender dynamic. By reproducing ancient beliefs about gender, he closed down the possibilities for girls to imagine themselves forward in the subject. In this way, design and technology remained an alien territory for girls.

It is most unlikely that Mr Hunt *meant* to pull these aspects of the historical legacy of gender into view while he was instructing boys or girls. The associative links that we have pointed to above lie beneath the surface of language and culture, lost in the condensed folds of the past. Therefore we can view Mr Hunt's activity as simultaneously located within different planes. On the personal plane he showed initiative in the way he drew on the symbolic resources of his discipline to interest the boys in a potentially boring topic and he retained his position of authority. At the same time, his pedagogic activity inadvertently reproduced images of masculinity as domineering and active. In the girls' lesson, sometimes despite his best efforts, and in part due to the provocation of the girls, he fell back on common sense beliefs of femininity as passive, lacking agency and in need of male support. By moving between planes of analysis, we have been able to demonstrate that Mr Hunt reproduced the cultural legacy of the subject, and at the same time pulled ancient beliefs about gender into view. Through his practice he projected boys and girls forward in line with the gendered history of design and technology. This can be identified therefore as a 'retrospective pedagogic' approach (Rose 1996; Bernstein 1996).

Through the empirical examples given in Chapters 3, 4 and 5 we suggested that in their efforts to adjust their pedagogic approaches to address boys and girls as they imagined them, teachers changed not just the activities but also the curriculum subject. Even when teachers explicitly said that they were treating boys and girls the same, for example when Mrs Young said that boys and girls should be taught *Romeo and Juliet*, things often went awry in the moment-by-moment enactments of everyday classroom practice. Classroom life takes place in atmospheres that are often stressful, intense and precarious simply because there are lots of people crammed into spaces in which they are obliged to achieve aims that are not necessarily of their own making. Within such pressurized environments teachers improvise, try out ideas and draw on cultural resources that have worked in the past. Our investigations showed that gender became a visible influence when teachers had to cope with unfamiliar situations, and these included: teaching single-sex classes, having to change rooms, not having the right equipment or trying to retrieve a bad lesson. *We recognized in these actions a pattern of practice in which teachers changed subjects that carry core feminine identities to accommodate masculinity. By removing some of the cultural tools of these subjects they removed obstacles that may have interfered with the reproduction of masculinity. Thus they refocused the subject towards the objective-masculine, knowledge-gender alignment.* We found that, in general, pedagogic practices and instruction addressed to boys gave them more autonomy than girls. Their ideas were validated more explicitly and their right to play was tolerated more than girls. In these imperceptible ways boys were treated as more agentive than girls and this revitalized historical legacies of masculinity as autonomous, competitive and individual.

We identified parallel practices in girls' classes, which have equally significant implications for their learning. These patterns of practice have been well documented (Walkerdine 1988; Walkerdine and Lucey 1989; Lloyd and Duveen 1992; Epstein *et al.* 1998) and our research shows that they still persist. It was through a combination of both the imperceptible and the repeated nature of these pedagogic practices that historical legacies of gender were reconstructed in contemporary classrooms. Such patterns created settings that demarcated the legitimate territory that boys and girls could occupy. They also gave boys and girls different versions of the disciplinary subject and, with that, different expectations. These repeated practices provided messages regarding participation within subjects, about the likelihood of success or failure, and therefore about the kinds of futures that students could imagine. Gender story 1 tells how the public domain invented by the social contract theorists of the seventeenth and eighteenth centuries was designated as masculine. It is possible to see that teachers' pedagogic instruction invited boys to operate within the public realm while girls were expected not to forget their role within the private domain.

The differences in practice between boys' and girls' classes that teachers enacted were imperceptible to them; they occurred below the radar of what was salient, except when a student overstepped the invisible knowledge-gender boundary. It was in the seemingly inconsequential minutiae of everyday practice that gender emerged. This is why we believe that the influence of gender was invisible to teachers. We all, in different ways, collude with the historical legacies of gender because none of us can resist them until they become visible to us and, when they do, they often threaten our professional and personal identities. In Chapter 3 we revealed how gender legacies were implicated in teachers' professional identities as subject specialists. Teachers' interview accounts showed that they drew on the knowledge-gender dynamic within their subject to make sense of their roles as teachers. Therefore, resistance to historical legacies of gender can challenge conceptions of the world created within disciplinary fields, the constitutive social order (including school arenas) and understandings of disciplinary knowledge as we have come to know them. What then can be done?

Opening up knowledge frontiers

There is a need to open up knowledge frontiers in a new way. One move in achieving this is to become reflexively aware of gender and encourage boundary-crossing in knowledge territories. This entails challenging what counts as knowledge, which in turn relies on our ability to imagine alternative futures. We encountered teachers who were reflexively aware of gender and who actively tried to counter its influence in the classroom – and yet, unintended consequences ensued that they could not explain. Therefore, employing overt strategies does not of itself ensure success. In some cases all that would have been required to achieve the desired ends was one more step in teachers' awareness. To illustrate this we shall return to an example from the science laboratory.

In science, Mr White imagined that his pedagogic instructions were aimed at 'the boy'. Yet, in line with discourses of equality he was committed to making science accessible to girls. Sophie's behaviour in the laboratory seemed to disturb a deep historical legacy of the curriculum subject. When Mr White reprimanded Sophie he indicated where the boundary between legitimate and illegitimate behaviour lay for girls. While we do not want to advocate that all girls be encouraged to play with fire in a laboratory, we do wish to encourage teachers to give girls more freedom, autonomy and agency. *In thinking about how to address girls as agentive in masculine subjects it would be worthwhile imagining addressing them as the builders, navigators and scientists of the future.* This would involve a shift in the way the pedagogic subject was imagined. We suspect that if the contradiction between the historical legacy of science and his convictions about equality had been pointed out to Mr White, he would have been able to recognize how in practice he inadvertently aligned girls with the private and boys with the public domain. Recognizing this knowledge-gender alignment would have enabled him to reflect on his future pedagogic practices.

In design and technology Mr Green showed an explicit awareness of gender by advocating equal access for boys and girls to gender territories that in the past they would not necessarily have occupied. Here too all that was required to achieve his aim would have been for Mr Green to have some understanding about students' investments in the artefacts they were creating. Some boys personally invested in the style of the cars as a way to create unique and distinctive designs. *The boys' aesthetic investment was invisible to Mr Green because it clashed with cultural legacies of masculinity. Yet boys are changing and their interest in style, designer labels and aesthetics is flourishing.* If Mr Green had known the importance of the aesthetic element of the design for boys, and indeed for girls, he would have had the insight he needed to achieve his aim to help both boys and girls to engage creatively and productively in the subject. Although we are never going to prevent gender emerging in practice, with some insight it becomes possible to shape pedagogy in ways that offset the narrowing influence of historical legacies of gender.

We have shown that removing the cultural tools of a subject and reducing tasks so that they align with boys' familiar and personal cultures can create unintended effects that do a disservice to boys in a number of ways. By removing the text *Buddy*, Mrs Young prevented the boys from accessing a source of ideas that would have mediated between them and their peer group. Had the boys had access to the text they would not have had to take personal responsibility for the ideas needed to create the radio script, and so could have blamed 'bad' ideas on the text. This would have freed them up to experiment a little more without the risk of exposing themselves. The need not to expose feelings and other aspects of their inner worlds was something that the boys articulated strongly to us when they explained why they did not write romance. We have argued elsewhere that girls also deserve to have access to cultural tools that enable them not to expose their personal experiences in the semi-public space of the classroom (Ivinson and Murphy 2003). To fully engage in classroom activities students have to find cultural resources that belong to the curriculum subject and teachers need to feel free to make a broad range of these available to students.

Making the cultural tools of a subject available to students in classroom settings gives them the possibility to try out gender-transgressive ideas, negotiate meanings, take risks and sometimes 'get it wrong'. To have the confidence to do this, students must feel that they have a legitimate right to belong to a community of practice as well as having access to the resources that mediate between their inner and outer worlds. Becoming a member is at the heart of learning and engaging more fully with the conventions, principles and know-how within the community without fear of exposure and humiliation allows students to develop agentive mastery.

Our study leads us to suggest that boys want teachers to open rather than close down access to imaginative territories. The difficulty that we recognize is that territories that align with masculinity have high status and those that align with femininity have low status. Boys will resist practices that place them in compromised positions (Berge with Ve 2000; Skelton 2001; Davies 2003) and will tend to limit their participation to communities in which masculinity is valued. Basil Bernstein (1974) taught us to think about the strength of the boundaries between inside and outside school, between inside and outside the classroom and between curriculum subjects. We can add to this a further consideration, namely the boundaries between inner and outer worlds. Our task as teachers is to maintain strong boundaries between imaginary worlds while helping students to connect with the conventions of subject communities of practice so that they can negotiate meanings within them.

Entering into a subject community of practice paradoxically requires students to leave something of themselves outside the classroom door. For example, according to historical accounts, scientific discourses suppress embodied knowledge, negate subjectivity and deny emotions. Curriculum subjects as communities of practice edit out aspects of the everyday cultural worlds that students live in. This is essential for learning because it requires students to participate in cultural worlds that are different to common sense domains of experience. Suppressing some aspects of personal desire goes hand in hand with accepting the conventions of the subject community of practice. We, as educators, can only justify this suppression if we show students that mastering the tools of the subject culture will open up new imaginative worlds to them. *A key step towards doing this is to make sure that our pedagogic discourses relay messages to all students that they are the legitimate inheritors of subject domains, irrespective of their gender or class.* We fully recognize the challenge involved in working against the core gender identities carried by curriculum subjects, yet believe that the way forward is to focus on the future.

Training our gaze on the future, rather than looking nostalgically to the past, requires that we re-imagine curriculum knowledge as dynamic, living and therefore open to change. The knowledge-gender alignments depicted in Chapter 3 was presented in order to emphasize that curriculum subjects are diverse, have various cultural legacies and place the emphasis on 'objective' and 'subjective' elements differently. In revisiting knowledge-gender alignments we wish to emphasize the dynamic nature of knowledge, even of scientific knowledge. This view of curriculum knowledge is contrary to that portrayed by National Curriculum documents that divide subjects into stages, phases and levels. When we think about knowledge as dynamic and socially constructed, albeit within limits set up by the conventions of the knowledge community, we can start to think about the kind of futures we would like our students to create. To re-imagine the pedagogic subject we need to re-imagine the future.

References

Abreu, G. (1995) Understanding how children experience the relationship between home and school mathematics, *Mind, Culture and Activity*, 2: 119–42.

Adam, B. (2004) *Time*. Cambridge and Malden, MA: Polity.

Alloway, N. and Gilbert, P. (1997) Boys and literacy: lessons from Australia, *Gender and Education*, 9(1): 49–58.

Alloway, N., Gilbert, P., Gilbert, R. and Henderson, R. (2003) Boys performing English, *Gender and Education*, 15(4): 49–58.

American Association of University Women (AAUW) (1992) *How Schools Short-change Girls*. Washington, DC: AAUW Educational Foundation.

American Association of University Women (AAUW) (1998) *Separated by Sex: A Critical Look at Single-sex Education for Girls*. Washington, DC: AAUW Educational Foundation.

Apple, M. (2000) *Official Knowledge: Democratic Education in a Conservative Age*. New York: Routledge.

Archer, R.L. (1921) *Secondary Education in the Nineteenth Century*. Cambridge: Cambridge University Press.

Arendt, H. ([1958] 1998) *The Human Condition*. Chicago: University of Chicago Press.

Arnot, M. (1983) A cloud over co-Education: an analysis of the forms of transmission of class and gender relations, in S. Walker and L. Barton (eds) *Gender, Class and Education*. London: Falmer Press.

Arnot, M., Gray, J., James, M., Rudduck, J. and Duveen, G. (1998) *Recent Research on Gender and Educational Performance*. London: Ofsted.

Arnot, M., David, M. and Weiner, G. (1999) *Closing the Gender Gap: Postwar Education and Social Change*. London: Polity.

Austin, S. (2005) *Women's Aggressive Fantasies: Post-Jungian Exploration of Self-Hatred, Love and Agency*. London: Routledge.

Bacon, F. (1620) *The New Organon*, trans. by J. Spedding, R.L. Ellis and D. Dennon Heath (1863). Boston, MA: Tagggard and Thompson.

Ball, S. (2003) *The More things Change ... Educational Research, Social Class and 'Interlocking' Inequalities.* London: Institute of Education, University of London.

Ball, S. and Vinvent, C. (2006) *Childcare, Choice and Class Practice: Middle Class Parents and their Children.* London: Routledge.

Ball, S., Maguire, M. and Macrae, S. (2000) *Choice, Pathways and Transitions Post-16: New Youth, New Economies in the Global City.* Washington, DC: Routledge.

Baudrillard, J. (1997) *The Consumer Society: Myth and Structures.* London: Sage.

Benson, C. (2001) *The Cultural Psychology of Self.* London: Routledge.

Berge, B-M. with Ve, H. (2000) *Action Research for Gender Equity.* Buckingham: Open University Press.

Bernstein, B. (1974) *Class, Codes and Control 1, Theoretical Studies Towards a Sociology of Language,* 2nd (revised) edn. London: Routledge.

Bernstein, B. (1996) *Pedagogy, Symbolic Control and Identity Theory, Research, Critique.* London: Taylor & Francis.

Bernstein, B. (1999) Vertical and horizontal discourse: an essay, *British Journal of Sociology of Education,* 20(2): 157–73.

Boaler, J. (1997) *Experiencing School Mathematics: Teaching Styles, Sex and Setting.* Buckingham: Open University Press.

Bone, A. (1983) *Girls and Girls-only Education: A Review of Evidence.* Manchester: Equal Opportunities Commission.

Brawn, R. (2000) The formal and intuitive in science and medicine, in T. Atkinson and G. Claxton (eds) *The Intuitive Practitioner.* Buckingham: Open University Press.

Bredo, E. (1994) Reconstructing educational psychology, *Educational Psychologist,* 29(1): 23–45.

Brehony, K. (1984) 'Co-educational perspectives and debates in the early twentieth century. In R. Deem (ed.) *Co-education Reconsidered.* Milton Keynes: Open University Press.

Bruner, J. (1996) *The Culture of Education.* London: Harvard University Press.

Brutsaert, H. and Van Houtte, M. (2002) Girls' and boys' sense of belonging in single-sex versus co-educational schools, *Research in Education,* 68: 48–56.

Burton, L. (ed.) (1986) *Girls into Maths Can Go.* London: Holt, Rinehart & Winston.

Burton, L. (1996) A socially just pedagogy for the teaching of maths, in P.F. Murphy and C.V. Gipps (eds) *Equity in the Classroom: Towards Effective Pedagogy for Girls and Boys.* London: Falmer Press/UNESCO.

Carr, L. (1985) Legislation and mediation: to what extent has the Sex

Discrimination Act changed girls' schooling? in J.Whyte, R. Deem, L. Kant and M. Cruickshank (eds) *Girl-friendly Schooling*. London: Methuen.

Claxton, G. (2000) The anatomy of intuition, in T. Atkinson and G. Claxton (eds) *The Intuitive Practitioner*. Buckingham: Open University Press.

Cohen, M. (1996) Is there a space for the achieving girl? in P.F. Murphy and C.V. Gipps (eds) *Equity in the Classroom: Towards Effective Pedagogy for Girls and Boys*. London: Falmer Press.

Colley, A., Comber, C. and Hargreaves, D. (1994) School subject preferences of pupils in single-sex and co-educational secondary schools, *Educational Studies*, 20(3): 379–85.

Comenius, J. A. (1631) *Janua Linguarum Reserata, The Gate of Tongues Unlocked*.

Connell, P. (2005) A critical review of recent developments in quantitative research on gender and achievement, paper presented at the fifth international gender and education conference, Cardiff University, March 2005.

Connell, R.W. (1987) *Gender and Power: Society, the Person and Sexual Politics*. Cambridge: Polity.

Connell, R.W. (1995) *Masculinities*. Cambridge: Polity.

Dale, R.R. (1969) *Mixed or Single-sex Schools, Vol 1, A Research Study About Pupil-teacher Relationships*. London: Routledge & Kegan Paul.

Dale, R.R. (1971) *Mixed or Single-sex Schools, Vol 2, Some Social Aspects*. London: Routledge & Kegan Paul.

Dale, R.R. (1974) *Mixed or Single-sex Schools, Vol 3, Attainment, Attitudes and Overview*. London: Routledge & Kegan Paul.

Datnow, A. and Hubbard, L. (2002) *Gender in Policy and Practice: Perspectives on Single-Sex and Coeducational Schooling*. New York: Routledge Falmer.

Davies, B. (2003) *Shards of Glass: Children Reading and Writing beyond Gendered Identities*. Cresskill, NJ: Hampton Press.

de Beauvoir, S. (1972) *The Second Sex*. Harmondsworth: Penguin.

Deem, R. (1984) (ed.) *Co-education Reconsidered*. Buckingham: Open University Press.

Delamont, S. and Duffin, L. (eds) (1978) *Nineteenth-Century Woman*. London: Croom Helm.

Department of Education and Science (DES) (1975) *Curricular Differences for Boys and Girls*, Educational Survey No. 21. London: HMSO.

Department of Education and Science (DES) (1985) *The Curriculum from 5 to 16*. London: HMSO.

Descartes, R. (1641) *Meditations*, trans J. Veitch. Cambridge: Cambridge University Press.

Dewey, J. (1934) *Art as Experience*. London: Allen & Unwin.

Dixon, C. (1998) Action, embodiment and gender in the design and technology classroom, in A. Clark and E. Millard (eds) *Gender in the Secondary Curriculum*. London: Routledge.

Duveen, G. (2001) Representations, identities, resitance, in K. Deaux and G. Philogène (eds) *Social Representations: Introductions and Explorations*. Oxford: Blackwell.

Duveen, G. and Lloyd, B. (1990) *Social Representations and the Development of Knowledge*. Cambridge: Cambridge University Press.

Dyehouse, (1981) *Girls Growing up in Late Victorian and Edwardian England*. London: Routledge & Kegan Paul.

Eagleton, T. (1983) *Literary Theory: An Introduction*. Oxford: Blackwell.

Eagley, A.H. (1987) *Sex Differences in Social Behaviour: A Social-Role*. London: Lawrence Erlbaum Associates.

Edgeworth, M. (1795)

Elwood, J. (2001) Examination techniques: issues of validity and effects on pupils' performance, in D. Scott (ed.) *Curriculum and Assessment*. Westport, CT: Ablex.

Elwood, J. and Gipps, C. (1999) *Review of Recent Research on the Achievement of Girls in Single-sex Schools*. London: Institute of Education University of London.

EOC 2007 Report

Epstein, D. (1998) Real boys don't work: 'underachievement' masculinity, and the harassment of 'sissies', in D. Epstein, J. Elwood, V. Hey and J. Maw (eds) *Failing Boys? Issues in Gender and Achievement*. Buckingham: Open University Press.

Epstein, D. and Johnson, R. (1997) *Schooling Sexualities*. Buckingham: Open University Press.

Epstein, D., Elwood, J., Hey, V. and Maw, J. (eds) (1998) *Failing Boys? Issues in Gender and Achievement*. Buckingham: Open University Press.

Filer, A. (1997) 'At least they were laughing', in A. Pollard, D. Thiessen and A. Filer (eds) *Children and their Curriculum*. London: Falmer Press.

Fox Keller, E. (1985) How gender matters or, why it's so hard to count past two, in J. Harding (ed.) *Perspectives on Gender and Science*. London: Falmer Press.

Francis, B. (2000) *Boys, Girls, and Achievement: Addressing the Classroom Issues*. London: RoutledgeFalmer.

Francis, B., Hutchings, M., Archer, L. and Melling, L. (2003) Subject choice and occupational aspirations among pupils at girls' schools, *Pedagogy, Culture & Society*, 11(3): 425–42.

Frosh, S., Phoenix, A. and Pattman, R. (2002) *Young Masculinities: Understanding Boys in Contemporary Society*. Basingstoke: Palgrave.

Gee, J. (1990) *Social Linguistics and Literacies: Ideology in Discourses*. London: Taylor & Francis.

Gibson, J.J. (1979) *The Ecological Approach to Visual Perception*. Boston, MA: Houghton Mifflin.

Gillborn, D. and Youdell, D. (1999) *Rationing Education: Policy, Practice, Reform and Equality*. Buckingham: Open University Press.

González, N. (2005) Beyond culture: the hybridity of funds of knowledge, in N. González, L.C. Moll and C. Amanti (eds) *Funds of Knowledge: Theorizing Practices in Households, Communities and Classrooms*. Mahwah, NJ: Lawrence Erlbaum Associates.

Gorard, S. (2000) *Education and Social Justice: The Changing Composition of Schools and its Implications*. Cardiff: University of Wales Press.

Greenfield, S. (2000) *The Private Life of the Brain*. London: Penguin.

Gulbrandsen, M. (2003) Peer relations as arenas for gender constructions among classroom teaching, *Pedagogy, Culture and Society*, 11(1): 113–31.

Gurian, M. (2001) *Boys and Girls Learn Differently!* San Fransisco: Jossey-Bass.

Halpern, D.F. (1992) *Sex Differences in Cognitive Abilities*. Hillsdale, NJ: Lawrence Erlbaum Associates.

Hannon, G. (1997) *The Gender Game and How to Win It*. London: G. Hannon.

Hawkes, T. (2001) *Boy Oh Boy: How to Raise and Educate Boys*. Sydney: Pearson Education.

Heider, F. (1958) *The Psychology of Interpersonal Relations*. New York: Wiley.

Hildebrand, G.H. (1996) Redefining achievement, in P.F. Murphy and C.V. Gipps (eds) *Equity in the Classroom: Towards Effective Pedagogy for Girls and Boys*. London: Falmer/UNESCO.

Hoffmann, L. (1997) An intervention project promoting girls' and boys' interest in physics: opening the door to physics for girls, paper presented at ESERA Symposium: 'Gender Issues in Physics', Rome, Italy.

Holland, D., Lachicotte Jr, W., Skinner, D. and Cain, C. (1998) *Identity and Agency in Cultural Worlds*. Cambridge, MA: Harvard University Press.

Hornbrook, D. (1998) *Education and Dramatic Art*. London: Routledge.

Ivinson, G. (2004) The social context of classroom art; collaboration, social identities and social consequences, in D. Miell and K. Littleton (eds) *Collaborative Creativity*. Milton Keynes: The Open University.

Ivinson, G. (2005) The development of young people's social representations of art, *Welsh Journal of Education*, 13(2): 47–67.

Ivinson, G. and Murphy, P. (2003) Boys don't write romance: the construction of knowledge and gender identities in English classrooms, *Pedagogy, Culture and Society*, 11(1): 89–111.

Jackson, C. (2002) Can single-sex classes in co-educational schools enhance the learning experiences of girls and/or boys? An exploration of pupils' perceptions, *British Educational Research Journal*, 28(1): 37–48.

Jackson, D. (1998) Breaking out of the binary trap, in D. Epstein, J. Elwood, V. Hey and J. Maw (eds) *Failing Boys? Issues in Gender and Achievement*. Buckingham: Open University Press.

Jardine, A. (1985) *Gynesis: Configurations of Woman and Modernity*. Ithaca, NY: Cornell University Press.

Jarman, T.L. (1963) *Landmarks in the History of Education*. London: John Murray.

Jodelet, D. (1991) *Madness and Social Representations*. Hemel Hempstead: Harvester Wheatsheaf.

Jodelet, J. and Willis, S. (1986) Feminist single-sex educational strategies: some theoretical flaws and practical fallacies, *Discourse*, 7(1): 1–30.

Joffe, H. (1999) *Risk and the Other*. Cambridge: Cambridge University Press.

Kelly, A. (1988) Gender differences in teacher-pupil interactions: a meta-analytic review, *Research in Education*, 39: 1–24.

Kenway, J. and Willis, S. with Blackmore, J. and Rennie, L. (1998) *Answering Back*. London: Routledge.

Kessler, S., Ashenden, D.J., Connell, R.W. and Dowsett, G.W. (1985) Gender relations in secondary schooling, *Sociology of Education*, 58: 34–48.

Kotthoff, H. and Baron, B. (2001) Preface, in B. Barron and H. Kotthoff (eds) *Gender in Interaction, Perspectives on Femininity and Masculinity in Ethnography and Discourse*. Amersterdam: John Benjamins.

Krogh, L.B. and Thomsen, P. (2005) Studying students' attitudes towards science from a cultural perspective but with a quantitative methodology: border crossing into the physics classroom, *International Journal of Science Education*, 27(3): 281–302.

Kruse, A-M. (1996) Single sex settings: pedagogies for boys and girls in Danish schools, in P.F. Murphy and C.V. Gipps (eds) *Equity in the Classroom: Towards Effective Pedagogy for Girls and Boys*. London: Falmer/UNESCO.

Kung, H. (2001) *Women in Christianity*. Aldershot: Continuum.

Lankshear, C. and McLaren, P (eds) (1993) *Critical Literacy: Policy, Praxis and the Postmodern*. Albany, NY: State University of New York Press.

Lave, J. (1988) *Cognition in Practice*. Cambridge: Cambridge University Press.

Lave, J. and Wenger, E. (1991) *Situated Learning: Legitimate Peripheral Participation*. Cambridge: Cambridge University Press.

Layton, D. (1993) *Technology's Challenge to Science Education*. Buckingham: Open University Press.

Lee, C.D. and Majors, Y.J. (2003) 'Heading up the street': localised opportunities for shared construction of knowledge, *Pedagogy, Culture and Society*, 11(1): 49–67.

Linguard, B. and Douglas, P. (1999) *Men Engaging Feminisms: Profeminisms, Black-lashes and Schooling*. Buckingham: Open University Press.

Lloyd, B. and Duveen, G. (1992) *Gender Identities and Education*. Hemel Hempstead: Harvester Wheatsheaf.

Lloyd, G. (1989) Man of reason, in A. Garry and M. Pearsall (eds) *Women, Knowledge and Reality: Explorations in Feminist Philosophy*. Boston, MA: Unwin Hyman.

Mac an Ghaill, M. (1994) *The Making of Men: Masculinities, Sexualities and Schooling*. Buckingham: Open University Press.

MacDonald, R.A.R., Hargreaves, D.J. and Miell, D. (eds) (2002) *Musical Identities*. Oxford: Oxford University Press.

Mael, F.A. (1998) Single-sex and coeducational schooling: relationships to socioemotional and academic development, *Review of Educational Research*, 68(2): 101–29.

Mahony, P. (1985) *Schools for the Boys? Co-education Reassessed*. London: Hutchinson.

Manthorpe, C. (1985) The value of an historical perspective on girls and science and technology: the English experience, Girls and Science and Technology (GASAT) contributions to the Third GASAT Conference, London, Chelsea College.

Marsh, H.W., Smith, I.D., Marsh, M. and Owens, L. (1988) The transition from single-sex to co-educational high schools: effects on multiple dimensions of self-concept and on academic achievement, *American Journal of Education*, 25: 237–69.

Martin, M. (2002) Single sex classes in English Trial in Year 9 (13–14-year-olds), 1997–2001 at Comberton Village College, *Educational Action Research*, 10(1): 105–21.

Martino, W. and Meyenn, B. (2002) War, guns and cool, tough things: interrogating single-sex classes as a strategy for engaging boys in English, *Cambridge Journal of Education*, 32(3): 303–24.

Mason, R. and Houghton, N. (2002) The educational value of making, in S. Sayers, J. Morley and B. Barnes (eds) *Issues in Design and Technology Teaching*. London: Routledge Falmer.

McDermott, R.P. (1996) The acquisition of a child by a learning disability, in S. Chaiklin and J. Lave (eds) *Understanding Practice: Perspectives on Activity and Context*. Cambridge: Cambridge University Press.

McDowell, L. (1990) Gender divisions, in C. Hamnett, L. McDowell and P. Sarre (eds) *Restructuring Britain: The Changing Social Structure*. London: Sage Publications in association with the Open University.

Merchant, C. (1983) Mining the earth's womb, in J. Rothschild, *Machina Ex Dea*. New York: Pergamon Press.

Mills, M. (2001) *Challenging Violence in Schools: An Issue of Masculinities*. Buckingham: Open University Press.

Mills, M. and Linguard, B. (1997) Masculinity politics: myths and boys' schooling: a review essay, *British Journal of Educational Studies*, 45(3): 276–92.

Moscovici, S. (1984) The phenomenon of social representations, in R.M. Farr and S. Moscovici (eds) *Social Representations*. Cambridge: Cambridge University Press.

Moscovici, S. (1988) Notes towards a description of social representations, *European Journal of Social Psychology*, 18: 211–150.

Moscovici, S. (2001) *Social Representations: Explorations in Social Psychology* (ed. G. Duveen). New York: New York University Press.

Murphy, P. (1999) Supporting collaborative learning: a gender dimension, in P. Murphy (ed.) *Learners, Learning & Assessment*. London: Paul Chapman in association with Open University Press.

Murphy, P. (2006) Gender and technology: gender mediation in school knowledge construction, in J.R. Dakers (ed.) *Defining Technological Literacy: Towards an Epistemological Framework*. New York: Palgrave Macmillan.

Murphy, P. and Elwood, J. (1998) Gendered experiences, choices and achievement: exploring the links, *International Journal of Inclusive Education*, 2(2): 95–118.

Murphy, P. and Ivinson, G. (2004) Gender differences in educational achievement: a socio-cultural analysis, in M. Olssen (ed.) *Culture and Learning*. Greenwich, CT: Information Age Publishing.

Murphy, P. and Ivinson, G. (2005) Assessment and students' literacy learning: implications for formative assessment, *Teacher Development*, 9(2): 185–200.

Murphy, P. and Whitelegg, E. (2006) *Girls in the Physics Classroom: A Review of the Research into the Participation of Girls in Physics*. London: Institute of Physics Publishing.

Ovitt, G. (1987) *The Restoration of Perfection: Labor and Technology in Medieval Culture*. London: Rutgers University Press.

Paechter, C. (1998) *Educating the Other: Gender, Power and Schooling*. London: Falmer.

Paechter, C. and Head, J.C. (1996) Gender, identity, status and the body: life in a marginal subject, *Gender and Education*, 8(1): 21–9.

Parker, L.H. and Rennie, L.J. (2002) Teachers' implementation of gender-inclusive instructional strategies in single-sex and mixed-sex science classrooms, *International Journal of Science Education*, 24(9): 881–97.

Pateman, C. (1988) *The Sexual Contract*. Cambridge: Polity Press.

Peim, N. (2004) Bernstein and curriculum politics: rethinking theory, English and English teaching. Paper presented at the Third International Bernstein Symposium, Cambridge, 15–17 July.

Penuel, W.R. and Wertsch, J.V. (1995) Vygotsky and identity formation: a sociocultural approach, *Education Psychologist*, 30(2): 83–92.

Peyton Young, J. (2000) Boy talk: critical literacy and masculinities, *Reading Research Quarterly*, 35(3): 312–37.

Plowden Report (1969) *Children: Their Primary Schools*. London: HMSO.

Portes, R.P. and Vadeboncoeur, J.A. (2003) Mediation in cognitive socialization: the influence of socioeconomic status, in A. Kozulin, B. Gindis, V.S. Ageyev and S.M. Miller (eds) *Vygotsky's Educational Theory in Cultural Context*. Cambridge: Cambridge University Press.

Purvis, J. (1991) *A History of Women's Education in England*. Buckingham: Open University Press.

Raphael Reed, L. (1999) Troubling boys and disturbing discourses on masculinity and schooling: a feminist exploration of current debates and interventions concerning boys in school, *Gender and Education*, 11: 93–110.

Renold, E. (2000) 'Coming out': gender, (hetro)sexuality and the primary school, *Gender and Education*, 12(3): 309–26.

Ringrose, J. (2006) A new universal mean girl: examining the discursive construction and social regulation of a new feminine pathology, *Feminism and Psychology*, 16(4): 405–24.

Riordan, C. (1997) *Equality and Achievement: An Introduction to the Sociology of Education*. New York: Addison-Wesley Longman.

Riordan, C. (2002) What do we know about the effects of single-sex schools in the private sector? in A. Datnow and L. Hubbard (eds) *Gender in Policy and Practice: Perspectives on Single-Sex and Coeducational Schooling*. London: Routledge Falmer.

Robinson, M. (2000) 'What is(n't) this subject called English?' in J. Davidson and J. Moss (eds) *Issues in English Teaching*. London and New York: Routledge.

Rogoff, B. (1990) *Apprenticeship in Thinking: Cognitive Development in Social Context*. Oxford: Oxford University Press.

Rogoff, B. (1995) Observing sociocultural activity on three planes:

participatory appropriation, guided participation, and apprenticeship, in J.V. Wertsch, P. Del Rio and A. Alvarez (eds) *Sociocultural Studies of Mind*. Cambridge: Cambridge University Press.

Rogoff, B. (2003) *The Cultural Nature of Human Development*. Oxford: Oxford University Press.

Rose, N. (1996) *Inventing our Selves: Psychology, Power and Personhood*. Cambridge: Cambridge University Press.

Roth, W.M. and Lee, Y.J. (2006) Contradictions in theorizing and implementing communities in education, *Educational Research Review*, 1(1): 27–40.

Rothschild, J. (1983) *Machina Ex Dea*. New York: Pergamon Press.

Rowan, L., Knobel, M., Bigum, C. and Lankshear, C. (2002) *Boys, Literacies and Schooling*. Buckingham: Open University Press.

Sarah, E., Scott, M. and Spender, D. (1980) The education of feminists: the case for single sex schools, in D. Spender and E. Sarah (eds) *Learning to Lose*. London: The Women's Press.

Schwartz Cowan, R. (1997) *A Social History of American Technology*. Oxford: Oxford University Press.

Sewell, T. (1997) *Black Masculinities and Schooling: How Black Boys Survive Modern Schooling*. Stoke on Trent: Trentham.

Sharp, G. (2004) A longitudinal study investigating pupil attitudes towards their science learning experiences from a gender perspective, unpublished Ph.D thesis, the Open University.

Shaw, J. (1984) Education and the individual: schooling for girls, or mixed schooling – a mixed blessing? in R. Deem (ed.) *Co-education Reconsidered*. Milton Keynes: Open University.

Shutz, A. (1962) *The Problem of Social Reality*, Vol. 1 of *Collected Papers*. The Hague: M. Nijhoff.

Skeggs, B. (2004) *Class, Self, Culture*. London: Routledge.

Skelton, C. (2001) *Schooling the Boys: Masculinities and Primary School Education*. Buckingham: Open University Press.

Smithers, A. and Robinson, P. (1995) *Co-educational and Single-sex Schooling*. Manchester: Centre for Education and Employment Research, University of Manchester.

Smithers, A. and Robinson, P. (1997) *Co-education and Single-sex – Revisited*. Uxbridge: Brunel University.

Smithers, A. and Robinson, P. (2006) *The Paradox of Single-Sex and Co-educational Schooling*. Buckingham: Carmichael Press.

Southern Examining Group (1998) *Inter-Group Statistics*. Guilford: SEG.

Spielhofer, T., O'Donnell, L., Benton, T., Schagen, S. and Schagen, I. (2002) *The Impact of School Size and Single-sex Education on Performance*. Slough: National Foundation for Educational Research/Local Government Association.

Stables, A. (1990) Differences between pupils from mixed and single-sex schools in their enjoyment of school subjects and in their attitudes to science and to school, *Educational Review*, 42(3): 221–30.

Streitmatter, J. (1999) *For Girls Only: Making a Case for Single Schooling*. Albany, NY: SUNY Press.

Sukhnandan, L., Lee, B. and Kelleher, S. (2000) *An Investigation into Gender Differences in Achievement. Phase 2: School and Classroom Strategies*. Slough: National Foundation for Educational Research.

Valsiner, J. (1998) *The Guided Mind. A Sociogenetic Approach to Personality*. Cambridge, MA: Harvard University Press.

Vygotsky, L.S. (1994) The problem of the environment, in R. van der Veer and J. Valsiner (eds) *The Vygotsky Reader*. Cambridge, MA: Blackwell.

Wajcman, J. (1991) *Feminism Confronts Technology*. University Park, PA: The Pennsylvania State University Press.

Walker, J. C. (1988) *Louts and Legends: Male Youth Culture in an Inner City School*. Sydney: Allen & Unwin.

Walkerdine, V. (1988) *The Mastery of Reason: Cognitive Development and the Production of Rationality*. London: Routledge.

Walkerdine, V. (1998) *Counting Girls Out: Girls and Mathematics*. London: Falmer Press.

Walkerdine, V. (2007) *Children, Gender, Video Games: Towards a Relational Approach to Multimedia*. Basingstoke: Palgrave Macmillan.

Walkerdine, V. and Lucey, H. (1989) *Democracy in the Kitchen? Regulating Mothers and Socialising Daughters*. London: Virago.

Warrington, M. and Younger, M. (2001) Single-sex classes and equal opportunities for girls and boys: perspectives through time from a mixed comprehensive school in England, *Oxford Review of Education*, 27(3): 339–56.

Watson, S. (1997) Single-sex education for girls: heterosexuality, gendered subjectivity and school choice, *British Journal of Sociology of Education*, 18(3): 371–83.

Weiner, G., Arnot, M. and David, M. (1997 Is the future female? Female success, male disadvantage and changing patterns in education, in A.H. Halsey, H. Lauder, P. Brown and A. Stuart Wells (eds) *Education, Economy, Culture and Society*. Oxford: Oxford University Press.

Wenger, E. (1998) *Communities of Practice: Learning, Meaning, and Identity*. Cambridge: Cambridge University Press.

Wertsch, J.V. (1991) *Voices of the Mind: A Sociocultural Approach to Mediated Activity*. Cambridge, MA: Harvard University Press.

Wertsch, J.V. and Stone, A. (1979) A social interactional analysis of learning disabilities remediation. Paper presented at the International Conference of the Association for Children with Learning Disabilities, San Francisco February 1979.

Whitelegg, (1996) The supported learning in physics project, *Physics Education*, 31(5): 291–6.

Whitty, G. (2002) *Making Sense of Educational Policy: Studies in the Sociology of Education*. London: Sage.

Whyte, J. (1985) Girl friendly science and the girl friendly school, in J. Whyte, R. Deem, L. Kant and M. Cruickshank (eds) *Girl-friendly Schooling*. London: Methuen.

Williams, J. (2006) Will the new GCSE really teach pupils how science works? *Education in Science*, 218(June): 14–15.

Williams, R. (1984) *Keywords: A Vocabulary of Culture and Society*, 2nd edn. New York: Oxford University Press.

Willis, P. (1977) *Learning to Labour*. Aldershot: Saxon House.

Woody, E.L. (2002) Constructions of masculinity in California's single-gender academies, in A. Datnow and L. Hubbard (eds) *Gender in Policy and Practice: Perspectives on Single-Sex and Coeducational Schooling*. New York: Routledge Falmer.

Yates, L. (1997) Gender equity and the boys debate: what sort of challenge is it? *British Journal of Sociology of Education*, 18(3): 337–47.

Younger, M. and Warrington, M. (2002) Single-sex teaching in a co-educational comprehensive school in England: an evaluation based upon students' performance and classroom interactions, *British Educational Research Journal*, 28(3): 353–74.

Younger, M., Warrington, M. and Williams, J. (1999) The gender gap and classroom interactions: reality and rhetoric, *British Journal of Sociology of Education*, 20(3): 325–41.

Younger, M. and Warrington, M. with McLelland, R. (2005) *Raising Boys' Achievement in Secondary Schools: Issues, Dilemmas and Opportunities*. Maidenhead: Open University Press.

Zittoun, T., Duveen, G., Gillespie, A., Ivinson, G. and Psaltis, C. (2003) The use of symbolic resources in developmental transitions, *Culture and Psychology*, 9(4): 415–48.

Index